LATIN AMERICAN HISTORY
A GUIDE TO THE LITERATURE
IN ENGLISH

LATIN AMERICAN HISTORY

A GUIDE TO THE LITERATURE
IN ENGLISH

by

R. A. HUMPHREYS

Professor of Latin American History
in the University of London

Issued under the auspices of the
Royal Institute of International Affairs

GREENWOOD PRESS, PUBLISHERS
WESTPORT, CONNECTICUT

Library of Congress Cataloging in Publication Data

Humphreys, Robert Arthur, 1907-
    Latin American history.

    Reprint of the 1958 ed. published by Oxford University
Press, London, New York.
    Includes indexes.
    1. Latin America--Bibliography. I. Title.
[Z1601.H853]   016.98   77-752
ISBN 0-8371-9490-3

Originally published in 1958 by Oxford University Press,
London, New York, under the auspices of the Royal
Institute of International Affairs

Reprinted with the permission of The Royal Institute of
International Affairs

Reprinted in 1977 by Greenwood Press, Inc.

Library of Congress catalog card number 77-752

ISBN 0-8371-9490-3

Printed in the United States of America

PREFACE

I have designed this Guide to serve the needs both of the university student of Latin American history and of the general reader. I hope also that it may be of some use to the professional scholar. It is, of course, selective, as all such guides must be, and it reflects, no doubt, errors of judgement both in what it includes and in what it omits. But it should at least help to unlock the doors to the great body of literature on Latin American history in the English language.

The literature in English, steadily as it has grown in the last half century, is, of course, only a sizeable proportion of the literature available in the major European languages. But though a thorough and complete guide to Latin American history is much needed, such a work can only be compiled by a team of experts, and I have preferred to deal with one language systematically, rather than to include necessarily fragmentary references to writings in French, German, Italian, Spanish, and Portuguese.

History I have interpreted in the widest possible sense. But I have not tried to cover the fields of archaeology or ethnology. Nor have I addressed myself to the professional student of geography or literature. The literature relating to the discovery of America, moreover, and the very substantial body of writings concerning Spanish territory now in the possession of the United States, have been treated more fully elsewhere, and I have not sought to duplicate work already done. Finally, I have not found it practicable to make this Guide a guide also to Parliamentary and Congressional papers. But the student should certainly be aware of these invaluable sources of information.

I wish to record my gratitude to Dr. C. J. Bartlett, who has assisted me with the checking of titles, to Professor Lewis Hanke, who has made many valuable suggestions, to Mrs. Audrey Munro, who has patiently typed and re-typed my manuscript, and to the Royal Institute of International Affairs, which, having published my earlier bibliography on Latin America in 1941 and a revised and enlarged edition of it in 1949, has yet had the generosity to sponsor this new, and, so far as I am concerned, final manual to accompany its series of monographs on the individual Latin American States.

R. A. H.

October 1957

CONTENTS

Contents

Contents

Contents

Contents

Contents

Contents

I

GENERAL REFERENCE WORKS

The most useful handbooks or guides to the Latin American countries taken together are [1] *The South American Handbook* (edited by Howell Davies, London, Trade and Travel Publications), which is published annually and embraces Mexico, Central America, and Cuba as well as South America, and [2] *The New World Guides to the Latin American Republics* (edited by E. P. Hanson, 3rd ed., rev., 3 vols., New York, Duell, Sloan and Pearce, 1950).

[3] Fitzgibbon, R. H., ed., *The Constitutions of the Americas* (Univ. of Chicago Press, 1948).

A useful compilation in which the constitutions of the Latin American states are translated with introductory notes. For an earlier compendium see [4] J. I. Rodríguez, *American Constitutions. A compilation of the political constitutions of the independent nations of the New World, with short historical notes and various appendixes* (2 vols., Washington, Govt. Printing Office, 1906-7).

[5] Hanson, E. P., *Index to Map of Hispanic America 1 : 1,000,000* (Washington, Govt. Printing Office, 1945).

A one-volume edition of the twelve-volume index to the American Geographical Society's millionth map of Hispanic America.

[6] Hilton, R., ed., *Who's Who in Latin America. A biographical dictionary of notable living men and women of Latin America* (3rd ed., rev., 7 vols., Stanford Univ. Press, 1945-51).

A revised and enlarged edition of a work first published in 1935. Part i, *Mexico*; Part ii, *Central America and Panama*; Part iii, *Colombia, Ecuador, and Venezuela*; Part iv, *Bolivia, Chile, and Peru*; Part v, *Argentina, Paraguay, and Uruguay*; Part vi, *Brazil*; Part vii, *Cuba, Dominican Republic, and Haiti*.

II
BIBLIOGRAPHIES AND GUIDES

1. GENERAL

[7] C. K. Jones, *A Bibliography of Latin American Bibliographies* (2nd ed., rev., Washington, Govt. Printing Office, 1942), and [8] the *Handbook of Latin American Studies*, published annually (Harvard Univ. Press, 1936–51; Univ. of Florida Press, 1951–), are indispensable tools. The former brings together more than 3,000 items. The latter, prepared by the Hispanic Foundation of the Library of Congress, provides a guide to current writings in almost every branch of Latin American studies, including anthropology, archaeology, art, economics, education, ethnology, geography, government, history, international relations, labour and social welfare, language, literature, law, music, philosophy, and sociology. In addition, the first eight volumes contain bibliographical articles and notes, together with a number of special subject bibliographies. Of great value, also, [9] Charmion Shelby, ed., *Latin American Periodicals currently received in the Library of Congress and in the Library of the Department of Agriculture* (Washington, Library of Congress, 1944 [1945]), lists some 1,500 items and provides information not easily accessible elsewhere.

Bibliographies of special subjects, as well as more general lists, are issued from time to time by the Pan American Union in Washington and by the United Nations Headquarters Library in New York. Reference should also be made to the list of publications of the Library of Congress. The Hispanic Foundation of the Library of Congress was not established till 1939, but the Library's publishing activities in the Latin American field extend over half a century.

[10] Goldsmith, P. H., *A Brief Bibliography of Books in English, Spanish and Portuguese, relating to the republics commonly called Latin American, with comments* (New York, Macmillan, 1915).
Still valuable for its critical remarks.

[11] Grismer, R. L., ed., *A New Bibliography of the Literatures of Spain and Spanish America, including many studies on anthropology, archaeology, art, economics, education, geography, history, law, music, philosophy and other subjects*

2

(vols. i–iv, Minneapolis, Perine Book Co., 1941–2; vol. v, St. Louis, John S. Swift, 1944; vols. vi– , Dubuque, Iowa, W. C. Brown, 1945–). The scale may be judged by vol. i, Aa-Ans (248 pp.) and vol. ii, Ant-Azz (509 pp.). Publication of this list has been in suspense since vol. vii, Cat-Cez (1946).

[**12**] Sabin, J., *A Dictionary of Books relating to America, from its discovery to the present time* . . . (29 vols., New York, J. Sabin, 1868–92; Bibliographical Society of America, 1927–36).

A monumental author catalogue, which includes pamphlets and periodicals as well as books, many relating to Latin America.

2. ARCHIVES, LIBRARIES, AND SPECIAL COLLECTIONS

[**13**] Ronald Hilton, *Handbook of Hispanic Source Materials and Research Organizations in the United States* (2nd ed., Stanford Univ. Press, 1956), surveys the holdings and activities of United States libraries, archives, and museums and the work of research institutes and organizations. [**14**] R. R. Hill, *The National Archives of Latin America* (Harvard Univ. Press, 1945), describes the history, organization, contents, and publications of the nineteen existing national archives in Latin America.[1] [**15**] A. E. Gropp, *Guide to Libraries and Archives in Central America and the West Indies, Panama, Bermuda, and British Guiana* (New Orleans, Tulane Univ. Press, 1941), covers the Central American and island republics.

MANUSCRIPTS IN AMERICAN AND LATIN AMERICAN DEPOSITORIES[2]

[**16**] Bolton, H. E., *Guide to Materials for the History of the United States in the Principal Archives of Mexico* (Washington, Carnegie Institution, 1913).

[1] See the author's supplementary articles in the *Handbook of Latin American Studies* [8], vol. xi (1948), *Hispanic American Historical Review*, xxx (1950), 115–39, xxxi (1951), 152–76, xxxii (1952), 458–82, xxxiv (1954), 256–79, and *Americas*, xii (July 1955), 51–75.

[2] A guide to Latin American materials in the National Archives of the United States is to be published shortly. For guides and calendars printed in periodical publications see, in the *Hispanic American Historical Review*, Woodrow Borah, 'The Cathedral Archive of Oaxaca', xxviii (1948), 640–5, and 'Notes on the Civil Archives in the City of Oaxaca', xxxi (1951), 723–49; J. P. Harrison, 'The Archives of the United States Diplomatic and Consular Posts in Latin America', xxxiii (1953), 168–83; R. D. Hussey, 'Manuscript Hispanic Americana in the Harvard College Library', xvii (1937), 259–77; Jac Nachbin, 'Descriptive Calendar of South American Manuscripts in the Northwestern University Library', xii (1932), 242–59, 376–86, 503–21, xiii (1933), 124–42, 267–80, 403–19, 524–42; J. E. Patterson, 'Manuscripts relating to Peru in

Bibliographies and Guides

[**17**] Butler, R. L., *A Check List of Manuscripts in the Edward E. Ayer Collection* (Chicago, Newberry Library, 1937).
Primarily relating to Mexico and the Spanish borderlands of the American southwest.

[**18**] Castañeda, C. E., and Dabbs, J. A., *Calendar of the Manual E. Gondra Manuscript Collection. The University of Texas Library* (Mexico, D.F., Ed. Jus, 1952).

[**19**] Castañeda, C. E., and Dabbs, J. A., *Guide to the Latin American Manuscripts in the University of Texas Library* (Harvard Univ. Press, 1939).

[**19a**] Castañeda, C. E., and Dabbs, J. A., *Independent Mexico in Documents: Independence, Empire and Republic. A calendar of the Juan E. Hernández y Dávalos manuscript collection. The University of Texas Library* (Mexico, D.F., Ed. Jus, 1954).

[**20**] Castañeda, C. E., *A Report on the Spanish Archives in San Antonio, Texas* (San Antonio, Yanaguana Society Pubns., vol. i, 1937).

[**21**] Clemence, Stella R., *The Harkness Collection in the Library of Congress. i. Calendar of Spanish Manuscripts concerning Peru, 1531-1651* (Washington, Govt. Printing Office, 1932).
Vol. ii of this work consists of *Documents from Early Peru* (1936).

[**21a**] Ewing, W. S., *Guide to the Manuscript Collections in the William L. Clements Library* (2nd ed., Ann Arbor, Clements Library, 1953).

[**22**] Geiger, M. J., *Calendar of Documents in the Santa Barbara Mission Archives* (Washington, Academy of American Franciscan History, 1947).

[**23**] Pérez, L. M., *Guide to Materials for American History in Cuban Archives* (Washington, Carnegie Institution, 1907).

[**24**] Twitchell, R. E., *The Spanish Archives of New Mexico* (2 vols., Cedar Rapids, Iowa, Torch Press, 1914).

[**24a**] Wright, Doris M., *A Guide to the Mariano Guadalupe Vallejo Documentos para la Historia de California, 1780-1875* (Univ. of California Press, 1953).
The Vallejo papers in the Bancroft Library.

Yale University Library', xxxvi (1956), 243-62; D. Van den Eynde, 'Catalogue of Spanish Documents in John Carter Brown Library', xvi (1936), 564-607; Schafer Williams, 'The G. R. G. Conway Collection in the Library of Congress: a checklist', xxxv (1955), 386-97; and Juan de Zengotita, 'The National Archive and the National Library of Bolivia at Sucre', xxix (1949), 649-76. The *Handbook of Latin American Studies* [8] contains, in vol. 2 (1937), R. S. Chamberlain, 'A Report on Colonial Materials in the Governmental Archives of Guatemala City', pp. 387-432, and in vol. 6 (1941), M. S. Cardozo, 'A Guide to the Manuscripts in the Lima Library, the Catholic University of America, Washington, D.C.', pp. 471-504, and R. C. West, 'The Municipal Archives of Parral, Chihuahua, Mexico', pp. 523-29. See also J. E. Patterson, 'Spanish and Spanish American Manuscripts in Yale University Library', *Yale University Library Gazette*, xxxi (1957), 110-33.

Archives, Libraries, and Special Collections
MANUSCRIPTS IN EUROPEAN DEPOSITORIES[1]

[25] Chapman, C. E., *Catalogue of Materials in the Archivo General de Indias for the History of the Pacific Coast and the American Southwest* (Univ. of California Press, 1919).

[26] Gayangos, Pascual de, *Catalogue of the Manuscripts in the Spanish Language in the British Museum* (4 vols., London, The Trustees, 1875–93). See, in particular, vols. ii and iv.

[27] Hill, R. R., *Descriptive Catalogue of the Documents relating to the History of the United States in the Papeles procedentes de Cuba deposited in the Archivo General de Indias at Seville* (Washington, Carnegie Institution, 1916).

[28] Nasatir, A. P., *French Activities in California: an archival calendar-guide* (Stanford Univ. Press, 1945).
Materials, principally in French archives, for French activities in California, Mexico, Central America.

[28a] Peña y Cámara, José María de la, *A List of the Spanish Residencias in the Archives of the Indies, 1516–1775* (Washington, Library of Congress, 1955).

[29] Robertson, J. A., *List of Documents in Spanish Archives relating to the History of the United States, which have been printed, or of which transcripts are preserved in American libraries* (Washington, Carnegie Institution, 1910).

[30] Shepherd, W. R., *Guide to the Materials for the History of the United States in Spanish Archives* (Washington, Carnegie Institution, 1907).

PRINTED MATERIALS

[31] Cole, G. W., *A Catalogue of Books relating to the Discovery and Early History of North and South America forming a part of the library of E. D. Church* (5 vols., New York, Dodd, Mead and Co., 1907. Reprinted New York, Peter Smith, 1951).
These books are now in the Henry E. Huntington Library, California.

[32] Holmes, Ruth E. V., *Bibliographical and Historical Description of the Rarest Books in the Oliveira Lima Collection at the Catholic University of America* (Washington, 1927).

[1] A guide to the manuscript materials for Latin American history in the archives and libraries of Great Britain is much needed. For Mexican transcripts in the Cambridge and Aberdeen University Libraries see John Street, 'The G. R. G. Conway Collection in Cambridge University Library: a checklist', *Hispanic American Historical Review*, xxxvii (1957), 60–68; and A. P. Thornton, 'The G. R. G. Conway MS. Collection in the Library of the University of Aberdeen', *ibid.*, xxxvi (1956), 345–7. For copies in American and Latin American libraries of documents in British and European depositories see the series of volumes published by the Comisión de Historia of the Instituto Panamericano de Geografía e Historia under the general title of *Misiones Americanos en los Archivos Europeos* (Mexico City, 1949–).

5

Bibliographies and Guides

[33] Luquiens, F. B., *Spanish American Literature in the Yale University Library: a bibliography* (Yale Univ. Press, 1939).

[33a] Manchester, A. K., 'Descriptive Bibliography of the Brazilian Section of the Duke University Library', *Hispanic American Historical Review*, xiii (1933), 238-66, 495-523.

[34] *Spain and Spanish America in the Libraries of the University of California: a catalogue of books* (2 vols., Berkeley, Calif., 1928-30).

[34a] Spell, Lota M., *Research Materials for the Study of Latin America at the University of Texas* (Univ. of Texas Press, 1954).

[35] Thomas, Henry, *Short-Title Catalogue of Spanish-American Books printed before 1601 now in the British Museum* (London, 1944).

[36] Welsh, Doris V., *A Catalog of the William B. Greenlee Collection of Portuguese History and Literature and the Portuguese Materials in the Newberry Library* (Chicago, Newberry Library, 1953).

3. OFFICIAL PUBLICATIONS

[37] Childs, J. B., *The Memorias of the Republics of Central America and of the Antilles* (Washington, Govt. Printing Office, 1932).

[38] *Guide to the Official Publications of the other American Republics* (19 vols., Washington, Library of Congress, Govt. Printing Office, 1945-8).
(i) *Argentina* (J. B. Childs, 1945); (ii) *Bolivia* (J. B. Childs, 1945); (iii) *Brazil* (John De Noia, 1948); (iv) *Chile* (Otto Neuburger, 1947); (v) *Colombia* (J. B. Childs, 1948); (vi) *Costa Rica* (H. V. Besso, 1947); (vii) *Cuba* (J. B. Childs, 1945); (viii) *Dominican Republic* (John De Noia, 1947); (ix) *Ecuador* (John De Noia, 1947); (x) *El Salvador* (John De Noia, 1947); (xi) *Guatemala* (H. V. Besso, 1947); (xii) *Haiti* (Otto Neuburger, 1947); (xiii) *Honduras* (Otto Neuburger, 1947); (xiv) *Nicaragua* (John De Noia, 1947); (xv) *Panama* (John De Noia, 1947); (xvi) *Paraguay* (J. B. Childs, 1947); (xvii) *Peru* (John De Noia, 1948); (xviii) *Uruguay* (John De Noia and Glenda Crevenna, 1948); (xix) *Venezuela* (Otto Neuburger, 1948).

[39] Ker, A. M., *Mexican Government Publications. A guide to the more important publications of the national government of Mexico, 1821-1936* (Washington, Govt. Printing Office, 1940).

4. CARTOGRAPHY

[40] American Geographical Society of New York, *A Catalogue of Maps of Hispanic America, including maps in scientific periodicals and books, and sheet and atlas maps . . .* (4 vols., New York, American Geographical Society, 1930-3).

Economics, Politics, Sociology

[41] Lowery, W., *The Lowery Collection. A descriptive list of maps of the Spanish possessions within the present limits of the United States, 1502–1820* (ed. P. L. Phillips, Washington, Govt. Printing Office, 1912). [41a] Wagner, H. R., ed., *The Cartography of the Northwest Coast of America to the year 1800* (2 vols., Univ. of California Press, 1937).

5. ECONOMICS, POLITICS, SOCIOLOGY

[42] *The Economic Literature of Latin America: a tentative bibliography*, compiled by the staff of the Bureau for Economic Research in Latin America, Harvard University (2 vols., Harvard Univ. Press, 1935–6), lists more than 12,000 items and is important to economists and economic historians. It is supplemented by [42a] T. B. Jones, E. A. Warburton, and A. Kingsley, *A Bibliography on South American Economic Affairs: articles in nineteenth-century periodicals* (Univ. of Minnesota Press, 1955), which indexes 229 periodicals published in three continents and in nine languages. [43] Richard F. Behrendt, *Modern Latin America in Social Science Literature: a selected, annotated bibliography of books, pamphlets, and periodicals in English in the fields of economics, politics, and sociology of Latin America* (Univ. of New Mexico Press, 1949), was primarily designed to assist the student of contemporary affairs.

[44] Bernstein, Sylvia P., *Bibliography on Labor and Social Welfare in Latin America* (Washington, Pan American Union, 1944).

[45] *Bibliography of Selected Statistical Sources of the American Nations* (Washington, Inter-American Statistical Institute, 1947).

[45a] *Bibliography on Public Administration in Latin America* (Columbus Memorial Library, Bibliographic Series, No. 43. Washington, Pan American Union, 1954).

[46] Pierson, Donald, *Survey of the Literature on Brazil of Sociological Significance published up to 1940* (Harvard Univ. Press, 1945).

[47] Taeuber, I. B., *General Censuses and Vital Statistics in the Americas* (Washington, Govt. Printing Office, 1943).

See also Morrison [64].

6. HISTORY

[48] H. Keniston, *List of Works for the Study of Hispanic-American History* (New York, Hispanic Society of America, 1920), is still worth consulting. [49] A. Curtis Wilgus, *Histories and Historians of Hispanic America* (New York, H. W. Wilson, 1942), is a useful

bibliographical essay. [**50**] R. L. Butler, *Guide to the Hispanic American Historical Review, 1918–1945* (Duke Univ. Press, 1950), is invaluable. See also Goldsmith [10], *The Economic Literature of Latin America* [42], Jones [42a] and Bemis and Griffin [60], and, in the field of biography, [**51**] Josefina del Toro, *A Bibliography of the Collective Biography of Spanish America* (Río Piedras, Puerto Rico, The University, 1938).

[**51a**] E. J. Burrus, 'An Introduction to Bibliographical Tools in Spanish Archives and Manuscript Collections relating to Hispanic America', *Hispanic American Historical Review*, xxxv (1955), 443–83, describes 'the more important printed and manuscript catalogues, guides, inventories, card-indexes and other bibliographical tools available in the key Spanish repositories'.

[**51b**] Charles Gibson and Benjamin Keen, 'Trends of United States Studies in Latin American History', *American Historical Review*, lxii (July 1957), 855–77, provides a useful survey with extensive bibliographical notes.

COLONIAL HISTORY

[**52**] P. A. Means, *Biblioteca Andina, Pt. 1. The chroniclers, or the writers of the 16th and 17th centuries who treated of the pre-Hispanic history and culture of the Andean countries* (New Haven, Connecticut Academy of Arts and Sciences [*Transactions*, xxix, 271–525], 1928), is the first part of an ambitious work which was never completed. See also Shelby [222]. [**53**] J. L. Mecham, 'The Northern Expansion of New Spain, 1522–1822. A selected descriptive bibliographical list', *Hispanic American Historical Review*, vii (1927), 233–76, is a useful early list. [**54**] F. B. Steck, *A Tentative Guide to Historical Materials on the Spanish Borderlands* (Philadelphia, Catholic Historical Society of Philadelphia, 1943), covers the history of Florida to 1819, of Texas to 1836, of New Mexico, Arizona, and California to 1846, and of Louisiana between 1763 and 1803.

[**55**] Adams, E. B., *A Bio-Bibliography of Franciscan Authors in Colonial Central America* (Washington, Pubns. of the Academy of American Franciscan History, 1953).

[**55a**] Cowan, R. E. and R. G., *A Bibliography of the History of California, 1510–1930* (3 vols., San Francisco, J. H. Nash, 1933).

[**56**] Cox, E. G., *A Reference Guide to the Literature of Travel, including voyages, geographical descriptions, adventures, shipwrecks and expeditions. Vol. ii.*

The New World (Seattle, Univ. of Washington Pubns. in Language and Literature, 1938).

[57] Geiger, M. J., *A Biographical Dictionary of the Franciscans in Spanish Florida and Cuba, 1528-1841* (Paterson, N.J., St. Anthony Guild Press, 1940).

[58] Harrisse, Henry, *Biblioteca Americana Vetustissima. A description of works relating to America, published between 1492 and 1551* (New York, G. P. Philes, 1866). *Additions* (Paris, Tross, 1872). Reprinted Leipzig, Schmidt and Guenther, 1921.

[58a] Medina, J. T., 'Critical Notes on Sources', *Hispanic American Historical Review*, iv (1921), 783-99.

Freely translated by C. K. Jones from the author's *Biblioteca Hispano-Americana (1493-1810)*.

[58b] Streeter, T. W., *Bibliography of Texas, 1795-1845* (2 vols., Harvard Univ. Press, 1955).

[59] Wagner, H. R., *The Spanish Southwest, 1542-1794. An annotated bibliography* (2 vols., Albuquerque, Quivira Society, 1937).

See also Cole [31] and Thomas [35].

DIPLOMATIC HISTORY

[60] S. F. Bemis and G. G. Griffin, *Guide to the Diplomatic History of the United States, 1775-1921* (Washington, Govt. Printing Office, 1935), is in part also a guide to the diplomatic history of Latin America.

[61] Bradley, P., *A Bibliography of the Monroe Doctrine, 1919-1929* (London, London School of Economics, 1929).

[62] Marchant, A., *Boundaries of the Latin American Republics, an annotated list of documents, 1493-1943* (Washington, Dept. of State, 1944).

[63] Meyer, H. H. B., *List of References on the Monroe Doctrine* (Washington, Govt. Printing Office, 1919).

[64] Morrison, H. A., *List of Books and of Articles in Periodicals relating to interoceanic canal and railway routes (Nicaragua; Panama, Darien, and the valley of the Atrato; Tehuantepec and Honduras; Suez Canal)* (Washington, Govt. Printing Office, 1900).

7. LAW AND LEGAL LITERATURE

[65] E. M. Borchard's *Guide to the Law and Legal Literature of Argentina, Brazil and Chile* (Washington, Govt. Printing Office) appeared in 1917. It has been supplemented by [66] H. L,

Clagett, *A Guide to the Law and Legal Literature of Argentina, 1917–1946* (Washington, Library of Congress, 1948), and her **[67]** *A Guide to the Law and Legal Literature of Chile, 1917–1946 (ibid.,* 1947). The Library of Congress has also produced guides to the law and legal literatures of the following countries: **[68]** *Bolivia* (H. L. Clagett, 1947); **[69]** *Colombia* (R. C. Backus and P. J. Eder, 1943); **[70]** *Cuba, the Dominican Republic and Haiti* (C. M. Bishop and A. M. Marchant, 1944); **[71]** *Ecuador* (H. L. Clagett, 1947); **[72]** *Mexico* (J. T. Vance and H. L. Clagett, 1945); **[73]** *the Mexican States* (H. L. Clagett, 1947); **[74]** *Paraguay* (H. L. Clagett, 1947); **[75]** *Peru* (H. L. Clagett, 1947); **[76]** *Uruguay* (H. L. Clagett, 1947); and **[77]** *Venezuela* (H. L. Clagett, 1947). The American Foreign Law Association published **[78]** Edward Schuster's *Guide to the Law and Legal Literature of Central American Republics* (New York) in 1937.

[79] Bishop, C. M., *Legal Codes of the Latin American Republics* (Washington, Govt. Printing Office, 1942).

8. LITERATURE, THE ARTS, FOLKLORE

[80] R. C. Smith and E. Wilder, *Guide to the Art of Latin America* (Washington, Library of Congress, 1948), and **[81]** Gilbert Chase, *A Guide to Latin American Music* (Washington, Library of Congress, 1945), are indispensable.

For the student of literature and letters there are **[82]** *A Working Bibliography of Latin American Literature* (St. Augustine, Fla., Inter-American Bibliographical and Library Association, 1952) by J. M. Topete and a series of bibliographies sponsored by the Harvard Council on Hispano-American Studies and published by the Harvard University Press. In this series **[83]** A. L. Coester, *A Tentative Bibliography of the Belles-Lettres of the Argentine Republic,* appeared in 1933, and there are similar volumes for **[84]** *Bolivia* (S. E. Leavitt, 1933); **[85]** *Brazil* (J. D. M. Ford, *et al.,* 1931); **[86]** *Central America* (H. G. Doyle, 1935); **[87]** *Chile* (A. Torres-Ríoseco, 1935); **[88]** *Colombia* (S. E. Leavitt and C. García Prada, 1934); **[89]** *Cuba* (J. D. M. Ford and M. I. Raphael, 1933); **[90]** *Ecuador* (G. Rivera, 1934); **[91]** *Panama* (H. G. Doyle, 1934); **[92]** *Paraguay* (M. I. Raphael and J. D. M. Ford, 1934); **[93]** *Peru* (S. E. Leavitt, 1932); **[94]** *Santo Domingo* (S. M. Waxman, 1931); **[95]** *Uruguay* (A. L. Coester, 1931), and **[96]** *Venezuela* (S. M. Waxman, 1935).

[97] Boggs, R. S., *Bibliography of Latin American Folklore* (New York, H. W. Wilson, 1940).

[98] Grismer, R. L., ed., *A Reference Index to Twelve Thousand Spanish-American Authors. A guide to the literature of Spanish America* (New York, H. W. Wilson, 1939).

[99] Jones, W. K., *Latin American Writers in English Translation, a tentative bibliography* (Washington, Pan American Union, 1944).

[100] Leavitt, S. E., *Hispano-American Literature in the United States. A bibliography of translations and criticism* (Harvard Univ. Press, 1932).

[101] Nichols, M. W., *A Bibliographical Guide to Materials on American Spanish* (Harvard Univ. Press, 1941).

See also Luquiens [33].

III

PERIODICALS

HISTORICAL, LITERARY, AND BIBLIOGRAPHICAL

[**102**] The *Hispanic American Historical Review* (Baltimore, 1918–22; Durham, North Carolina, 1926–) has been the major instrument in promoting the professionalization of Latin American historical studies in the United States. There is a guide to its contents between 1918 and 1945 in Butler, *Guide* [50]. [**103**] *The Americas. A Quarterly Review of Inter-American Cultural History* (Washington, 1944–) is the journal of the Academy of American Franciscan History. [**104**] *Inter-American Economic Affairs* (Washington, 1947–) caters for the economic historian as well as for the economist.

[**105**] *Bulletin of Hispanic Studies* [formerly *Bulletin of Spanish Studies*] (Liverpool, Institute of Hispanic Studies, 1923–).

[**106**] *Hispania* (Wallingford, Conn., American Association of Teachers of Spanish and Portuguese, 1918–).

[**107**] *Hispanic Review* (Philadelphia, Univ. of Pennsylvania Press, 1933–).

[**108**] *Review of Inter-American Bibliography* (Washington, Pan American Union, 1951–).

CURRENT AFFAIRS

[**109**] The *Hispanic American Report* [formerly *Hispanic World Report*] (Stanford Univ. Press, 1948–) provides a monthly survey of current developments in Latin America. *Inter-American Economic Affairs* [104] is issued quarterly and [**109a**] *The Economic Bulletin for Latin America* (United Nations, 1956–) is a semiannual publication. [**110**] The monthly *Américas* and [**111**] the quarterly *Annals of the Organization of American States* replaced in 1949 the former *Bulletin* of the Pan American Union (Washington, D.C., 1893–1948). Useful articles appear from time to time in [**112**] *Foreign Affairs* (New York, Council on Foreign Relations, 1922–), in [**113**] *Foreign Policy Reports* (New York, Foreign Policy Association, 1931–), in [**114**] *International Conciliation* (New York, Carnegie Endowment for International Peace,

1907–), and in the two journals of the Royal Institute of International Affairs, London, namely [**115**] *International Affairs* (1922–39; 1944–) and [**116**] *The World Today* (1945–), which continues the *Bulletin of International News* (1922–45). See also the publications of the United States Departments of State, Agriculture, and Commerce, together with those of the various agencies of the United Nations organization and of the Organization of American States. For Bank reports, Chamber of Commerce publications, and commercial periodicals [**117**] D. M. Phelps, 'Sources of Current Economic Information on Latin America', *Handbook of Latin American Studies*, iii, for 1937 [8], provides a still helpful list.

IV

GENERAL HISTORIES
AND COMPREHENSIVE WORKS

TEXT-BOOKS AND GENERAL HISTORIES

Among general text-books [**118**] J. F. Rippy, *Historical Evolution of Hispanic America* (3rd ed., rev., New York, Crofts, 1945), is one of the more original, and [**119**] F. A. Kirkpatrick, *Latin America: a brief history* (Cambridge Univ. Press, 1938), one of the more stimulating. For further examples see [**120**] J. F. Bannon and P. M. Dunne, *Latin America: an historical survey* (Milwaukee, Bruce Publishing Co., 1947), [**121**] D. G. Munro, *The Latin American Republics: a history* (2nd ed., rev., New York, Appleton-Century, 1950), [**122**] W. S. Robertson, *History of the Latin American Nations* (3rd ed., rev., New York, Appleton-Century, 1943), [**122a**] A. B. Thomas, *Latin America. A history* (New York, Macmillan, 1956); [**123**] A. Curtis Wilgus, *The Development of Hispanic America* (New York, Farrar and Rinehart, 1941), [**124**] M. W. Williams, R. J. Bartlett, and R. E. Miller, *The People and Politics of Latin America* (4th ed., Boston, Ginn and Co., 1955), and [**124a**] D. E. Worcester and W. G. Schaeffer, *The Growth and Culture of Latin America* (New York, Oxford Univ. Press, 1956). Older volumes include [**125**] T. C. Dawson, *The South American Republics* (2 vols., New York and London, Putnam's, 1903-4), and [**126**] W. R. Shepherd's short sketch, *Central and South America* (London, Williams and Norgate: New York, Holt, 1914).

[**127**] J. A. Crow, *The Epic of Latin America* (New York, Doubleday, 1946), and [**128**] Hubert Herring, *A History of Latin America from the beginnings to the present* (New York, Knopf, 1955: London, Cape, 1956), are comprehensive surveys addressed to the general reader.

[**128a**] W. L. Schurz, *This New World: The Civilization of Latin America* (New York, Dutton, 1954: London, Allen and Unwin, 1956), is primarily concerned with the three centuries of Spanish colonial rule.

Source Books

SOURCE BOOKS

[**129**] Arciniegas, Germán, ed., *The Green Continent. A comprehensive view of Latin America by its leading writers* (New York, Knopf, 1944).

[**130**] Cleven, N. A. N., ed., *Readings in Hispanic American History* (Boston, Ginn and Co., 1927).

[**130a**] Keen, Benjamin, ed., *Readings in Latin-American Civilization* (New York, Houghton Mifflin, 1955).

[**131**] Plenn, Abel, *The Southern Americas: a new chronicle* (New York, Creative Age Press, 1948).

[**132**] Wilgus, A. C., ed., *Readings in Latin American Civilization* (New York, Barnes and Noble, 1946).

COLLECTED ESSAYS

[**133**] H. E. Bolton, *Wider Horizons of American History* (New York, Appleton-Century, 1939), contains four of the author's previously published essays, including his well-known 'The Epic of Greater America' and 'The Mission as a Frontier Institution in the Spanish American Colonies', both of which originally appeared in the *American Historical Review*. [**134**] *Greater America. Essays in honor of Herbert Eugene Bolton* (Univ. of California Press, 1945) consists of twenty-seven essays by different hands, ranging, in area, from Patagonia to Alaska, and, in time, from the sixteenth century to the end of the nineteenth century, and includes, besides, a bibliography of Bolton's writings and a bibliography of the writings of Bolton's pupils. The twenty essays in [**135**] *Hispanic American Essays: a memorial to James Alexander Robertson* (edited by A. Curtis Wilgus, Univ. of North Carolina Press, 1942) also range over the whole field of Hispanic American history and are a tribute to the scholar and bibliographer who edited the *Hispanic American Historical Review* for its first eighteen years. Reference should also be made to the valuable papers collected together in [**136**] *Concerning Latin American Culture* (edited by C. C. Griffin, Columbia Univ. Press, 1940), and to the essays in English, as well as in Spanish and Portuguese, in the two volumes issued by the Comisión de Historia of the Instituto Panamericano de Geografía e Historia, namely, [**137**] *Estudios de Historia de América* (Mexico, D.F., 1948), and [**138**] *Ensayos sobre la Historia del Nuevo Mundo* (Mexico, D.F., 1951).

V

THE LAND AND THE ENVIRONMENT

[**139**] Preston E. James, *Latin America* (2nd ed., rev., New York, Odyssey Press, 1950), and [**140**] Robert S. Platt, *Latin America: countrysides and united regions* (New York and London, McGraw-Hill, 1942), are outstanding. [**141**] J. L. Rich, *The Face of South America: an aerial traverse* (New York, American Geographical Society, 1942), is an excellent collection of photographs with descriptive notes, and [**142**] A. C. Wilgus, *Latin America in Maps* (New York, Barnes and Noble, 1943), is a compilation designed to illustrate the history as well as the geography and economy of the Latin American area. [**142a**] Hans Mann, *South America* (London, Thames and Hudson, 1957), is notable for its illustrations.

For the effects of high altitudes see Monge [1594], and, for the environment of the tropics, Price [1151] and [**142b**] Marston Bates, *Where Winter Never Comes: a study of man and nature in the tropics* (New York, Scribner's, 1952).

[**143**] Carlson, F. A., *Geography of Latin America* (3rd ed., rev., New York, Prentice-Hall, 1952).

[**144**] Jones, C. F., *South America* (New York, Holt: London, Allen and Unwin, 1930).

[**145**] Shanahan, E. W., *South America: an economic and regional geography* . . . (9th ed., rev., London, Methuen, 1953).

[**146**] Whitbeck, R. H., Williams, F. E., and Christians, W. F., *Economic Geography of South America* (3rd ed., New York and London, McGraw-Hill, 1940).

VI
ANCIENT PEOPLES AND CULTURES

THE AMERICAN INDIAN: GENERAL

The work done in the fields of archaeology, anthropology, and ethnology is too extensive and too specialized for adequate treatment here. There is an excellent guide to much of it in [147] Juan Comas, *Bibliografía Selectiva de las Culturas Indígenas de América* (Instituto Panamericano de Geografía e Historia, Comisión de Historia, Mexico, 1953), which lists more than 2,000 items. The *Handbook of Latin American Studies* [8] records current investigations. [148] The *Handbook of South American Indians*, edited by Julian H. Steward (6 vols., Bureau of American Ethnology, Smithsonian Institution, Washington, 1946–50), is a major work of reference.

[149] Hannah M. Wormington, *Origins* (Program of the History of America, Instituto Panamericano de Geografía e Historia, Comisión de Historia, Mexico, 1953), provides a brief but elegant summary of the present state of knowledge on the origins of the American Indian, and [150] E. H. Sellards, *Early Man in America. A study in prehistory* (Univ. of Texas Press, 1952), discusses early 'locality records'. [151] Clark Wissler, *The American Indian. An introduction to the anthropology of the New World* (3rd ed., New York, Oxford Univ. Press, 1938), has attained the status of a classic. [152] John Collier, *The Indians of the Americas* (New York, W. W. Norton, 1947), is concerned both with pre-conquest history and with post-conquest history. [153] Rafael Karsten deals with *The Civilization of the South American Indians, with special reference to magic and religion* (New York, Knopf: London, Kegan Paul, 1926), and [154] Pál Kelemen surveys the field of pre-Colombian art in *Medieval American Art* (2 vols., New York, Macmillan, 1943; new edition in one vol., 1956), magnificent and indispensable volumes.

[155] Jenness, Diamond, ed., *The American Aborigines. Their origin and antiquity* (Univ. of Toronto Press, 1933).

[156] MacGowan, Kenneth, *Early Man in the New World* (New York, Macmillan, 1950).

[156a] McQuown, N. A., 'The Indigenous Languages of Latin America', *American Anthropologist*, lvii (June 1955), 501–70.

[157] Nordenskiöld, Erland, 'Origin of the Indian Civilizations in South America', *Comparative Ethnographical Studies*, ix (Göteborg, 1931).

[158] Radin, Paul, *Indians of South America* (New York, Doubleday, 1942).

MEXICO AND CENTRAL AMERICA

The greater contributions of the nineteenth century include [159] Edward King, Viscount Kingsborough, *Antiquities of Mexico* (9 vols. in folio, London, 1830–48), eccentric in purpose and ruinous in publication; the classic works of J. L. Stephens, illustrated by Frederick Catherwood, [160] *Incidents of Travel in Central America, Chiapas and Yucatan* (2 vols., New York, 1841. New edition by R. L. Predmore, 2 vols., Rutgers Univ. Press, 1949), and [161] *Incidents of Travel in Yucatan* (2 vols., New York, 1843); and, in the vast *Biologia Centrali-Americana*, edited by F. D. Godman and Osbert Salvin, the researches of [162] A. P. Maudslay, *Archaeology. Biologia Centrali-Americana* (5 vols., London, Porter and Dulau, 1889–1902). On Stephens and Catherwood as the pioneers of Maya studies see [163] Victor W. von Hagen, *The Maya Explorer: John Lloyd Stephens and the lost cities of Central America and Yucatan* (Univ. of Oklahoma Press, 1947), and, by the same author, [164] *Frederick Catherwood, Archt.* (New York, Oxford Univ. Press, 1950), which reproduces [165] Catherwood's splendid *Views of Ancient Monuments in Central America, Chiapas and Yucatan*, originally published in 1844.

Of early Spanish sources [166] the famous *Relación de las Cosas de Yucatan* of Bishop Diego de Landa is available in a splendidly annotated translation by A. M. Tozzer (Cambridge, Mass., *Papers* of the Peabody Museum, vol. xviii, 1941), and [167] in an edition by William Gates, *Yucatan before and after the Conquest by Friar Diego de Landa* (Baltimore, The Maya Society, 1937). A part of [168] Bernardino de Sahagún's sixteenth-century *Historia General de las Cosas de Nueva España* has been translated by Mrs. F. Bandelier under the title of *A History of Ancient Mexico* (Nashville, Fisk Univ. Press, 1932). The definitive modern edition is [169] Bernardino de Sahagún, *General History of the Things of New Spain. Florentine Codex* (translated from the Aztec into English, with notes and illustrations by Arthur J. O. Anderson and Charles E. Dibble. Salt Lake City, Univ. of Utah Press, and Santa Fe, New

Mexico, School of American Research, 1950–). For Fray Toribio de Benavente, or Motolinía, *History of the Indians of New Spain*, see no. 269 and, for the account of the Anonymous Conqueror, no. 270.

[**170**] *Popol Vuh. The sacred book of the ancient Quiché Maya* (English version by Delia Goetz and Sylvanus G. Morley, from the Spanish translation of Adrián Recinos. Univ. of Oklahoma Press, 1950: London, William Hodge, 1951) is a remarkable example of ancient Indian literature, committed to writing, from oral tradition, in the mid-sixteenth century. Compare [**171**] *The Book of Chilam Balam of Chumayel* (translated and edited by R. L. Roys. Washington, Carnegie Institution, 1933).

[**172**] H. J. Spinden, *Ancient Civilizations of Mexico and Central America* (3rd ed., rev., New York, American Museum of Natural History, 1928), provides a general introduction to a field of study in which new discoveries are constantly taking place. For the Valley of Mexico and adjacent regions see more particularly [**173**] J. E. S. Thompson, *Mexico before Cortez. An account of the daily life, religion and ritual of the Aztecs and kindred peoples* (New York and London, Scribner's, 1933), which was itself complementary to [**174**] T. A. Joyce, *Mexican Archaeology* (London, Philip Lee Warner, 1914), and, a later and authoritative summation, [**175**] G. C. Vaillant, *Aztecs of Mexico* (New York, Doubleday, Doran, 1941). For the advances made in the interpretation of Mayan history compare the excellent monographs of [**176**] S. G. Morley, *The Ancient Maya* (3rd ed., rev., Stanford Univ. Press, 1956), and [**177**] J. E. S. Thompson, *The Rise and Fall of Maya Civilization* (Univ. of Oklahoma Press, 1954). See also Roys [263a].

Tatiana Proskouriakoff, [**178**] *An Album of Maya Architecture* (Washington, Carnegie Institution, 1946), and [**179**] *A Study of Classic Maya Sculpture* (Washington, Carnegie Institution, 1950), are outstanding. [**180**] H. J. Spinden, *A Study of Maya Art* (Cambridge, Mass., *Memoirs* of the Peabody Museum, vol. vi, 1913), and [**181**] T. A. Joyce, *Maya and Mexican Art* (London, Studio, 1927), are well known among older studies. [**182**] M. H. Saville, *The Goldsmith's Art in Ancient Mexico* (Museum of the American Indian, Heye Foundation, New York, 1920), is one of three books which the author devoted to Mexican arts and crafts.

[**183**] Barlow, R. H., *The Extent of the Empire of the Culhua Mexica* (Ibero-Americana, 28, Univ. of California Press, 1949). The Aztec empire.

[184] Joyce, T. A., *Central American and West Indian Archaeology* (London, Philip Lee Warner, 1916).

[185] *The Maya and their Neighbours* (New York and London, Appleton-Century, 1940). A symposium.

THE ANDEAN AREA

[186] W. C. Bennett and Junius B. Bird, *Andean Culture History* (New York, American Museum of Natural History, 1949), [186a] J. A. Mason, *The Ancient Civilizations of Peru* (Harmondsworth, Middlesex, Penguin Books, 1957), which contains an excellent bibliography, and the older volume of [187] P. A. Means, *Ancient Civilisations of the Andes* (New York and London, Scribner's, 1931), afford the best introductions to the pre-Spanish civilizations of the Andean area. See also [187a] G. H. S. Bushnell, *Peru* (London, Thames and Hudson, 1956), and, for Andean art, [188] W. C. Bennett, *Ancient Arts of the Andes* (New York, Museum of Modern Art: London, Putnam, 1954), and [189] H. Ubbelohde-Doering, *The Art of Ancient Peru* (London, Zwemmer, 1952).

[190] C. R. Markham, ed., *Narratives of the Rites and Laws of the Yncas* (Hakluyt Soc. Pubns., 1st series, No. 48, London, 1873), contains the accounts of Cristóbal de Molina of Cuzco, Juan de Santa Cruz Pachacuti, Francisco de Avila, and the Licentiate Juan Polo de Ondegardo. For the contrasting histories of the Inca Garcilaso de la Vega and of Pedro Sarmiento de Gamboa see nos. 313 and 314, and, for [191] the seventeenth-century *Memorias Antiguas Historiales del Peru* of Fernando Montesinos, the edition by P. A. Means (Hakluyt Soc. Pubns., 2nd series, No. 48, London, 1920). See also nos. 308–12.

[192] Bandelier, A. F. A., *The Islands of Titicaca and Koati* (New York, Hispanic Society of America, 1910).

[193] Bingham, H., *Machu Picchu: a citadel of the Incas* (Yale Univ. Press, 1930).

[194] Joyce, T. A., *South American Archaeology* (London, Macmillan and Philip Lee Warner, 1912).

[194a] Posnansky, A., *Tihuanacu. The cradle of American man* (2 vols., New York, J. J. Augustin, 1945).
Valuable for its descriptive qualities, not for its theoretical discussions.

VII
THE SPANISH EMPIRE IN AMERICA

1. GENERAL

HISTORIES AND ESSAYS

[**195**] William Robertson's classic *History of America* (2 vols., London, 1777; 5th and definitive edition, 3 vols., London, 1788) was the first modern history of Spanish America in the English language. It is primarily concerned with the great age of discovery and conquest, but Book VIII contains a review of Spanish colonial policy and administration from the foundation of the empire to the Bourbon reforms of the eighteenth century. See [**196**] R. A. Humphreys, *William Robertson and his History of America* (The Canning House Annual Lecture, London, Hispanic and Luso-Brazilian Councils, 1954). Among nineteenth-century works [**197**] R. G. Watson, *Spanish and Portuguese South America during the Colonial Period* (2 vols., London, 1884), should not be entirely forgotten, and [**198**] Justin Winsor, ed., *Narrative and Critical History of America* (8 vols., Boston, 1884–9), contains a wealth of bibliographical and critical information.

[**199**] R. B. Merriman, *The Rise of the Spanish Empire in the Old World and the New* (4 vols., New York, Macmillan, 1918–34), is a magisterial work covering the reigns of Ferdinand and Isabella, Philip I, Charles V, and Philip II. [**200**] E. G. Bourne's admirable *Spain in America, 1450–1580* ('American Nation Series', vol. iii, New York and London, Harper, 1904) is wider in scope than its title implies. [**201**] C. H. Haring, *The Spanish Empire in America* (rev. ed., New York, Oxford Univ. Press, 1952), is an important 'institutional' history, which sums up recent research and is itself the fruit of long years of research and teaching, and [**202**] Bailey W. Diffie's very useful *Latin American Civilization: colonial period* (Harrisburg, Pa., Stackpole Sons, 1945), covering all aspects of the colonial period, though a text-book, is also something more. Salvador de Madariaga's two volumes, [**203**] *The Rise of the Spanish American Empire*, and [**204**] *The Fall of the Spanish American Empire* (London, Hollis and Carter, 1947), are almost in the nature of a sustained *apologia*. The empire is briefly placed in its

larger setting by [**205**] J. H. Parry, *Europe and a Wider World,
1415–1715* (London, Hutchinson's Univ. Library, 1949).

[**206**] Bernard Moses, *The Establishment of Spanish Rule in
America* (New York and London, Putnam's, 1898), was a pioneer
work designed 'to offer an introduction to the neglected half of
American history'. [**207**] His *The Spanish Dependencies in South
America* (2 vols., New York, Harper: London, Smith, Elder,
1914) consists of studies of various phases and aspects of colonial
life and [**208**] his last brief book, *Spain Overseas* (New York,
Hispanic Society of America, 1929), is a 'marginal commentary
on some sections of the general history of Spanish America', more
particularly during the colonial period. [**209**] Silvio Zavala, *New
Viewpoints on the Spanish Colonization of America* (Univ. of Pennsylvania Press, 1943), is a suggestive collection of essays, and
[**210**] Wilhelm Roscher, *The Spanish Colonial System* (New York,
Holt, 1914; G. E. Stechert, 1944), is a chapter, translated by
E. G. Bourne, from Roscher's *Kolonien, Kolonialpolitik und Aus-
wanderung* (3rd ed., Leipzig, 1885). See also Griffin [136] and
Schurz [128a].

[**210a**] Bishko, C. J., 'The Iberian Background of Latin American
History: Recent Progress and Continuing Problems', *Hispanic American
Historical Review*, xxxvi (1956), 50–80.
An invaluable historiographical and bibliographical survey.

[**211**] Chapman, C. E., *Colonial Hispanic America: a history* (New York,
Macmillan, 1933).

[**212**] Wilgus, A. C., ed., *Colonial Hispanic America* (Washington, George
Washington Univ. Press, 1936).

CONTEMPORARY NARRATIVES, HISTORIES,
AND DESCRIPTIONS

The great series of publications issued by [**213**] the Hakluyt
Society (London), which celebrated its centenary in 1946, contains translations of a number of the most important early
chronicles and histories relating to Spanish America, as well as
narratives of voyages and collections of documents. The Society
has also reprinted [**214**] Richard Hakluyt, *The Principal Naviga-
tions, Voyages, Traffiques and Discoveries of the English Nation made
by sea or over-land to the remote and farthest distant quarters of the earth
at any time within the compasse of these 1600 yeeres* (12 vols., Glasgow,
1903–5), originally published between 1598 and 1600, and [**215**]

the 1625 edition of Samuel Purchas, *Hakluytus Posthumus, or Purchas his Pilgrimes, contayning a history of the world in sea voyages and land travells by Englishmen and others* (20 vols., Glasgow, 1905–7). For other collections of voyages and for the literature of travel in general see Cox [56].

[**216**] The Cortés Society published five volumes at New York between 1917 and 1924 in its series of *Documents and Narratives concerning the Discovery and Conquest of Latin America,* and the series was revived at the University of California in 1942. [**217**] The Quivira Society, now also at the University of California, began life in 1929 and has concerned itself with sources for the history of the American southwest.

Possibly to be regarded as the first history of America, [**218**] *De Orbe Novo, the Eight Decades of Peter Martyr d'Anghera* (Pietro Martire d'Anghiera) is available in a translation by F. A. MacNutt (2 vols., New York and London, Putnam's, 1912). The great sixteenth-century histories of Gonzalo Fernández de Oviedo and of Bartolomé de Las Casas and the seventeenth-century history of Antonio de Herrera still await modern translations, though of Herrera there is an eighteenth-century English version by John Stevens, [**219**] *The General History of the Vast Continent and Islands of America* (6 vols., London, 1725–6). [**220**] José de Acosta's *The Natural and Moral History of the Indies* (1590), in the 1604 version of Edward Grimston, has been edited for the Hakluyt Society (2 vols., 1st series, Nos. 60 and 61, London, 1880) by Sir Clements R. Markham, and [**221**] Antonio Vázquez de Espinosa's *Compendium and Description of the West Indies,* which reviews the empire in the early seventeenth century, has been translated and edited by C. U. Clark (Washington, Smithsonian Institution, 1942). On the former see [**221a**] T. Hornberger, 'Acosta's *Historia Natural y Moral de las Indias:* a guide to the source and the growth of the American scientific tradition', *Studies in English, 1939* (Univ. of Texas Press, 1939), pp. 139–62. For guides to contemporary literature in general consult Wilgus [49], Means [52], and [**222**] Charmion Shelby, 'The *Cronistas* and their Contemporaries: recent editions of works of the sixteenth and seventeenth centuries', *Hispanic American Historical Review,* xxix (1949), 295–317.

For an understanding of the empire at the end of the eighteenth century [**223**] Alexander von Humboldt's monumental *Political Essay on the Kingdom of New Spain* (translated and edited by John

Black, 4 vols., London, 1811), and [**224**] his *Personal Narrative of Travels to the Equinoctial Regions of the New Continent during the years 1799–1804* (translated by Helen Maria Williams, 7 vols., London, 1814–29) are indispensable.

WORKS OF REFERENCE

[**225**] Davenport, F. G., ed., *European Treaties bearing on the History of the United States and its Dependencies* (4 vols., Washington, 1917–37). Vol. iv, covering the years 1716–1815, edited by C. O. Paullin.

[**226**] Thompson, G. A., *The Geographical and Historical Dictionary of America and the West Indies* (5 vols., London, 1812–15). A translation, with additions, of the great *Diccionario* of Antonio de Alcedo (5 vols., Madrid, 1786–9).

2. DISCOVERY AND CONQUEST

GENERAL

See Robertson [195], Merriman [199], Bourne [200], and Diffie [202]. The classic story is the splendid narrative of W. H. Prescott, [**227**] *History of the Conquest of Mexico* (3 vols., New York, 1843), and [**228**] *History of the Conquest of Peru* (2 vols., New York, 1847). There is a short account in [**229**] I. B. Richman, *The Spanish Conquerors* ('Chronicles of America', vol. ii, Yale Univ. Press, 1919), and a brilliant summary in [**230**] F. A. Kirkpatrick, *The Spanish Conquistadores* (London, Black, 1934; reprinted 1946). [**231**] Sir Arthur Helps, *The Spanish Conquest in America* (4 vols., 1855–61; new ed., with notes by M. Oppenheim, New York and London, Lane, 1900–4), is particularly concerned with the problems of the status of the Indians and of slavery.

THE 'ENTERPRISE OF THE INDIES'

On the European background of American discovery see [**232**] C. R. Beazley, *The Dawn of Modern Geography* (3 vols., Oxford, Clarendon Press, 1897–1906; reprinted New York, Peter Smith, 1949), [**233**] A. H. Lybyer, 'The Ottoman Turks and the Routes of Oriental Trade', *English Historical Review*, xxx (1915), 577–88, together with [**234**] his 'The Influence of the Rise of the Ottoman Turks upon the Routes of Oriental Trade', American Historical Association, *Annual Report*, 1914 (2 vols., Washington, Govt. Printing Office, 1916), i, 127–33, which dissipate a hoary legend, [**235**] Charles Verlinden, 'Italian Influence in Iberian Colonization', *Hispanic American Historical Review*, xxxiii (1953), 199–211, and Bishko [210a]. [**236**] *Portuguese Voyages to America in the Fifteenth Century* are examined by S. E. Morison (Harvard Univ. Press, 1940), and [**237**] Edgar Prestage, *The Portuguese Pioneers* (London, Black, 1933), discusses the general movement of Portuguese expansion.

For the letters and journals of Columbus see [**238**] Cecil Jane, *Select Documents illustrating the Four Voyages of Columbus* (2 vols., Hakluyt Soc. Pubns., 2nd series, Nos. 65 and 70, London, 1930, 1933), and [**239**] his edition of *The Voyages of Christopher Columbus* (London, Argonaut Press, 1930), together with [**240**] S. E. Morison's discussion of *The Second Voyage of Christopher Columbus* (Oxford, Clarendon Press, 1939), and [**241**] J. B. Thacher's monumental *Christopher Columbus: his life and work* (3 vols., New York and London, Putnam's, 1903–4). [**241a**] *The Geographical Conceptions of Columbus* are discussed by G. E. Nunn (New York, American Geographical Society, 1924).

[**242**] Washington Irving, *The History of the Life and Voyages of Christopher Columbus* (4 vols., London, 1828), provoked the remark of Southey that it presented 'a most remarkable portion of history in a popular form' and was 'therefore likely to succeed'. Only with the years were its pretensions to independent scholarship exposed. The most distinguished modern biography, among many biographies, is [**243**] S. E. Morison, *Admiral of the Ocean Sea: a life of Christopher Columbus* (2 vols., Boston, Little, Brown; also 1 vol. ed., abridged; 1942). But see also [**244**] Salvador de Madariaga, *Christopher Columbus* (rev. ed., London, Hollis and Carter, 1949), and [**245**] C. E. Nowell, 'The Columbus Question. A survey of recent literature and present opinion', *American Historical Review*, xliv (July 1939), 802–22. [**246**] Otto Schoenrich, *The Legacy of Christopher Columbus* (2 vols., Glendale, Calif., Arthur H. Clark, 1949–50), is concerned with disputes and litigation among the heirs of Columbus in respect of the privileges and rights granted to him.

[**247**] *The Letters of Amerigo Vespucci*, who gave his name to the New World, have been edited by Sir Clements R. Markham (Hakluyt Soc. Pubns., 1st series, No. 90, London, 1894). For modern biographies of Vespucci see [**248**] F. J. Pohl, *Amerigo Vespucci. Pilot Major* (Columbia Univ. Press, 1944), and [**248a**] Germán Arciniegas, *Amerigo and the New World: the life and times of Amerigo Vespucci* (New York, Knopf, 1955), and for further

references to the literature of discovery in general [**249**] Oscar Handlin, *et al.*, *Harvard Guide to American History* (Belknap Press, Harvard Univ. Press, 1954).

MEXICO AND MIDDLE AMERICA

See Prescott [227], Bourne [200], and [**250**] H. I. Priestley, *The Coming of the White Man, 1492–1848* (New York, Macmillan, 1929). H. H. Bancroft, [**251**] *History of Mexico* (6 vols., San Francisco, 1883–8), and [**252**] *History of Central America* (3 vols., San Francisco, 1883–7), contain abundant bibliographical notes and are invaluable as works of reference.

[**253**] C. L. G. Anderson, *Life and Letters of Vasco Núñez de Balboa* (New York, F. H. Revell, 1941), is a semi-popular treatment, supplemented by [**253a**] Kathleen Romoli, *Balboa of Darién. Discoverer of the Pacific* (New York, Doubleday, 1953). On Cortés see [**254**] F. A. MacNutt, *Fernando Cortés and the Conquest of Mexico* (New York and London, Putnam's, 1908), which is addressed to the general reader, [**255**] Salvador de Madariaga, *Hernan Cortés, conqueror of Mexico* (2nd ed., London, Hodder and Stoughton, 1955), a semi-fictionalized biography, and [**256**] H. R. Wagner, *The Rise of Fernando Cortés* (Berkeley, Calif., The Cortés Society, 1944). [**256a**] C. H. Gardiner, *Naval Power in the Conquest of Mexico* (Univ. of Texas Press, 1956), examines the reduction of the island city of Tenochtitlán. The work of Alvarado in Mexico and Guatemala is discussed by [**257**] J. E. Kelly, *Pedro de Alvarado, conquistador* (Princeton Univ. Press, 1932). Sauer [385] treats of the conquest of Colima.

[**258**] H. R. Wagner, 'Three Studies on the Same Subject', *Hispanic American Historical Review*, xxv (1945), 155–211, discusses the life, family, and writings of Bernal Díaz del Castillo, and there is a characteristic 'literary' biography, [**259**] by R. B. Cunninghame Graham, *Bernal Díaz del Castillo* (London, Nash: New York, Dodd, Mead, 1915).

[**260**] R. S. Chamberlain, *The Conquest and Colonization of Yucatan, 1517–1550* (Washington, Carnegie Institution, 1948), and [**261**] his *The Conquest and Colonization of Honduras, 1502–1550* (Washington, Carnegie Institution, 1953), are important detailed studies. See also [**262**] P. A. Means, *History of the Spanish Conquest of Yucatan and the Itzas* (Cambridge, Mass., *Papers* of the Peabody Museum, vol. vii, 1917), [**263**] F. Blom, *The Conquest of Yucatan* (Boston, Houghton Mifflin, 1936), and [**263a**] R. L. Roys, *The*

Indian Background of Colonial Yucatan (Washington, Carnegie Institution, 1943). [**264**] Ricardo Fernández Guardia, *History of the Discovery and Conquest of Costa Rica* (New York, Crowell, 1913), covers in part also the later colonial period.

Among contemporary narratives [**265**] Bernal Díaz del Castillo, *The True History of the Conquest of New Spain*, is available in A. P. Maudslay's translation for the Hakluyt Society (5 vols., 2nd series, Nos. 23, 24, 25, 30, and 40, London, 1908–16), and [**266**] in Maudslay's abridged edition, *The Discovery and Conquest of Mexico, 1517–1521* (London, Routledge, 1928: New York, Farrar, Straus, and Cudahy, 1956). [**267**] *The Letters of Cortés* have been edited by F. A. MacNutt (2 vols., New York and London, Putnam's, 1908). [**268**] Francisco López de Gómara's *The Conquest of the Weast India* (a sixteenth-century translation of that part of Gómara's history which relates to the conquest of Mexico) has been reproduced in facsimile by H. I. Priestley (New York, Scholars' Facsimiles and Reprints, 1940), and [**269**] *Motolinía's History of the Indians of New Spain* has been translated and edited by F. B. Steck (Washington, Academy of American Franciscan History, 1951). See also the *Documents and Narratives concerning the Discovery and Conquest of Latin America* published by the Cortés Society, which include [**270**] M. H. Saville's edition of the *Narrative of some things of New Spain . . .* written by the Anonymous Conqueror (New York, 1917), [**271**] *An Account of the Conquest of Guatemala in 1524 by Pedro de Alvarado*, ed. S. J. Mackie (New York, 1924), [**272**] *The Discovery of New Spain in 1518, by Juan de Grijalva*, ed. H. R. Wagner (Berkeley, Calif., 1942), and [**273**] *The Discovery of Yucatan, by Francisco Hernández de Córdoba*, ed. H. R. Wagner (Berkeley, Calif., 1942).

[**274**] Of the famous seventeenth-century history of Antonio de Solís there is a partial eighteenth-century translation. *The History of the Conquest of Mexico by the Spaniards* (London, 1724).

NORTHERN EXPLORATION TO 1542

See Mecham [53] and Steck [54]. [**275**] H. E. Bolton, *The Spanish Borderlands* ('Chronicles of America', vol. xxiii, Yale Univ. Press, 1921), [**276**] J. B. Brebner, *The Explorers of North America, 1492–1806* (London, Black: New York, Macmillan, 1933; reprinted 1955), and Priestley [250], all deal with the later as well as with the earlier history of exploration to the north of the Valley of Mexico. See also [**277**] W. Lowery, *The Spanish Settle-*

ments within the Present Limits of the United States (2nd ed., 2 vols., New York and London, Putnam's, 1911), which covers the years 1513 to 1574, [**278**] H. R. Wagner, *Spanish Voyages to the Northwest Coast of America in the Sixteenth Century* (San Francisco, California Historical Society, 1929), and [**279**] the brief essay of Carl Sauer, *The Road to Cíbola* (Ibero-Americana, 3, Univ. of California Press, 1932).

[**280**] Morris Bishop, *The Odyssey of Cabeza de Vaca* (New York and London, Century, 1933), is a general biography. [**281**] Cleve Hallenbeck, *Alvar Núñez Cabeza de Vaca* (Glendale, Calif., A. H. Clark, 1940), is a detailed study of 'the journey and route of the first European to cross the continent of North America, 1534–1536'. For the De Soto expedition of 1538–43 see [**282**] E. G. Bourne's edition of the *Narratives of the Career of Hernando de Soto in the Conquest of Florida*... (2 vols., New York, A. S. Barnes, 1904). There is a biography of De Soto [**283**] by T. Maynard, *De Soto and the Conquistadores* (New York, Longmans, Green, 1930), and another, of a still more popular kind, [**284**] by R. B. Cunninghame Graham, *Hernando de Soto* (London, Heinemann, 1903). [**285**] Cleve Hallenbeck discusses *The Journey of Fray Marcos de Niza* (Dallas, Univ. Press in Dallas, 1949). On the Coronado expedition see the early and important treatise [**286**] of G. P. Winship, *The Coronado Expedition, 1540–1542* (14th Annual Report of the Bureau of Ethnology, Washington, D.C., Govt. Printing Office, 1896), the massive study [**287**] of H. E. Bolton, *Coronado on the Turquoise Trail: knight of pueblos and plains* (Coronado Cuarto Centennial Pubns., vol. i, Univ. of New Mexico Press, 1949: also New York, Whittlesey House, 1949), and [**288**] A. G. Day, *Coronado's Quest. The discovery of the south-western states* (Univ. of California Press, 1940).

Besides Bourne [282] and Winship [286], the documentary sources include [**289**] F. W. Hodge and T. H. Lewis, eds., *Spanish Explorers in the Southern United States, 1528–1543* (Original Narratives of Early American History, New York, Scribner's, 1907; reprinted Barnes and Noble, 1953), [**290**] G. P. Hammond and Agapito Rey, eds., *Narratives of the Coronado Expedition, 1540–1542* (Coronado Cuarto Centennial Pubns., vol. ii, Univ. of New Mexico Press, 1940), and [**291**] Garcilaso de la Vega, *The Florida of the Inca. A history of the Adelantado, Hernando de Soto*... (edited by J. G. and J. J. Varner, Univ. of Texas Press, 1951). See also [**292**] the translation by J. A. Robertson of the Gentleman of Elvas, *True Relation of the Hardships suffered by Governor Fernando de Soto and certain Portuguese Gentlemen during the Discovery of the Province of Florida* . . . (2 vols., Deland, Florida State Historical Society, 1932–3).

PERU AND SOUTH AMERICA

See Prescott [228]. [**293**] R. C. Murphy discusses 'The Earliest Spanish Advances Southward from Panama along the West Coast of South America', *Hispanic American Historical Review*, xxi (1941), 3–28. Three articles by George Kubler deal respectively with [**294**] 'A Peruvian Chief of State: Manco Inca (1515–1545)', [**295**] 'The Behaviour of Atahualpa, 1531–1533', and [**295a**] 'The Neo-Inca State (1537–1572)', *ibid.*, xxiv (1944), 253–76, xxv (1945), 413–27, and xxvii (1947), 189–203. [**296**] P. A. Means, *Fall of the Inca Empire and the Spanish Rule in Peru, 1530–1780* (New York and London, Scribner's, 1932), is a standard work. For the part played by De Soto see Maynard [283] and Graham [284], and for later Inca history [**296a**] J. H. Rowe, 'The Incas under Spanish Colonial Institutions', *Hispanic American Historical Review*, xxxvii (1957), 155–99. See also no. 386.

[**297**] Germán Arciniegas, *Germans in the Conquest of America: a sixteenth century venture* (New York, Macmillan, 1943), is principally, though not exclusively, concerned with the Welsers and Venezuela. [**298**] Sir Clements R. Markham tells, for the general reader, the story of *The Conquest of New Granada* (London, Smith, Elder, 1912), and this is also the theme of two popular biographies, [**299**] R. B. Cunninghame Graham, *The Conquest of New Granada, being the life of Gonzalo Jiménez de Quesada* (London, Heinemann, 1922), and [**300**] Germán Arciniegas's somewhat fictionalized *The Knight of El Dorado: the tale of Don Gonzalo Jiménez de Quesada and his conquest of New Granada* . . . (New York, Viking Press, 1942).

For the conquest in southern South America see [**301**] R. B. Cunninghame Graham, *Pedro de Valdivia, conqueror of Chile* (London, Heinemann, 1926), [**302**] a slight, academic biography, *Pedro de Valdivia, conquistador of Chile*, by I. S. W. Vernon (Univ. of Texas Press, 1946), [**303**] R. B. Cunninghame Graham, *The Conquest of the River Plate* (London, Heinemann, 1924), and [**304**] M. W. Nichols, 'Colonial Tucumán', *Hispanic American Historical Review*, xviii (1938), 461–85. See also [**305**] C. E. Nowell, 'Aleixo Garcia and the White King', *ibid.*, xxvi (1946), 450–66.

The Spanish Empire in America

The voyage of Magellan through the straits that bear his name is told in [**306**] F. H. H. Guillemard, *The Life of Ferdinand Magellan and the First Circumnavigation of the Globe, 1480–1521* (London, George Philip, 1890), and by [**307**] C. M. Parr, *So Noble a Captain. The life and times of Ferdinand Magellan* (New York, Crowell, 1953).

For contemporary sources see Means [52], Shelby [222], and Clemence [21]. *The Documents and Narratives concerning the Discovery and Conquest of Latin America* published by the Cortés Society contain [**308**] Pedro Sancho, *An Account of the Conquest of Peru*, ed. P. A. Means (New York, 1917), and [**309**] Pedro Pizarro, *Relation of the Discovery and Conquest of the Kingdoms of Peru*, ed. P. A. Means (2 vols., New York, 1921). [**310**] *The Conquest of Peru as recorded by a Member of the Pizarro Expedition* has been translated by J. H. Sinclair (New York Public Library, 1929), and there is a modern edition [**310a**], edited by D. B. Thomas, of A. de Zárate, *A History of the Discovery and Conquest of Peru. Books I–IV, translated out of the Spanish by T. Nicholas, anno 1581* (London, Penguin Press, 1933). The Hakluyt Society publications include [**311**] *Reports on the Discovery of Peru*, ed. C. R. Markham (1st series, No. 47, London, 1872), by Francisco de Xeres, Miguel de Estete and Hernando Pizarro, and Markham's editions of [**311a**] *The Life and Acts of Don Alonzo Enríquez de Guzmán* (1st series, No. 29, London, 1862), [**312**] Pedro de Cieza de León's *Chronicle of Peru* (5 vols., various titles, 1st series, Nos. 33 and 68; 2nd series, Nos. 31, 42, and 54, London, 1864, 1883, 1913, 1918, 1923), [**313**] *The First Part of the Royal Commentaries of the Yncas*, by the Inca Garcilaso de la Vega (2 vols., 1st series, Nos. 41 and 45, London, 1869, 1871), and [**314**] Pedro Sarmiento de Gamboa's *History of the Incas* (2nd series, No. 22, Cambridge, 1907). On these translations see [**315**] B. W. Diffie, 'A Markham Contribution to the *Leyenda Negra*', *Hispanic American Historical Review*, xvi (1936), 96–103, and [**316**] H. Bernstein and B. W. Diffie, 'Sir Clements R. Markham as a Translator', *ibid.*, xvii (1937), 546–57.

[**317**] Pascual de Andagoya, *Narrative of the Proceedings of Pedrarias Dávila in the Provinces of Tierra Firme or Castilla del Oro ...*, ed. C. R. Markham, is in the Hakluyt Society publications (1st series, No. 34, London, 1865). [**318**] There is an edition by H. C. Heaton of *The Discovery of the Amazon according to the account of Friar Gaspar de Carvajal* (translated by B. T. Lee, with an introduc-by J. T. Medina. New York, American Geographical Society,

1934) and another [**318a**] by William Bollaert of *The Expedition of Pedro de Ursua and Lope de Aguirre in search of El Dorado and Omagua in 1560–1* (Hakluyt Soc. Pubns., 1st series, No. 28, London, 1861). See also no. 353. The voyage of Ulrich Schmidt and the commentaries of Alvar Núñez Cabeza de Vaca are contained in [**319**] *The Conquest of the River Plate, 1535–1555*, ed. Luis L. Domínguez (Hakluyt Soc. Pubns., 1st series, No. 81, London, 1891), and [**320**] a version of Alonso de Ercilla y Zúñiga's epic poem, *La Araucana*, is to be found in C. M. Lancaster and P. T. Manchester, *The Araucaniad* (Nashville, Vanderbilt Univ. Press, 1945).

Special Aspects

[**321**] H. Vander Linden, 'Alexander VI and the Demarcation of the Maritime and Colonial Domains of Spain and Portugal, 1493–1494', *American Historical Review*, xxii (Oct. 1916), 1–20, is the standard monograph on this subject. See also Davenport [225] and Zavala [209].

The theoretical and practical problems raised by the conquest are discussed in [**322**] J. H. Parry's essay, *The Spanish Theory of Empire in the Sixteenth Century* (Cambridge Univ. Press, 1940), in [**323**] Silvio Zavala, *The Political Philosophy of the Conquest of America* (Mexico, Editorial Cultura, 1953), a book which is not confined to sixteenth-century ideas alone, in [**323a**] J. M. van der Kroef, 'Francisco de Vitoria and the Nature of Colonial Policy', *Catholic Historical Review*, xxxv (July 1949), 129–62, and in the detailed and illuminating analysis of [**324**] Lewis Hanke, *The Spanish Struggle for Justice in the Conquest of America* (Univ. of Pennsylvania Press, 1949). See also [**325**] Lewis Hanke, *The First Social Experiments in America* (Harvard Univ. Press, 1935), and, by the same author, [**326**] 'Pope Paul III and the American Indians', *Harvard Theological Review*, xxx (1937), 65–102, [**327**] 'The "Requerimiento" and its Interpreters', *Revista de Historia de América*, Núm. 1 (1938), 25–34, and [**328**] 'Free Speech in Sixteenth-Century Spanish America', *Hispanic American Historical Review*, xxvi (1946), 135–49. [**329**] Silvio Zavala, *Sir Thomas More in New Spain. A utopian adventure of the renaissance* (The Canning House Annual Lecture, London, Hispanic and Luso-Brazilian Councils, 1955), discusses the ideas and work of Bishop Vasco de Quiroga, and [**330**] C. S. Braden deals generally with *Religious Aspects of the Conquest of Mexico* (Duke Univ. Press, 1930).

On Las Casas, 'the Apostle to the Indians', see [**331**] F. A.

MacNutt, *Bartholomew de Las Casas* (New York and London, Putnam's, 1909), which is a popular treatment, and the three later works of Lewis Hanke: [**332**] *Bartolomé de Las Casas. An interpretation of his life and writings* (The Hague, Martinus Nijhoff, 1951), [**333**] *Bartolomé de Las Casas. Bookman, scholar and propagandist* (Univ. of Pennsylvania Press, 1952), and [**334**] *Bartolomé de Las Casas. Historian. An essay in Spanish historiography* (Univ. of Florida Press, 1952).

[**335**] I. A. Leonard, *Books of the Brave; being an account of books and of men in the Spanish conquest and settlement of the sixteenth-century new world* (Harvard Univ. Press, 1949), discusses the popular literature of the novels of chivalry read by the conquistadores and settlers. [**336**] P. M. Ashburn, *The Ranks of Death. A medical history of the conquest of America* (New York, Coward McCann, 1947), deals, by groups of diseases, with early contacts between whites, Indians, and negroes. [**337**] V. Aubrey Neasham, 'Spain's Emigrants to the New World, 1492–1592', *Hispanic American Historical Review*, xix (1939), 147–60, examines regional origins.

For the beginnings of royal government see [**338**] C. H. Haring, 'The Genesis of Royal Government in the Spanish Indies', *Hispanic American Historical Review*, vii (1927), 141–91, [**339**] C. W. Hackett, 'The Delimitation of Political Jurisdictions in Spanish North America to 1535', *ibid.*, i (1918), 40–69, and Haring [201].

3. THE EMPIRE UNDER THE HABSBURGS
GENERAL

See nos. 195 to 212, together with Bancroft's *History of Mexico* [251] and *History of Central America* [252].

An illuminating commentary on the colonial history of Mexico is contained in [**340**] L. B. Simpson, *Many Mexicos* (3rd ed., rev., Univ. of California Press, 1952). [**341**] I. A. Wright tells the story of *The Early History of Cuba, 1492–1586* (New York, Macmillan, 1916), and continues her Cuban studies in [**342**] *Santiago de Cuba and its District (1607–1640)* (Madrid, Felipe Peña Cruz, 1918). The Spanish régime in Peru from 1530 to 1780 is covered by Means [296] and in the older work [**343**] of Sir Clements R. Markham, *A History of Peru* (Chicago, Sergel and Co., 1892). [**344**] Agustín Edwards, *Peoples of Old* (London, Benn, 1929), is a popular history of colonial Chile. Consult also, for Chile, [345] Luis Galdames, *A History of Chile* (translated and edited by I. J. Cox, Univ. of North Carolina Press, 1941), for the Provinces of the Río de la Plata, [346] Ricardo Levene, *A History of Argentina* (translated and edited by W. S. Robertson, Univ. of North Carolina Press, 1937), and [347] H. G. Warren, *Paraguay. An informal history* (Univ. of Oklahoma Press, 1949), and less satisfactory, for New Granada, [348] J. M. Henao and G. Arrubla, *History of Colombia* (translated and edited by J. F. Rippy, Univ. of North Carolina Press, 1938).

For Acosta's late sixteenth-century history and Vázquez de Espinosa's early seventeenth-century survey see nos. 220 and 221.

[349] The celebrated work of Thomas Gage, *The English-American his Travail by Sea and Land; or, a New Survey of the West India's containing a journall of three thousand and three hundred miles within the main land of America*, which principally concerns Central America and Mexico, was first published in 1648, and there is a modern, abridged edition by A. P. Newton (London, Routledge, 1928). See also [350] William Dampier, *A New Voyage Round the World* (1697), edited by N. M. Penzer with an introduction by Sir Albert Gray (London, Black, 1937), and [351] Lionel Wafer, *A New Voyage and Description of the Isthmus of America* (1699), edited by L. E. Elliott Joyce (Hakluyt Soc. Pubns., 2nd series, No. 73, Oxford, 1934). [352] The *Voyages and Discoveries in South America* printed at London in 1698 contain Acarete du Biscay's account of his travels up the Río de la Plata and thence by land to Potosí, together with Cristóbal de Acuña's account of his journey up the Amazon. The latter is also reproduced in [353] C. R. Markham's *Expeditions into the Valley of the Amazons, 1539, 1540, 1639* (Hakluyt Soc. Pubns., 1st series, No. 24, London, 1859).

Regional histories include the late eighteenth-century history of [354] J. I. Molina, *The Geographical, Natural, and Civil History of Chile* . . . (2 vols., London, 1809), translated from the Italian, and an abridged translation [355] of Domingo Juarros's early nineteenth-century work, *A Statistical and Commercial History of the Kingdom of Guatemala* (London, 1823).

ADMINISTRATIVE ORGANIZATION

See Haring [201] and [338], Merriman [199], Moses [207] and Roscher [210]. The viceroy and the audiencia, the two chief agents of royal government are discussed in [356] L. E. Fisher, *Viceregal Administration in the Spanish-American Colonies* (Univ. of California Press, 1926), [357] C. H. Cunningham, *The Audiencia in the Spanish Colonies as illustrated by the Audiencia of Manila, 1583–1800* (Univ. of California Press, 1919), and [358] the excellent monograph of J. H. Parry, *The Audiencia of New Galicia in the Sixteenth Century* (Cambridge Univ. Press, 1948). [359] C. E. Castañeda, 'The Corregidor in Spanish Colonial Administration', *Hispanic American Historical Review*, ix (1929), 446–70, treats of provincial government. Compare [360] R. S. Chamberlain, 'The Corregidor in Castile in the Sixteenth Century . . .', *ibid.*, xxiii (1943), 222–57. Municipal institutions are dealt with by [361] W. W. Pierson, 'Some Reflections on the Cabildo as an Institution', *ibid.*, v (1922), 573–96, [362] H. I. Priestley, 'Spanish Colonial Municipalities', *Louisiana Historical Quarterly*, v (1922), 125–43, [363] F. A. Kirkpatrick, 'Municipal Administration in the Spanish Dominions in America', Royal Historical Society, *Transactions*, 3rd series, ix (1915), 95–109, and [364] J. P. Moore, *The Cabildo in Peru under the Hapsburgs* (Duke Univ. Press, 1954).

[365] J. H. Parry, *The Sale of Public Office in the Spanish Indies under the Hapsburgs* (Ibero-Americana, 37, Univ. of California Press, 1953), examines a practice of which the end result was 'less a sale than an abdication of control, so complete that only the extinction of the Hapsburg line and the accession of a more vigorous dynasty could redeem it, and then only in part'.

[366] Aiton, A. S., *Antonio de Mendoza, first viceroy of New Spain* (Duke Univ. Press, 1927).

[367] Cunningham, C. H., 'The Institutional Background of Spanish American History', *Hispanic American Historical Review*, i (1918), 24–39.

[368] Gibson, Charles, 'Rotation of Alcaldes in the Indian *Cabildo* of Mexico City', *Hispanic American Historical Review*, xxxiii (1953), 212–23.

[369] Hill, R. R., 'The Office of Adelantado', *Political Science Quarterly*, xxviii (1913), 646–68.

[370] Mecham, J. L., 'The *Real de Minas* as a Political Institution', *Hispanic American Historical Review*, vii (1927), 45–83.

[371] Nuttall, Zelia, 'Royal Ordinances concerning the Laying Out of New Towns', *Hispanic American Historical Review*, iv (1921), 743–53; v (1922), 249–54.

[371a] Stanislawski, Dan, 'Early Spanish Town Planning in the New World', *Geographical Review*, xxxvii (1947), 94–107.

The Empire under the Habsburgs

[372] Zimmerman, A. F., *Francisco de Toledo, the fifth viceroy of Peru, 1569–1581* (Caldwell, Idaho, Caxton Printers, 1938).

See also Gibson [386].

THE LAND SYSTEM, THE LABOUR SUPPLY, AND THE NATIVE PEOPLES

For the great debates in Castile on the status and treatment of the Indian and the effects of these debates on royal policy see Hanke [324] and nos. 322 to 334 in general. [373] L. B. Simpson, *Studies in the Administration of the Indians in New Spain: I. The Laws of Burgos of 1512; II. The Civil Congregation; III. The Repartimiento System of Forced Native Labor in New Spain and Guatemala; IV. The Emancipation of the Indian Slaves and the Resettlement of the Freedmen, 1548–1553* (Ibero-Americana, 7, 13, 16, Univ. of California Press, 1934–40), and [374] *The Encomienda in New Spain: the beginning of Spanish Mexico* (Univ. of California Press, 1950), are indispensable. The 1950, extensively revised, edition of this last book should be compared with the first edition published in 1929. On the institutions of *encomienda, repartimiento*, and the *congregaciones*, see also F. A. Kirkpatrick, [375] 'Repartimiento-Encomienda', and [376] 'The Landless Encomienda', *Hispanic American Historical Review*, xix (1939), 372–9, xxii (1942), 765–74, [377] E. R. Service, 'The *Encomienda* in Paraguay', *ibid.*, xxxi (1951), 230–52, [377a] the same author's *Spanish-Guarani Relations in Early Colonial Paraguay* (Ann Arbor, Univ. of Michigan, Museum of Anthropology, 1954), and [378] H. F. Cline, 'Civil Congregations of the Indians in New Spain, 1598–1606', *Hispanic American Historical Review*, xxix (1949), 349–69. See also Zavala [209].

Demographic and ecological studies which emphasize the importance of population decline in New Spain include [379] George Kubler, 'Population Movements in Mexico, 1520–1600', *Hispanic American Historical Review*, xxii (1942), 606–43, [380] S. F. Cook and L. B. Simpson, *The Population of Central Mexico in the Sixteenth Century* (Ibero-Americana, 31, Univ. of California Press, 1948), [381] L. B. Simpson, *Exploitation of Land in Central Mexico in the Sixteenth Century* (Ibero-Americana, 36, Univ. of California Press, 1952), and [382] Woodrow Borah, *New Spain's Century of Depression* (Ibero-Americana, 35, Univ. of California Press, 1951), which reaches the conclusion that 'the sharp and long-continued

D

decrease of Mexico's Indians from the Conquest until the beginning of the eighteenth century must be accounted one of the most important factors in Mexican history'. Consult also [383] S. F. Cook, *Soil Erosion and Population in Central Mexico* (Ibero-Americana, 34, Univ. of California Press, 1949).

[384] Charles Gibson, *Tlaxcala in the Sixteenth Century* (Yale Univ. Press, 1952), is a detailed investigation of the relations between conquerors and conquered. Compare, among regional studies, [385] Carl Sauer, *Colima of New Spain in the Sixteenth Century* (Ibero-Americana, 29, Univ. of California Press, 1948), [385a] F. V. Scholes and R. L. Roys, *The Maya Chontal Indians of Acalan-Tixchel: a contribution to the history and ethnography of the Yucatan Peninsula* (Washington, Carnegie Institution, 1948), and Roys [263a], and, for South America, [386] Charles Gibson, *The Inca Concept of Sovereignty and the Spanish Administration in Peru* (Univ. of Texas Press, 1948). See also Nichols [304] and the *Handbook of South American Indians* [148].

[387] Barber, R. K., *Indian Labor in the Spanish Colonies* (Univ. of New Mexico Press, 1932).

[387a] Douglas-Irvine, H., 'The Landholding System of Colonial Chile', *Hispanic American Historical Review*, viii (1928), 449–95.

[388] Marshall, C. E., 'The Birth of the Mestizo in New Spain', *Hispanic American Historical Review*, xix (1939), 161–84.

[388a] Scholes, W. V., *The Diego Ramírez Visita* (Columbia, Mo., Univ. of Missouri Studies, 1946).

THE NEGRO AND NEGRO SLAVERY

[389] Wilbur Zelinsky, 'The Historical Geography of the Negro Population of Latin America', *Journal of Negro History*, xxxiv (1949), 153–221, is an outstanding contribution. [390] G. Aguirre Beltrán discusses 'The Slave Trade in Mexico', *Hispanic American Historical Review*, xxiv (1944), 412–31, and [391] Fernando Romero 'The Slave Trade and the Negro in South America', *ibid.*, xxiv (1944), 368–86. See also [391a] H. A. Wyndham, *The Atlantic and Slavery* (Oxford Univ. Press, 1935), [392] J. F. King, 'Negro History in Continental Spanish America', *Journal of Negro History*, xxix (1944), 7–23, and, for further references, [392a] J. F. King, 'The Negro in Continental Spanish America: a select bibliography', *Hispanic American Historical Review*, xxiv (1944), 547–59, and [392b] M. N. Work, *A Biblio-*

graphy *of the Negro in Africa and America* (New York, H. W. Wilson, 1928). See also Donnan [597].

THE CHURCH AND THE MISSIONS

See Braden [330] and nos. 322 to 334 in general. A comprehensive 'history of politico-ecclesiastical relations' in Latin America is provided by [393] J. L. Mecham, *Church and State in Latin America* (Univ. of North Carolina Press, 1934).

[394] 'The Origins of *Real Patronato de Indias*' are examined by J. L. Mecham, *Catholic Historical Review*, n.s., viii (1928), 205–27, and [395] the establishment of 'The First Episcopal Sees in Spanish America' by E. W. Loughran, *Hispanic American Historical Review*, x (1930), 167–87. Woodrow Borah deals with [396] 'The Collection of Tithes in the Bishopric of Oaxaca in the Sixteenth Century' and with [397] 'Tithe Collection in the Bishopric of Oaxaca, 1601–1867', *Hispanic American Historical Review*, xxi (1941), 386–409, xxix (1949), 498–517.

On the rivalry between clerics born in Europe and clerics born in Spanish America see [397a] Antonine Tibesar, 'The Alternativa: a study in Spanish-Creole Relations in Seventeenth-Century Peru', *Americas*, xi (Jan. 1955), 229–83, and on that between regulars and seculars [397b] R. C. Padden, 'The Ordenanza del Patronazgo, 1574: an interpretative essay', *ibid.*, xii (April 1956), 333–54.

[398] H. C. Lea, *The Inquisition in the Spanish Dependencies* (New York and London, Macmillan, 1908), is still the fullest treatment of this subject in English. [399] G. R. G. Conway, ed., *An Englishman and the Mexican Inquisition, 1556–1560* (Mexico, privately printed, 1927)—the Englishman is Robert Tomson—and, by the same editor, [400] *The Rare Travailes of Job Hortop* (Mexico, privately printed, 1928), record the trials of two English 'heretics'. See also Aydelotte [512].

[401] H. E. Bolton, 'The Mission as a Frontier Institution in the Spanish American Colonies', *American Historical Review*, xxiii (Oct. 1917), 42–61, emphasizes its protective, civilizing, and pioneering rôles. For a general, semi-popular survey of the mission field in South America (but excluding the famous Jesuit reductions) see [402] J. F. Rippy and J. T. Nelson, *Crusaders of the Jungle* (Univ. of North Carolina Press, 1936).

THE FRANCISCANS

[**403**] Barth, P. J., *Franciscan Education and the Social Order in Spanish North America, 1502–1821* (Univ. of Chicago Press, 1945).

[**404**] Geiger, Maynard, *The Franciscan Conquest of Florida (1573–1618)* (Washington, Catholic Univ. of America, 1937).

[**405**] Lanning, J. T., *The Spanish Missions of Georgia* (Univ. of North Carolina Press, 1935).

[**406**] Oré, Luis Gerónimo, *The Martyrs of Florida (1513–1616)* (edited by Maynard Geiger. New York, Joseph F. Wagner, 1936).

[**406a**] Phelan, J. L., *The Millennial Kingdom of the Franciscans in the New World. A study of the writings of Gerónimo de Mendieta (1525–1604)* (Univ. of California Press, 1956).

[**407**] Tibesar, Antonine, *Franciscan Beginnings in Colonial Peru* (Washington, Academy of American Franciscan History, 1953).

THE JESUITS

[**408**] Magnus Mörner, *The Political and Economic Activities of the Jesuits in the La Plata Region. The Hapsburg era* (Stockholm, Ibero-Amerikanska Biblioteket och Institutet, 1953), is a sound and scholarly examination, and [**409**] R. B. Cunninghame Graham, *A Vanished Arcadia: some account of the Jesuits in Paraguay, 1607–1767* (rev. ed., London, Heinemann, 1924), is a popular treatment. There is an abridged translation of the eighteenth-century history of [**410**] Pierre François Xavier de Charlevoix entitled *The History of Paraguay* (2 vols., London, 1769). See also *Handbook of South American Indians*, vol. v [148]. On the work of the Jesuits in North America consult *Greater America* [134], *Lanning* [405], and the following studies:

[**411**] Bannon, J. F., 'Black-Robe Frontiersman: Pedro Méndez, S. J.', *Hispanic American Historical Review*, xxvii (1947), 61–86.

[**411a**] Bannon, J. F., *The Mission Frontier in Sonora, 1620–1687* (New York, United States Catholic Historical Society, 1955).

[**412**] Bolton, H. E., *Rim of Christendom: a biography of Eusebio Francisco Kino, Pacific coast pioneer* (New York, Macmillan, 1936).

[**413**] Burrus, E. J., ed., *Kino Reports to Headquarters: correspondence of Eusebio F. Kino, S.J., from New Spain with Rome* (Rome, Institutum Historicum Societatis Jesu, 1954).

[**414**] Dunne, P. M., *Pioneer Black Robes on the West Coast* (Univ. of California Press, 1940).

[**415**] Dunne, P. M., *Pioneer Jesuits in Northern Mexico* (Univ. of California Press, 1944).

[**416**] Dunne, P. M., *Early Jesuit Missions in Tarahumara* (Univ. of California Press, 1948).

[**417**] Jacobsen, J. V., *Educational Foundations of the Jesuits in Sixteenth-Century New Spain* (Univ. of California Press, 1938).

[**418**] Lewis, C. M., and Loomie, A. J., *The Spanish Jesuit Mission in Virginia, 1570-1572* (Univ. of North Carolina Press, 1953).

[**419**] Shiels, W. E., *Gonzalo de Tapia, (1561-1594), founder of the first permanent Jesuit mission in North America* (New York, United States Catholic Historical Society, 1934).

TRADE AND INDUSTRY

[**420**] C. H. Haring, *Trade and Navigation between Spain and the Indies in the time of the Hapsburgs* (Harvard Univ. Press, 1918), is fundamental. For the convoy system see also [**420a**] José de Veitia Linage, *Norte de la Contratación de las Indias Occidentales* (1672), of which there is an English version by John Stevens, *The Spanish Rule of Trade to the West Indies, containing an account of the Casa de Contratacion or India House . . .* (London, 1702).

[**421**] A. E. Sayous discusses 'Partnerships in the Trade between Spain and America and also in the Spanish Colonies in the Sixteenth Century', *Journal of Economic and Business History*, i (Feb. 1929), 282–301, and [**422**] Woodrow Borah, *Early Colonial Trade and Navigation between Mexico and Peru* (Ibero-Americana, 38, Univ. of California Press, 1954). [**423**] 'The Puerto Bello Fairs' are described by A. C. Loosley, *Hispanic American Historical Review*, xiii (1933), 314–35. [**424**] R. S. Smith, 'The Institution of the Consulado in New Spain', *ibid.*, xxiv (1944), 61–83, traces the history of the merchant guilds from the establishment in 1594 of the first American *consulado*. [**425**] I. A. Wright, 'Rescates: with special reference to Cuba, 1599–1610', *ibid.*, iii (1920), 333–61, discusses early contraband trade. For the trans-Pacific trade with Manila consult [**426**] W. L. Schurz, 'Mexico, Peru, and the Manila Galleon', *Hispanic American Historical Review*, i (1918), 389–402, and [**427**] his *The Manila Galleon* (New York, Dutton, 1939).

[**428**] Woodrow Borah, *Silk Raising in Colonial Mexico* (Ibero-Americana, 20, Univ. of California Press, 1943), is a model of careful investigation, and [**429**] M. Carrera Stampa, 'The Evolution of Weights and Measures in New Spain', *Hispanic American*

Historical Review, xxix (1949), 2–24, a valuable work of reference.

[**429a**] Bishko, C. J., 'The Peninsular Background of Latin American Cattle Ranching', *Hispanic American Historical Review*, xxxii (1952), 491–515.

[**430**] Bruman, H. J., 'Early Coconut Culture in Western Mexico', *Hispanic American Historical Review*, xxv (1945), 212–23.

[**431**] Bruman, H. J., 'The Culture History of Mexican Vanilla', *Hispanic American Historical Review*, xxviii (1948), 360–76.

[**432**] Dusenberry, W. H., 'The Regulation of Meat Supply in Sixteenth-Century Mexico City', *Hispanic American Historical Review*, xxviii (1948), 38–52.

[**433**] Guthrie, C. L., 'Colonial Economy. Trade, Industry, and Labor in Seventeenth Century Mexico City', *Revista de Historia de América*, Núm. 7 (1939), 103–34.

[**434**] Hussey, R. D., 'Spanish Colonial Trails in Panama', *Revista de Historia de América*, Núm. 6 (1939), 47–74.

[**435**] Lee, R. L., 'Grain Legislation in Colonial Mexico, 1575–1585', *Hispanic American Historical Review*, xxvii (1947), 647–60.

[**436**] Meek, W. T., *The Exchange Media of Colonial Mexico* (New York, King's Crown Press, 1948).

[**437**] Ratekin, Mervyn, 'The Early Sugar Industry in Española', *Hispanic American Historical Review*, xxxiv (1954), 1–19.

[**437a**] Rodríguez, Mario, 'The Genesis of Economic Attitudes in the Río de la Plata', *Hispanic American Historical Review*, xxxvi (1956), 171–89.

[**438**] Smith, R. S., 'Sales Taxes in New Spain, 1575–1770', *Hispanic American Historical Review*, xxviii (1948), 2–37.

Mining and the Precious Metals

[**439**] H. R. Wagner, 'Early Silver Mining in New Spain', *Revista de Historia de América*, Núm. 14 (1942), 49–71, is a preliminary survey, which pays incidental attention to the introduction of the patio process of amalgamation. This is also further examined in [**440**] R. C. West's excellent study of seventeenth-century developments, *The Mining Community of Northern New Spain: the Parral mining district* (Ibero-Americana, 30, Univ. of California Press, 1949). Compare, by the same author, [**441**] *Colonial Placer Mining in Colombia* (Baton Rouge, Louisiana State Univ. Press, 1942). [**442**] 'Supply and Transportation for the Potosí Mines, 1545–1640', are discussed by Gwendolin B. Cobb, *Hispanic American Historical Review*, xxix (1949), 25–45. See also,

for Potosí, *Greater America* [134] and [**442a**] Lewis Hanke, *The Imperial City of Potosí. An unwritten chapter in the history of Spanish America* (The Hague, Martinus Nijhoff, 1956). [**443**] A. P. Whitaker, in a book primarily concerned with the eighteenth century, outlines also the earlier history of *The Huancavelica Mercury Mine* (Harvard Univ. Press, 1941).

[**444**] C. H. Haring, 'American Gold and Silver Production in the first half of the Sixteenth Century', *Quarterly Journal of Economics*, xxix (1915), 433–79, and [**445**] E. J. Hamilton, 'Imports of American Gold and Silver into Spain, 1503–1660', *ibid.*, xliii (1929), 436–72, are important articles, and [**446**] B. W. Diffie, 'Estimates of Potosí Mineral Production, 1541–1555', *Hispanic American Historical Review*, xx (1940), 275–82, is a valuable note. For further discussion and for the larger significance of American gold and silver production see [**447**] E. J. Hamilton's important *American Treasure and the Price Revolution in Spain, 1501–1650* (Harvard Univ. Press, 1934), together with [**448**] his 'American Treasure and the Rise of Capitalism, 1500–1700', *Economica*, ix (1929), 338–57.

THE ROYAL EXCHEQUER

[**449**] Aiton, A. S., 'Real Hacienda in New Spain under the First Viceroy', *Hispanic American Historical Review*, vi (1926), 232–45.

[**450**] Aiton, A. S., and Wheeler, B. W., 'The First American Mint', *Hispanic American Historical Review*, xi (1931), 198–215.

[**451**] Haring, C. H., 'The Early Spanish Colonial Exchequer', *American Historical Review*, xxiii (July 1918), 779–96.

[**452**] Haring, C. H., 'Ledgers of the Royal Treasurers in Spanish America in the Sixteenth Century', *Hispanic American Historical Review*, ii (1919), 173–87.

[**452a**] Nesmith, R. S., *The Coinage of the First Mint of the Americas at Mexico City, 1536–1572* (New York, American Numismatic Soc., 1955).

EDUCATION, LITERATURE, THE ARTS

Barth [403] and Jacobsen [417] are specifically concerned with the educational work of the Franciscans and the Jesuits respectively. [**453**] J. T. Lanning, *Academic Culture in the Spanish Colonies* (New York, Oxford Univ. Press, 1940), though primarily a contribution to the history of the 'enlightenment' in the eighteenth century, traces the foundation and examines the functioning of the colonial universities. A vivid picture of town and gown is contained in [**454**] *Life in the Imperial and Loyal City of Mexico in New Spain and the Royal and Pontifical University of Mexico as Described in the Dialogues for the Study of the Latin Language prepared by Francisco Cervantes de Salazar and printed in 1554 by Juan Pablos*, ed. by M. L. B. Shepard with an introduction and notes by C. E. Castañeda (Univ. of Texas Press, 1953), and a detailed account of the University de San Carlos de Guatemala in [**454a**] J. T. Lanning, *The University in the Kingdom of Guatemala* (Cornell Univ. Press, 1955).

[**455**] Pedro Henríquez-Ureña, *Literary Currents in Hispanic America* (Harvard Univ. Press, 1945), is much more than a brilliant survey of Latin American literature from the sixteenth century to the twentieth: it opens up the whole field of arts and letters. [**456**] Bernard Moses, *Spanish Colonial Literature in South America* (New York, Hispanic Society of America, 1922), describes writers and their works. I. A. Leonard has broken fresh ground with his *Books of the Brave* [**335**] and [**457**] his *Romances of Chivalry in the Spanish Indies* (Univ. of California Press, 1933), and in [**458**] *Don Carlos de Sigüenza y Góngora* (Univ. of California Press, 1929), he has provided also an illuminating biography of a distinguished seventeenth-century Mexican savant. See also [**458a**] Franchón Royer, *The Tenth Muse, Sor Juana Inés de la Cruz* (Paterson, N.J., St. Anthony Guild Press, 1952).

[**459**] Pál Kelemen, *Baroque and Rococo in Latin America* (New York, Macmillan, 1951), is a major contribution to the history of architecture, sculpture, woodcarving, and painting. [**460**] George A. Kubler, *Mexican Architecture of the Sixteenth Century* (2 vols., Yale Univ. Press, 1948), is also a major contribution, not only to art history but to the economic history of the sixteenth century. See also [**461**] E. W. Weismann, *Mexico in Sculpture, 1521–1821* (Harvard Univ. Press, 1950), and [**462**] W. H. Kilham, *Mexican Architecture of the Vice-Regal Period* (New York, Longmans, 1927). [**463**] H. E. Wethey, *Colonial Architecture and Sculpture in Peru* (Harvard Univ. Press, 1949), and [**464**] Lawrence Anderson, *The Art of the Silversmith in Mexico, 1519–1936* (2 vols., New York, Oxford Univ. Press, 1941), are both outstanding.

THE NORTHERN EXPANSION OF NEW SPAIN AND FLORIDA

See Bolton [**275**], Brebner [**276**], Priestley [**250**], and Wagner [**278**], and, for bibliographies and guides, Mecham [**53**], Steck

[54], Wagner [59], and *Harvard Guide* [249]. H. H. Bancroft, *History of Mexico* [251], [**465**] *History of the North Mexican States and Texas* (2 vols., San Francisco, 1884–9), and [**466**] *History of Arizona and New Mexico, 1530–1888* (San Francisco, 1889), are a mine of information. [**467**] *New Spain and the Anglo-American West; historical contributions presented to Herbert Eugene Bolton* (2 vols., Los Angeles, privately printed, 1932) is 'a documentary collection', of which the contributions in the first volume all relate to the colonial period. See also *Greater America* [134].

[**468**] P. W. Powell, *Soldiers, Indians, and Silver. The northward advance of New Spain, 1550–1600* (Univ. of California Press, 1952), tells the story of 'the Spanish-Indian struggle on the silver frontier' in New Galicia, beginning with the discovery of the Zacatecas mines in 1546. See also, for New Galicia, Parry [358]. The founding of the province of New Vizcaya is dealt with by [**469**] J. L. Mecham, *Francisco Ibarra and Nueva Vizcaya* (Duke Univ. Press, 1927), and the advance into New Mexico at the end of the sixteenth century by [**470**] G. P. Hammond, *Don Juan de Oñate and the Founding of New Mexico* (Santa Fe, El Palacio Press, 1927). See also [**471**] Hammond's article on 'Oñate's Effort to Gain Political Autonomy for New Mexico', *Hispanic American Historical Review*, xxxii (1952), 321–30.

On the missionary and exploratory work of the Jesuits after their first entry into Sinaloa in 1591 see Shiels [419], Bannon [411, 411a], Dunne [414, 415], and, in the later years of the seventeenth century, Dunne [416] and Bolton's *Rim of Christendom* [412], which is a masterly account of the work of Father Kino in northern Sonora and southern Arizona.

The seventeenth-century history of New Mexico is covered by F. V. Scholes, [**472**] *Church and State in New Mexico, 1610–1650* (Univ. of New Mexico Press, 1937), and [**473**] *Troublous Times in New Mexico, 1659–1670* (Univ. of New Mexico Press, 1942). The re-conquest, after the revolt of the Pueblo Indians in 1680, is dealt with by [**474**] J. M. Espinosa, *Crusaders of the Rio Grande: the story of Don Diego de Vargas and the reconquest and refounding of New Mexico* (Chicago, Institute of Jesuit History, 1942), and [**475**] J. B. Bailey, *Diego de Vargas and the Reconquest of New Mexico, 1692–1704* (Univ. of New Mexico Press, 1940).

For the expeditions into Texas at the end of the seventeenth century see [**476**] C. E. Castañeda, *Our Catholic Heritage in Texas, 1519–1936. I. The Finding of Texas, 1519–1693; II. The Winning* *of Texas*, 1693–1731 (2 vols., Austin, Von Boeckmann-Jones Co., 1936). **[477]** W. E. Dunn, *Spanish and French Rivalry in the Gulf Region of the United States, 1678–1702* (Austin, Univ. of Texas Studies in History, 1917), is concerned with the beginnings of Texas and the occupation of Pensacola, and **[478]** *The Triangular Struggle for Spanish Pensacola, 1689–1739* is also examined by L. C. Ford (Washington, Catholic Univ. of America, 1939).

[479] H. I. Priestley, *Tristán de Luna: Conquistador of the Old South; a study of Spanish imperial strategy* (Glendale, Calif., A. H. Clark, 1936; reprinted 1952), gives a full account of the unsuccessful attempt to colonize Florida with the expedition to Pensacola of 1559 to 1561. The work of Pedro Menéndez de Avilés, landing at St. Augustine in 1565, is covered in the second volume of Lowery, *Spanish Settlements within the Present Limits of the United States* [277]. See also Parkman [502]. Geiger [404], Lewis and Loomie [418], and Lanning [405] are devoted to the work of the Jesuits and Franciscans. There is a highly specialized study of **[480]** *The Defenses of Spanish Florida, 1565 to 1763* by V. E. Chatelain (Washington, Carnegie Institution, 1941), and the beginnings of 'the Anglo-Spanish contest for the Georgia country' are dealt with in **[481]** H. E. Bolton and Mary Ross, *The Debatable Land* (Univ. of California Press, 1925), which is the introduction to no. 663 separately printed, and **[482]** V. W. Crane, *The Southern Frontier, 1670–1732* (Duke Univ. Press, 1928).

[483] H. E. Bolton, *Spanish Exploration in the Southwest, 1542–1706* (Original Narratives of Early American History, New York, Scribner's, 1916; reprinted Barnes and Noble, 1952), continues Hodge and Lewis [289]. **[484]** *Barcia's Chronological History of the Continent of Florida*, which covers, from 1512 to 1722, the whole of North America north of the settled area of New Spain, has been edited by Anthony Kerrigan (Univ. of Florida Press, 1951), and **[485]** *Obregón's History of Sixteenth Century Explorations in Western America* . . . , printed in 1584 and embracing the foundation of New Galicia and New Vizcaya and the earlier expeditions into New Mexico, by G. P. Hammond and Agapito Rey (Los Angeles, Wetzel Pub. Co., 1928). See also **[486]** C. W. Hackett's important *Historical Documents relating to New Mexico, Nueva Vizcaya, and approaches thereto, to 1773* (3 vols., Washington, Carnegie Institution, 1923–37).

For the early history of New Mexico consult, in addition, the texts published by the Quivira Society[1] and the rich documentation provided in [**487**] G. P. Hammond and Agapito Rey, eds., *Don Juan de Oñate, Colonizer of New Mexico, 1595–1628* (2 vols., Coronado Cuarto Centennial Pubns., vols. v, vi, Univ. of New Mexico Press, 1953), [**488**] F. W. Hodge, G. P. Hammond, and Agapito Rey, eds., *Fray Alonso de Benavides' Revised Memorial of 1634* (*ibid.*, vol. iv, 1945), which is a description of New Mexico in 1630, [**489**] C. W. Hackett and Charmion Shelby, eds., *Revolt of the Pueblo Indians of New Mexico and Otermín's Attempted Reconquest, 1680–1682* (2 vols., *ibid.*, vols. viii, ix, 1942), and [**490**] J. M. Espinosa, ed., *First Expedition of Vargas into New Mexico, 1692* (*ibid.*, vol. x, 1940).

[**491**] H. E. Bolton, ed., *Kino's Historical Memoir of Pimería Alta* (2 vols., Cleveland, A. H. Clark, 1919), is 'a contemporary account of the beginnings of California, Sonora and Arizona by Father Eusebio Francisco Kino . . . 1683–1711'. See also Burrus [413]. [**492**] A. B. Thomas, ed., *After Coronado* (Univ. of Oklahoma Press, 1935), illustrates 'Spanish exploration northeast of New Mexico, 1697–1727'.

[**493**] H. I. Priestley, ed., *The Luna Papers* (2 vols., Deland, Florida State Historical Society, 1928), [**494**] J. T. Connor, ed., *Pedro Menéndez de Avilés, Adelantado, Governor and Captain-General of Florida, Memorial by Gonzalo Solís de Merás* (*ibid.*, 1923), and [**495**] J. T. Connor, ed., *Colonial Records of Spanish Florida* (2 vols., *ibid.*, 1925, 1930), all relate to the history of Florida between 1559 and 1580. For the Florida 'martyrs' see no. 406, for documents on the Franciscan missions in West Florida at the end of the seventeenth century [**496**] M. F. Boyd, H. G. Smith, and J. W. Griffin, *Here They Once Stood. The tragic end of the Apalachee missions* (Univ. of Florida Press, 1951), and, for the Spanish occupation of Pensacola, [**497**] I. A. Leonard, ed., *Spanish Approach to Pensacola, 1689–1693* (Albuquerque, Quivira Society, 1939). See also Ribaut [513].

[1] E.g. G. P. Hammond and Agapito Rey, eds., *Expedition into New Mexico made by Antonio de Espejo, 1582–1583* . . . (Los Angeles, 1929); by the same editors, *New Mexico in 1602. Juan de Montoya's Relation of the Discovery of New Mexico* (Albuquerque, 1938); Gilbert Espinosa, ed., *History of New Mexico by Gaspar Pérez de Villagrá* (Los Angeles, 1933); I. A. Leonard, ed., *The Mercurio Volante of Don Carlos de Sigüenza y Góngora. An account of the first expedition of Don Diego de Vargas into New Mexico in 1692* (Los Angeles, 1932).

INTERNATIONAL RIVALRIES
GENERAL

See Brebner [276] and Haring [420]. [**498**] A. P. Newton, *The European Nations in the West Indies, 1493–1688* (London, Black, 1933), and [**499**] P. A. Means, *The Spanish Main, Focus of Envy, 1492–1700* (New York and London, Scribner's, 1935), are both concerned with international rivalries in the Caribbean area, though Means emphasizes the Spanish point of view and Newton the non-Spanish. [**500**] Violet Barbour, 'Privateers and Pirates of the West Indies', *American Historical Review*, xvi (April 1911), 529–66, is a general discussion which covers the sixteenth and seventeenth centuries, and [**501**] R. D. Hussey provides a brief sketch of 'Spanish Reaction to Foreign Aggression in the Caribbean to about 1680', *Hispanic American Historical Review*, ix (1929), 286–302.

THE SIXTEENTH CENTURY

[**502**] Francis Parkman, *Pioneers of France in the New World* (rev. ed., 1885: London, Macmillan, 1905), tells the story of the Huguenots in Florida, and [**503**] J. A. Williamson, *The Age of Drake* (rev. ed., London, Black, 1946), provides an excellent survey of English maritime enterprise in the Indies in the Elizabethan period.

[**504**] 'The First Recorded English Voyage to the West Indies' —the visit of an English ship to Santo Domingo in 1527—is examined by F. A. Kirkpatrick, *English Historical Review*, xx (1905), 115–24. [**505**] R. G. Marsden contributes a note on 'The Voyage of the *Barbara* of London' to Brazil and the Caribbean in 1540, *ibid.*, xxiv (1909), 96–100. See also no. 733a. [**506**] G. Connell-Smith, 'English Merchants Trading to the New World in the Early Sixteenth Century', *Bulletin of the Institute of Historical Research*, xxiii (May 1950), 53–67, revises conventional ideas. For Hawkins there are two studies by J. A. Williamson, [**507**] *Sir John Hawkins: the time and the man* (Oxford, Clarendon Press, 1927), and [**508**] *Hawkins of Plymouth* (London, Black, 1949). To these should be added the classic work of [**509**] Sir Julian Corbett, *Drake and the Tudor Navy* (2 vols., London, Longmans, Green, 1898), and [**510**] H. R. Wagner's abundantly documented *Sir Francis Drake's Voyage around the World* (San Francisco, J. Howell, 1926). See also [**511**] W. J. Harte, 'Some Recent Views on Drake's Voyage round the World', *History*, n.s., xx (March 1936), 348–53.

[**512**] Frank Aydelotte, 'Elizabethan Seamen in Mexico and Ports of the Spanish Main', *American Historical Review*, xlviii (Oct. 1942), 1–19, exploits to good effect the records of the Holy Office. [**512a**] D. B. Quinn examines 'Some Spanish Reactions to Elizabethan Colonial Enterprises', Royal Historical Society, *Transactions*, 5th series, i (1951), 1–23.

[**513**] Jean Ribaut, *The Whole and True Discouerye of Terra Florida*, has been reprinted from the London edition of 1563 by H. M. Biggar and J. T. Connor (Deland, Florida State Historical Society, 1927). An invaluable series, for the most part translations of Spanish documents, all edited by I. A. Wright, [**514**] *Spanish Documents concerning English Voyages to the Caribbean, 1527–1568*, [**515**] *Documents concerning English Voyages to the Spanish Main, 1569–1580*, and [**516**] *Further English Voyages to Spanish America, 1583–1594; documents from the Archives of the Indies at Seville*, is contained in the publications of the Hakluyt Society (2nd series, Nos. 62, 71, and 99, London, 1929, 1932, 1951), and the Hakluyt Society has also published [**517**] Zelia Nuttall's important collection, also in translation, of Spanish documents relating to the famous voyage of circumnavigation of 1577 to 1580, *New Light on Drake* (2nd series, No. 34, London, 1914). See also [**518**] *The World Encompassed and analogous contemporary documents concerning Sir Francis Drake's circumnavigation of the World*, edited by N. M. Penzer with an introduction by Sir Richard Temple (London, Argonaut Press, 1926). [**519**] *The Observations of Sir Richard Hawkins* on his voyage of 1593–4 have been edited by J. A. Williamson (London, Argonaut Press, 1933) and are also contained, in an uncorrected text, along with other voyages of the Hawkins family, in [**520**] *The Hawkins' Voyages during the Reigns of Henry VIII, Queen Elizabeth, and James I*, edited by C. R. Markham (Hakluyt Soc. Pubns., 1st series, No. 57, London, 1878). On Drake's last voyage see [**521**] *Sir Francis Drake his voyage, 1595, by Thomas Maynarde . . .* edited by W. D. Cooley (Hakluyt Soc. Pubns., 1st series, No. 4, 1849), and for [**522**] *The Discoverie of the Large and Bewtiful Empire of Guiana by Sir Walter Ralegh* the edition so entitled by V. T. Harlow (London, Argonaut Press, 1928).

THE SEVENTEENTH CENTURY

Engel Sluiter, [**523**] 'Dutch Maritime Power and the Colonial Status Quo, 1585–1641', *Pacific Historical Review*, xi (1942), 29–41, and [524] 'Dutch-Spanish Rivalry in the Caribbean Area, 1594–1609', *Hispanic American Historical Review*, xxviii (1948), 165–96, and [524a] I. A. Wright, 'The Dutch and Cuba, 1609–1643', *ibid.*, iv (1921), 597–634, are important articles, with which should be coupled G. Edmundson, [525] 'The Dutch in Western Guiana', *English Historical Review*, xvi (1901), 640–75, and, though relating to Portuguese territory, [526] 'The Dutch on the Amazon and Negro in the Seventeenth Century', *ibid.*, xviii (1903), 642–63, xix (1904), 1–25.

For French activities in the West Indies an outline, but not more than an outline, is available in [527] N. M. Crouse, *French Pioneers in the West Indies, 1624–1664* (Columbia Univ. Press, 1940), and [528] his *The French Struggle for the West Indies, 1665–1713* (Columbia Univ. Press, 1943). See also [529] S. L. Mims, *Colbert's West India Policy* (Yale Univ. Press, 1912).

[530] The attempt to establish *English Colonies in Guiana and on the Amazon, 1604–1668* is discussed by J. A. Williamson (Oxford, Clarendon Press, 1923). [531] A. P. Newton, *Colonising Activities of the English Puritans* (Yale Univ. Press, 1914), is concerned with the story of the Providence Company and of 'organised opposition to Spain in the Caribbean'. See also [532] D. Rowland, 'Spanish Occupation of the Island of Old Providence, or Santa Catalina, 1641–1670', *Hispanic American Historical Review*, xv (1935), 298–312. [533] I. A. Wright deals with 'The Spanish Resistance to the English Occupation of Jamaica, 1655–1660', *Royal Historical Society, Transactions*, 4th series, xiii (1930), 117–47, and [533a] A. P. Thornton with *West-India Policy under the Restoration* (Oxford, Clarendon Press, 1956). See also [534] his 'Spanish Slave-Ships in the English West Indies, 1660–1685', *Hispanic American Historical Review*, xxxv (1955), 374–85. For the buccaneers see [535] C. H. Haring, *The Buccaneers in the West Indies in the XVII Century* (London, Methuen, 1910), and [536] the classic *History of the Buccaneers of America* by James Burney (London, Allen and Unwin, 1949; reprinted from the London edition of 1816), and, for the ill-fated Darien scheme, [537] F. R. Hart, *The Disaster of Darien; the story of the Scots settlement and the causes of its failure, 1699–1701* (Boston and New York, Houghton Mifflin, 1929), [538] G. P. Insh, *The Company of Scotland trading to Africa and the Indies* (New York and London, Scribner's, 1932), and [539] G. P. Insh, *The Darien Scheme* (Historical Association Pamphlets, London, Staples Press, 1947).

See also Bolton and Ross [481], Crane [482], Dunn [477], Ford [478], Leonard [497], and, for further references to the literature on North America and the West Indies, *Harvard Guide to American History* [249].

[**540**] Esquemeling, John, *The Buccaneers of America* (edited by W. S. Stallybrass, London, Routledge: New York, Dutton, 1923).

[**541**] Firth, Sir Charles, ed., *The Narrative of General Venables, with an appendix of papers relating to the West Indies and the conquest of Jamaica, 1654–1655* (Royal Historical Society, Camden New Series, No. 60, London, 1900).

[**542**] Harlow, V. T., ed., *Colonising Expeditions to the West Indies and Guiana, 1623–1667* (Hakluyt Society Pubns., 2nd series, No. 56, London, 1925).

[**543**] Harlow, V. T., ed., 'The Voyages of Captain Christopher Jackson, 1642–1645', *Camden Miscellany, xiii* (Royal Historical Society, Camden Third Series, No. 34, London, 1924).

[**544**] Insh, G. P., ed., *Papers relating to the Ships and Voyages of the Company of Scotland trading to Africa and the Indies, 1696–1707* (Scottish Historical Society Pubns., 3rd series, No. 6, Edinburgh, 1924).

[**545**] Wilbur, M. E., ed., *Raveneau de Lussan, Buccaneer of the Spanish Main and early French Filibuster of the Pacific; a translation into English of his Journal of a Voyage into the South Seas in 1684* . . . (Cleveland, A. H. Clark, 1930).

[**546**] Wilmere, A., and Shaw, N. eds., *Narrative of a Voyage to the West Indies and Mexico in the years 1599–1602* . . . *by Samuel Champlain* (Hakluyt Soc. Pubns., 1st series, No. 23, London, 1859).

[**547**] Wright, I. A., ed., 'The English Conquest of Jamaica, 1655–56', *Camden Miscellany, xiii* (Royal Historical Society, Camden Third Series, No. 34, London, 1924).

[**548**] Wright, I. A., ed., 'Narrative of the English Attack on St. Domingo (1655)', *Camden Miscellany, xiv* (Royal Historical Society, Camden Third Series, No. 37, London, 1926).

See also Dampier [350] and Wafer [351].

4. THE EMPIRE UNDER THE BOURBONS

GENERAL

For general histories and special studies covering the Bourbon as well as the Habsburg period see nos. 195, 197–8, 201–4, 207–8, 210, and 211–12, and, for regional histories, nos. 251–2, 296, 340, and 343–8.

Bernard Moses, [**549**] *South America on the Eve of Emancipation* (New York and London, Putnam's, 1908), and [**550**] *Spain's Declining Power in South America, 1730–1806* (Univ. of California Press, 1919), bring together a widely ranging series of studies on various aspects of Spanish American life and institutions. [**551**] R. A. Humphreys, 'The Fall of the Spanish American Empire', *History*, n.s., xxxvii (1952), 213–27, is a general essay.

[**552**] L. E. Fisher, *The Background of the Revolution for Mexican Independence* (Boston, Christopher Publishing House, 1934), contains much ill-digested information. [**553**] W. S. Robertson, *The Life of Miranda* (2 vols., Univ. of North Carolina Press, 1929), is a masterly biography of the 'precursor' of Venezuelan independence which elaborates Robertson's earlier work, [**554**] *Francisco de Miranda and the Revolutionizing of Spanish America* (reprinted from the *Annual Report* of the American Historical Association for 1907, Washington, Govt. Printing Office, 1909). [**555**] H. G. Warren, 'The Early Revolutionary Career of Juan Mariano Picornell', *Hispanic American Historical Review*, xxii (1942), 57–81, discusses subversive propaganda in Venezuela in the closing decades of the empire, and [**556**] John Rydjord, *Foreign Interest in the Independence of New Spain* (Duke Univ. Press, 1935), is concerned with English (and American) designs and French activities. See also Rydjord [621].

[**557**] *A Voyage to South America: describing at large the Spanish cities, towns, provinces, etc., on that extensive continent*, by the two young Spanish naval officers, Jorge Juan and Antonio de Ulloa (London, 1758; 5th ed., 2 vols., London, 1807), is justly celebrated. On Ulloa, the real author, see [**558**] A. P. Whitaker, 'Antonio de Ulloa', *Hispanic American Historical Review*, xv (1935), 155–94, and [**559**] Lewis Hanke, 'Dos Palabras on Antonio de Ulloa and the *Noticias Secretas*', *ibid.*, xvi (1936), 479–514). [**560**] *An Account of the European Settlements in America* (3rd ed., rev., 2 vols., London, 1760), though not first-hand, makes use of first-hand evidence. For the researches of Alexander von Humboldt, who spent nearly five years in Spanish America, exploring, collecting, and describing, see the *Political Essay on the Kingdom of New Spain* [223], and the *Personal Narrative of Travels to the Equinoctial Regions of the New Continent* [224], which also contains Humboldt's 'Political Essay on the Island of Cuba'.

[**561**] Thomas Falkner, *A Description of Patagonia, and the adjoining parts of South America . . .* (Hereford, 1774; reprinted with an

introduction and notes by A. E. S. Neumann, Chicago, Armann and Armann, 1935), and [**562**] Martin Dobrizhoffer, *An Account of the Abipones, an equestrian people of Paraguay* (1784. 3 vols., London, 1822), are remarkable works by Jesuit missionaries. [**563**] A. Z. Helms, *Travels from Buenos Ayres, by Potosi, to Lima* (London, 1806), has its uses, though, as a contemporary review complained, the information which it contains is 'wonderfully scanty'. [**564**] François R. J. de Pons, *Travels in South America, during the years 1801, 1802, 1803 and 1804; containing a description of the captain-generalship of Caraccas* . . . (2 vols., London, 1807), is valuable. [**565**] *The Voyages and Travels of Captain Nathaniel Uring* (1726; edited by Alfred Dewar, London, Cassell, 1928), are noteworthy in that they contain, *inter alia*, an account of the methods of contraband trading. See also [**565a**] A. F. Frézier, *A Voyage to the South Sea and along the coasts of Chili and Peru in* . . . *1712, 1713 and 1714* (London, 1717), [**565b**] *The Narrative of* . . . *the Honourable John Byron* . . . *containing an account of the great distresses suffered by himself and his companions on the coast of Patagonia from the year 1740, till their arrival in England, 1746* . . . (London, 1768), *Anson's Voyage Round the World* [755], Molina [354], and Juarros [355].

ADMINISTRATIVE REORGANIZATION

See Haring [201], Roscher [210], Fisher [356], nos. 359, 361–3, and Moses [550].

[**566**] A. S. Aiton, 'Spanish Colonial Reorganization under the Family Compact', *Hispanic American Historical Review*, xii (1932), 269–80, examines French influence upon, and French interest in, the reform of the Spanish empire, also explored by [**567**] Allan Christelow, 'French Interest in the Spanish Empire during the Ministry of the Duc de Choiseul, 1759–1771', *ibid.*, xxi (1941), 515–37.

[**568**] H. I. Priestley, *José de Gálvez, Visitor-General of New Spain, 1765–1771* (Univ. of California Press, 1916), provides a detailed examination of conditions in New Spain and of the reforms which Gálvez initiated. It may be supplemented, so far as the Provincias Internas of New Spain are concerned, by Thomas [627], Bobb [628], and Worcester [629]. See also [**569**] L. N. McAlister, 'The Reorganization of the Army of New Spain, 1763–1766', *Hispanic American Historical Review*, xxxiii (1953), 1–32, together with [**569a**] his *The 'Fuero Militar' in New Spain, 1764–1800* (Univ. of Florida Press, 1957), and, for the operation of the

viceregal system in the late eighteenth century, [**570**] D. E. Smith, *The Viceroy of New Spain* (Univ. of California Press, 1913). For Peru there is no administrative study comparable to Priestley's *José de Gálvez*. Two useful articles, however, are [**571**] E. J. Gates, 'Don José Antonio de Areche: his own defense', *Hispanic American Historical Review*, viii (1928), 14–42, which discusses Areche's unsuccessful visitation from 1776 to 1783, and, on the administration of Teodoro de Croix from 1784 to 1790, [**572**] L. E. Fisher, 'Teodoro de Croix', *ibid.*, ix (1929), 488–504. Compare also Whitaker [443]. On the Viceroyalty of the Río de la Plata see Moses [549, 550] and Levene [346].

The intendancy system, first tried out in Cuba in 1764 and in time applied generally, is examined in [**573**] L. E. Fisher, *The Intendant System in Spanish America* (Univ. of California Press, 1929), and [**574**] her summary article under the same title in the *Hispanic American Historical Review*, viii (1928), 3–13. [**575**] W. W. Pierson, ed., *Studies in Hispanic American History* (Univ. of North Carolina Press, 1927), discusses 'The Establishment and Early Functioning of the *Intendencia* of Cuba', and [**576**] John Lynch throws new light on the relations of the intendants and the cabildos in the Río de la Plata, 'Intendants and Cabildos in the Viceroyalty of La Plata, 1782–1810', *Hispanic American Historical Review*, xxxv (1955), 337–62.

[**577**] A. P. Whitaker, 'The Pseudo-Aranda Memoir of 1783', *Hispanic American Historical Review*, xvii (1937), 287–313, and [**578**] A. R. Wright, 'The Aranda Memorial: Genuine or Forged?', *ibid.*, xviii (1938), 445–60, differ in their views on the authenticity of a document which proposed a drastic reorganization of the empire.

TRADE AND COMMERCIAL POLICY
GENERAL

On the Bourbon commercial reforms in general see Haring [201] and Diffie [202]. R. D. Hussey examines [**579**] 'Antecedents of the Spanish Monopolistic Overseas Trading Companies (1624–1728)', *Hispanic American Historical Review*, ix (1929), 1–30, and provides a detailed study of [**580**] *The Caracas Company, 1728–1784* (Harvard Univ. Press, 1934). [**581**] W. L. Schurz discusses the foundation, in 1785, of 'The Royal Philippine Company', *Hispanic American Historical Review*, iii (1920), 491–508. On the merchant guilds see [**582**] R. S. Smith, 'Origins of the Consulado of Guatemala', *ibid.*, xxvi (1946), 150–61, and his earlier article [424]. [**583**] J. F. King, 'Evolution of the Free Slave Trade Principle in Spanish Colonial Administration', *Hispanic American Historical Review*, xxii (1942), 34–56, throws light on 'a generally neglected aspect' of Bourbon commercial policy. [**584**] A. P. Whitaker, 'The Commerce of Louisiana and the Floridas at the end of the Eighteenth Century', *ibid.*, viii (1928), 190–203, examines the commercial history of a particular area 'evolving from monopoly through contraband to partial freedom, then greater freedom, and finally to separation from Spain'. [**585**] R. F. Nichols, 'Trade Relations and the Establishment of the United States Consulates in Spanish America, 1779–1809', *ibid.*, xiii (1933), 289–313, discusses concessions made to neutral traders, and [**586**] Harry Bernstein, *Origins of Inter-American Interest, 1700–1812* (Univ. of Pennsylvania Press, 1945), treats, *inter alia*, of commercial relations between New York, New England, and Pennsylvania and Spanish America. See also [**586a**] R. F. Nichols, *Advance Agents of American Destiny* (Univ. of Pennsylvania Press, 1956), for the career, in particular, of William Shaler.

Allan Christelow's two articles on 'French Interest in the Spanish Empire during the Ministry of the Duc de Choiseul, 1759–1771' [567], and [**587**] 'Great Britain and the Trades from Cadiz and Lisbon to Spanish America and Brazil, 1759–1783', *Hispanic American Historical Review*, xxvii (1947), 2–29, are alike important.

[**588**] Chandler, C. L., 'The River Plate Voyages, 1798–1800', *American Historical Review*, xxiii (July 1918), 816–26.

[**589**] Chandler, C. L., 'United States Merchant Ships in the Río de la Plata (1801–8), as shown by early Newspapers', *Hispanic American Historical Review*, ii (1919), 26–54.

[**590**] Nichols, R. F., 'Cuban Commercial Regulations in 1805', *Hispanic American Historical Review*, xvi (1936), 213–19.

[**591**] Smith, R. S., 'Shipping in the Port of Veracruz, 1790–1821', *Hispanic American Historical Review*, xxiii (1943), 5–20.

[**592**] Whitaker, A. P., ed., *Documents relating to the Commercial Policy of Spain in the Floridas with incidental reference to Louisiana* (Deland, Florida State Historical Society, 1931). [Relating to the years 1779–1808.]

See also Schurz [426, 427], Carrera Stampa [429], and Smith [438].

The Spanish Empire in America

[**593**] V. L. Brown, 'Contraband Trade: a Factor in the Decline of Spain's Empire in America', *Hispanic American Historical Review*, viii (1928), 178–89, is a short general discussion.

[**594**] Curtis Nettels, 'England and the Spanish American Trade, 1680–1715', *Journal of Modern History*, iii (1931), 1–32, discusses trade between Jamaica and the mainland. Compare [**595**] his *The Money Supply of the American Colonies before 1720* (Madison, Wis., Univ. of Wisconsin Studies in the Social Sciences and History, 1934).

[**596**] Elizabeth Donnan deals with 'The Early Days of the South Sea Company, 1711–1718', *Journal of Economic and Business History*, ii (May 1930), 419–50. Note also [**597**] her *Documents Illustrative of the History of the Slave Trade to America* (4 vols., Washington, Carnegie Institution, 1930–5), though these mostly relate to British possessions. On the contraband activities of the Company see [**598**] A. S. Aiton, 'The Asiento Treaty as Reflected in the Papers of Lord Shelburne', *Hispanic American Historical Review*, viii (1928), 167–77, [**599**] V. L. Brown, 'The South Sea Company and Contraband Trade', *American Historical Review*, xxxi (July 1926), 662–78, and the important contribution of [**600**] G. H. Nelson, 'Contraband Trade under the Asiento, 1730–1739', *ibid.*, li (Oct. 1945), 55–67. Compare [**601**] L. M. Penson, 'The West Indies and the Spanish American Trade, 1713–1748', *Cambridge History of the British Empire, I. The Old Empire* (Cambridge Univ. Press, 1929), pp. 330–45, [**602**] H. W. V. Temperley, 'The Relations of England with Spanish America, 1720–1744', American Historical Association, *Annual Report*, 1911 (2 vols., Washington, Govt. Printing Office, 1913), i, 231–7, Pares [691], and McLachlan [692].

On the later history of the contraband trade [**603**] A. Christelow, 'Contraband Trade between Jamaica and the Spanish Main and the Free Port Act of 1766', *Hispanic American Historical Review*, xxii (1942), 309–43, and [**604**] D. B. Goebel, 'British Trade to the Spanish Colonies, 1796–1823', *American Historical Review*, xliii (Jan. 1938), 288–320, do much to elucidate a difficult story. [**605**] Frances Armytage provides a detailed examination of the working of *The Free Port System in the British West Indies. A study in commercial policy, 1766–1822* (London, Longmans, Green, 1953). See also Whitaker [584], Bernstein [586], and Brown [696].

[606] Humphreys, R. A., 'Economic Aspects of the Fall of the Spanish American Empire', *Revista de Historia de América*, Núm. 30 (1950), 450–6.

MONEY AND MONETARY PROBLEMS

[607] Hamilton, E. J., 'Money and Economic Recovery in Spain under the first Bourbon, 1701–46', *Journal of Modern History*, xv (1943), 192–206.

[608] Hamilton, E. J., 'Monetary Problems in Spain and Spanish America, 1751–1800', *Journal of Economic History*, iv (1944), 21–48.

[609] Hamilton, E. J., *War and Prices in Spain, 1651–1800* (Harvard Univ. Press, 1947).

MINING

[610] C. G. Motten's brief study, *Mexican Silver and the Enlightenment* (Univ. of Pennsylvania Press, 1950), examines the state of the Mexican mining industry in the eighteenth century, the attempts to improve it, and, in particular, the work of Fausto de Elhuyar as director-general of the Real Cuerpo de Minería. [611] Walter Howe, *The Mining Guild of New Spain and its Tribunal General, 1770–1821* (Harvard Univ. Press, 1949), is a full and detailed administrative study which makes an important contribution to Mexican economic history. [612] A. P. Whitaker, 'The Elhuyar Mining Missions and the Enlightenment', *Hispanic American Historical Review*, xxxi (1951), 558–85, examines the inception of these missions, ending with their sailing, in 1788, to New Spain, Peru, and New Granada.

For the decadence of the Huancavelica mercury mine in the eighteenth century and the attempts at rehabilitation see Whitaker [443], and, for placer mining in Colombia, West [441].

THE CHURCH AND THE MISSIONS

For a general account see Diffie [202]. Many of the works which relate to ecclesiastical and mission history during the Habsburg period also refer to the Bourbon era. See, for example, Borah [397], Lea [398], Rippy and Nelson [402], Barth [403], Lanning [405], Graham [409], Charlevoix [410], Bolton [412], and Dunne [416]. The mission 'as a frontier institution' is, moreover, closely associated with the history of the Californias in the eighteenth century, and reference should therefore be made to such works as those of Wilbur [650], Bolton [658], and Geiger [658a]. Specifically eighteenth-century studies are not numerous. But [**613**] P. M. Dunne, *Black Robes in Lower California* (Univ. of California Press, 1952), is a notable contribution, and [**614**] Z. Engelhardt, *The Missions and Missionaries of California* (5 vols., San Francisco, J. H. Barry, 1908–16), is a standard work. For New Mexico see Adams and Chávez [644a]. [**615**] Mary Watters, 'The Colonial Missions in Venezuela', *Catholic Historical Review*, xxiii (1937), 129–52, is principally, though not exclusively, concerned with the eighteenth century. For a brief account of the expulsion of the Jesuits in 1767 see Moses [550]. [**616**] L. E. Fisher, *Champion of Reform. Manuel Abad y Queipo* (New York, Library Publishers, 1955), is a biography of the enlightened ecclesiastic who became bishop-elect of Michoacán in 1810.

SOCIAL AND INTELLECTUAL LIFE

[**617**] A. P. Whitaker, ed., *Latin America and the Enlightenment* (New York and London, Appleton-Century, 1942), and Lanning, *Academic Culture in the Spanish Colonies* [453], dispel the ancient legend of 'l'abrutissement de tous par un despotisme royal et la "sombre théocratie" '. See also [**617a**] J. T. Lanning, *The Eighteenth-Century Enlightenment in the University of San Carlos de Guatemala* (Cornell Univ. Press, 1956), and compare [**618**] the brief study of Bernard Moses, *The Intellectual Background of the Revolution in South America, 1810–1824* (New York, Hispanic Society of America, 1926), Lanning [454a], and Henríquez-Ureña [455].

Zavala [323] is in part concerned with the persistence of traditional Spanish-Catholic liberal ideas. Bernstein [586] discusses intellectual contacts with New York, Boston, and Philadelphia. [**619**] J. R. Spell sketches the influence of 'Rousseau in Spanish America', *Hispanic American Historical Review*, xv (1935), 260–7, and [**620**] discusses, with greater elaboration, *Rousseau in the Spanish World before 1833* (Univ. of Texas Press, 1938). [**621**] John Rydjord, 'The French Revolution and Mexico', *Hispanic American Historical Review*, ix (1929), 60–98, examines, *inter alia*, the impact of French revolutionary doctrines.

On the mining and botanical expeditions of the eighteenth century, see Whitaker [612] and Motten [610], together with [**622**] H. W. Rickett, *The Royal Botanical Expedition to New Spain, 1788–1820* (Waltham, Mass., Chronica Botanica, 1947), and [**623**] Hipólito Ruiz, *Travels of Ruiz, Pavón, and Dombey in Peru* *and Chile (1777–1788)*, translated by B. E. Dahlgren (Chicago, Field Museum of Natural History, 1940). For the arts consult Kelemen [459] and nos. 461–4.

Social conditions are discussed in Haring [201], Diffie [202], and Moses [207, 549, and 550]. [**624**] P. A. Means writes on 'The Rebellion of Tupac-Amaru II, 1780–1781', *Hispanic American Historical Review*, ii (1919), 1–25, and [**625**] M. W. Nichols on 'The Historic Gaucho', *ibid.*, xxi (1941), 417–24. Compare [**626**] her *The Gaucho. Cattle hunter, cavalryman, ideal of romance* (Duke Univ. Press, 1942).

THE NORTHERN FRONTIERS OF NEW SPAIN, 1700–1819

GENERAL

See Bolton [275], Brebner [276], Priestley [250], and *New Spain and the Anglo-American West* [467]. For bibliographies and guides consult Mecham [53], Steck [54], Wagner [59], and *Harvard Guide* [249].

[**627**] A. B. Thomas, *Teodoro de Croix and the Northern Frontier of New Spain, 1776–1783* (Univ. of Oklahoma Press, 1941), is concerned with the problems of administration and of defence against Indian warfare in the Commandancy-General of the Provincias Internas (Texas, Coahuila, New Vizcaya, Sonora, Sinaloa, New Mexico, and the Californias), which was organized in 1776. Compare [**628**] B. E. Bobb, 'Bucareli and the Interior Provinces', *Hispanic American Historical Review*, xxxiv (1954), 20–36, and [**629**] the edition by D. E. Worcester of Bernardo de Gálvez's *Instructions for Governing the Interior Provinces of New Spain, 1786* (Berkeley, Quivira Society, 1951).

For a description of the eastern interior provinces in 1811 see [**630**] the *Report of Ramos Arizpe to the Spanish Cortes*, ed. by N. L. Benson (Univ. of Texas Press, 1950), with which may be compared the *exposición*, also to the Spanish Cortes, of Pedro Bautisto Pino in [**631**] H. B. Carroll and J. V. Haggard, eds., *Three New Mexico Chronicles* (Albuquerque, Quivira Society, 1942).

TEXAS

See Bancroft [465] and Dunn [477]. C. E. Castañeda, *Our Catholic Heritage in Texas, 1519–1936. II. The Winning of Texas, 1693–1731* [476], deals with the occupation of eastern Texas and the foundation in 1718 of San Antonio. The history is continued in [**632**] *III. The Mission Era: the Missions at Work, 1731–1761*; [**633**] *IV. The Mission Era: the Passing of the Missions, 1762–1782*; [**634**] *V. The Mission Era: the End of the Spanish Régime, 1780–1810*; and [**635**] *VI. Transition Period: the Fight for Freedom, 1810–1836* (Austin, Von Boeckmann-Jones Co., 1938–50).

[**636**] L. F. Hill, *José de Escandón and the Founding of Nuevo Santander* (Columbus, Ohio State Univ. Press, 1926), is concerned with the consolidation of Spanish rule to the south of Texas. [**637**] H. E. Bolton, *Texas in the Middle Eighteenth Century* (Univ. of California Press, 1915), is one of his most able books. [**638**] J. K. Garrett, *Green Flag over Texas* (New York and Dallas, Cordova Press, 1939), deals with the early repercussions in Texas of revolutionary movements in New Spain between 1810 and 1813. See also Warren [881]. [**639**] *Pichardo's Treatise on the Limits of Louisiana and Texas* (edited by C. W. Hackett, C. C. Shelby, and M. R. Splawn, 4 vols., Univ. of Texas Press, 1931–46), is a monumental work written between 1808 and 1812 to refute the contention that Texas was included within the limits of the Louisiana purchase of 1803. For the Adams-Onís treaty of 1819 defining these limits see Brooks [690].

[**640**] Céliz, Francisco de, *Diary of the Alarcón Expedition into Texas, 1718–1719* (ed. by F. L. Hoffmann, Los Angeles, Quivira Society, 1935).

[**641**] Morfi, J. A., *History of Texas, 1673–1779* (ed. by C. E. Castañeda, 2 vols., Albuquerque, Quivira Society, 1935).

NEW MEXICO

See Bancroft [466], Thomas [492], and Hackett [486]. [**642**] A. B. Thomas, ed., *The Plains Indians and New Mexico, 1751–1778* (Coronado Cuarto Centennials Pubns., vol. xi, Univ. of New Mexico Press, 1940), and [**643**] the same editor's *Forgotten Frontiers: a study of the Spanish Indian policy of Don Juan Bautista de Anza, Governor of New Mexico, 1777–1787* (Univ. of Oklahoma Press, 1932), are principally concerned with the defence of the Pueblo Indians against the Plains Indians. [**644**] H. E. Bolton, ed., *Pageant in the Wilderness, the story of the Escalante expedition to the interior basin, 1776* . . . (Salt Lake City, Utah State Historical Society, 1950, i.e. 1951), records the itinerary of an expedition setting out from Santa Fe to open a route to the newly established port of Monterey in Upper California, and [**644a**] E. B. Adams and A. Chávez, eds., *The Missions of New Mexico, 1776. A descrip-*

tion by *Fray Francisco Atanasio Domínguez* (Univ. of New Mexico Press, 1956), is the report of a canonical visitor drawn up in 1776–7. For a report on New Mexico in 1811 see Carroll and Haggard [631].

SONORA, PIMERÍA ALTA, AND LOWER CALIFORNIA

See Bancroft [465, 466] and Bolton [412, 491]. Dunne, *Black Robes in Lower California* [613], covers the years 1691 to 1768. [645] S. F. Cook examines *The Extent and Significance of Disease among the Indians of Baja California, 1697–1773* (Ibero-Americana, 12, Univ. of California Press, 1937).

[646] Baegert, J. J., *Observations in Lower California* (ed. by M. M. Brandenburg and C. L. Baumann, Univ. of California Press, 1952).

[647] Clavigero, F. J., *The History of (Lower) California* (ed. by S. E. Lake and A. A. Gray, Stanford Univ. Press, 1938).

[648] Pfefferkorn, Ignaz, *Sonora. A description of the province* (ed. by T. E. Treutlein, Coronado Cuarto Centennial Pubns., vol. xii, Univ. of New Mexico Press, 1949).

[649] Taraval, Sigismundo, *The Indian Uprising in Lower California 1734–1737, as described by Father Sigismundo Taraval* (ed. by M. E. Wilbur, Los Angeles, Quivira Society, 1931).

[650] Venegas, Miguel, *Juan María de Salvatierra of the Company of Jesus; missionary in the province of New Spain, and apostolic conqueror of the Californias* (ed. by M. E. Wilbur, Cleveland, A. H. Clark, 1929).

UPPER CALIFORNIA AND THE NORTHWEST COAST

See Bancroft [465], together with [651] his monumental *History of California* (6 vols., San Francisco, 1884–9) and [652] *History of the Northwest Coast* (2 vols., San Francisco, 1884). C. E. Chapman, [653] *The Founding of Spanish California: the north-westward expansion of New Spain, 1687–1783* (New York, Macmillan, 1916), and [654] *A History of California: the Spanish period* (New York, Macmillan, 1921), are standard works. [655] H. E. Bolton, *Outpost of Empire* (New York, Knopf, 1931; reprinted 1939), tells 'the story of the founding of San Francisco' in 1776. On the missions see the massive work of Engelhardt [614] and note also [656] S. F. Cook, *The Conflict between the California Indian and White Civilization* (Pts. I and II, Ibero-Americana, 21, 22, Univ. of California Press, 1943).

[657] Bolton, H. E., ed., *Anza's California Expeditions* (5 vols., Univ. of California Press, 1930).

[**658**] Bolton, H. E., ed., *Fray Juan Crespi, missionary explorer on the Pacific coast, 1769–1774* (Univ. of California Press, 1927).

[**658a**] Geiger, M. J., ed., *Palóu's Life of Fray Junípero Serra* (Washington, Academy of American Franciscan History, 1955).

[**659**] Jane, Cecil, ed., *A Spanish Voyage to Vancouver and the Northwest Coast of America; being the narrative of the voyage made in 1792 by the schooners 'Sutil' and 'Mexicana' to explore the Strait of Fuca* (London, Argonaut Press, 1930).

[**660**] Palóu, Francisco, *Historical Memoirs of New California* (ed. by H. E. Bolton, 4 vols., Univ. of California Press, 1926).

[**660a**] Tibesar, Antonine, ed., *Writings of Junípero Serra* (4 vols., Washington, Academy of American Franciscan History, 1956–7).

[**661**] Wagner, H. R., *Spanish Explorations in the Strait of Juan de Fuca* (Santa Ana, California, Fine Arts Press, 1933).

LOUISIANA AND THE FLORIDAS

Florida, 1700–1763
For the Pensacola settlement at the end of the seventeenth century see Ford [478], for the *Defenses of Spanish Florida*, Chatelain [480], and, for the missions, Lanning [405]. The Anglo-Spanish conflict over the Georgia country is dealt with in Bolton and Ross, *The Debatable Land* [481]. See also Crane [482] and [**662**] J. T. Lanning, *The Diplomatic History of Georgia* (Univ. of North Carolina Press, 1936).

[**663**] Bolton, H. E., ed., *Arredondo's Historical Proof of Spain's Title to Georgia* . . . (Univ. of California Press, 1925).

Louisiana, 1763–1803
The cession of Louisiana by France to Spain in 1762–3 is considered in [**664**] A. S. Aiton, 'The Diplomacy of the Louisiana Cession', *American Historical Review*, xxxvi (July 1931), 701–20, and [**665**] E. W. Lyon's useful *Louisiana in French Diplomacy, 1759–1804* (Univ. of Oklahoma Press, 1934). Contrast [**666**] W. R. Shepherd, 'The Cession of Louisiana to Spain', *Political Science Quarterly*, xix (1904), 439–58. The revolt against the first Spanish governor, Antonio de Ulloa, who arrived in 1766, is described in [**667**] J. E. Winston, 'The Cause and Results of the Revolution of 1768 in Louisiana', *Louisiana Historical Quarterly*, xv (1932), 181–213, and the taking possession by Alexander O'Reilly in [**668**] D. K. Bjork, 'Alexander O'Reilly and the

The Empire under the Bourbons

Spanish Occupancy of Louisiana, 1769–70', *New Spain and the Anglo-American West* [467].

The classic history of Louisiana is [**669**] C. Gayarré, *History of Louisiana* (4th ed., 4 vols., New Orleans, Hansell, 1903). Special aspects and periods of Spanish administration are examined in [**670**] J. W. Caughey, *Bernardo de Gálvez in Louisiana, 1776–1783* (Univ. of California Press, 1934), and [**671**] C. M. Burson, *The Stewardship of Don Esteban Miró, 1782–1792* (New Orleans, American Printing Co., 1940), as also in [**672**] the collection of documents edited by H. E. Bolton, *Athanase de Mézières and the Louisiana-Texas Frontier, 1768–1780* (2 vols., Cleveland, A. H. Clark, 1914).

Two brilliant studies by A. P. Whitaker, [**673**] *The Spanish-American Frontier, 1783–1795: the westward movement and the Spanish retreat in the Mississippi Valley* (New York and Boston, Houghton Mifflin, 1927), and [**674**] *The Mississippi Question, 1795–1803. A study in trade, politics, and diplomacy* (New York, Appleton-Century, 1934), clarify the story of the relations between Spanish Louisiana and the United States. Compare, on the Treaty of San Lorenzo of 1795, which, *inter alia*, conceded to the United States the free navigation of the Mississippi, [**675**] S. F. Bemis, *Pinckney's Treaty; a study of America's advantage from Europe's distress* (Johns Hopkins Press, 1926), and, on Spanish commercial policy generally, Whitaker [584, 592].

For the retrocession of Louisiana to France in 1800 and its purchase by the United States in 1802 see Lyon [665], Whitaker [674], and Whitaker's articles on [**676**] 'The Retrocession of Louisiana in Spanish Policy', *American Historical Review*, xxxix (April 1934), 454–76, and [**677**] 'France and the American Deposit at New Orleans', *Hispanic American Historical Review*, xi (1931), 485–502. For further references consult Bemis and Griffin, *Guide* [60].

[**678**] Houck, L., ed., *The Spanish Régime in Missouri* (2 vols., Chicago, R. R. Donnelley, 1909).

[**679**] Kinnaird, L., ed., *Spain in the Mississippi Valley, 1765–1794* (3 vols., American Historical Association, *Annual Report*, 1945, Washington, Govt. Printing Office, 1949).

[**680**] Robertson, J. A., ed., *Louisiana under the Rule of Spain, France, and the United States, 1785–1807* (2 vols., A. H. Clark, Cleveland, 1911).

The Floridas, 1783–1819

On British policy in the Floridas after their cession by Spain in 1763 see [**681**] C. L. Mowat, *East Florida as a British Province, 1763–1784* (Univ. of California Press, 1943), and [**682**] C. Johnson, *British West Florida, 1763–1783* (Yale Univ. Press, 1943). [**683**] K. T. Abbey deals with 'Spanish Projects for the Reoccupation of the Floridas during the American Revolution', *Hispanic American Historical Review*, ix (1929), 265–85, and [**684**] J. B. Lockey's documentary collection, *East Florida, 1783–1785* (Univ. of California Press, 1949), relates to the transfer of the province from England to Spain. [**685**] R. K. Murdock discusses *The Georgia-Florida Frontier, 1793–1796* (Univ. of California Press, 1951). For commercial policy see Whitaker [584, 592].

On the disputed territory of West Florida consult Whitaker [674] and [**686**] I. J. Cox, *The West Florida Controversy, 1798–1813: a study in American diplomacy* (Johns Hopkins Press, 1918). See also [**687**] J. W. Pratt, *Expansionists of 1812* (New York, Macmillan, 1925). [**688**] R. K. Wyllys deals with 'The East Florida Revolution of 1812–1814', *Hispanic American Historical Review*, ix (1929), 415–45. See also [**688a**] R. W. Patrick, *Florida Fiasco: rampant rebels on the Georgia-Florida border, 1810–1815* (Univ. of Georgia Press, 1954). On the final purchase of Florida by the United States in 1819 see [**689**] C. C. Griffin, *The United States and the Disruption of the Spanish Empire, 1810–1822* (Columbia Univ. Press, 1937), and [**690**] P. C. Brooks, *Diplomacy and the Borderlands: the Adams-Onis treaty of 1819* (Univ. of California Press, 1939). For further references consult Bemis and Griffin, *Guide* [60].

INTERNATIONAL RIVALRIES[1]

The outstanding study for the first half of the eighteenth century is [**691**] Richard Pares, *War and Trade in the West Indies, 1739–1763* (Oxford, Clarendon Press, 1936). See also [**692**] Jean O. McLachlan, *Trade and Peace with Old Spain, 1667–1750* (Cambridge Univ. Press, 1940), which emphasizes the importance of British trade with Spain as distinct from British trade with Spanish America, and two short essays on the causes of the War of Jenkins' Ear, [**693**] H. W. V. Temperley, 'The Causes of the War of Jenkins' Ear, 1739', Royal Historical Society, *Transactions*,

[1] Colonial rivalries in North America, the problems of the Spanish-American frontier, and the relations between Spain and the United States are dealt with in the preceding sections on Texas and on Louisiana and the Floridas.

3rd series, iii (1909), 197–236, and [**694**] E. G. Hildner, 'The Rôle of the South Sea Company in the Diplomacy leading to the War of Jenkins' Ear, 1729–1739', *Hispanic American Historical Review*, xviii (1938), 322–41. [**695**] N. V. Russell describes 'The Reaction in England and America to the Capture of Havana, 1762', *ibid.*, ix (1929), 303–16, and [**695a**] F. R. Hart, *The Siege of Havana* (Boston and New York, Houghton Mifflin, 1931).

[**696**] V. L. Brown, 'Anglo-Spanish Relations in America in the Closing Years of the Colonial Era', *Hispanic American Historical Review*, v (1922), 327–483, covers the years 1763 to 1774 and ranges from the Mosquito Shore to the Falkland Islands. On the Mosquito Shore and the Belize settlement see also Pares [691] and [**697**] Sir John Burdon's very indifferently edited *Archives of British Honduras* (3 vols., London, Sifton, Praed, 1931–5), and, on the Falkland Islands, [**698**] Julius Goebel, *The Struggle for the Falkland Islands* (Yale Univ. Press, 1927). [**699**] *The Nootka Sound Controversy* of 1790 is dealt with by W. R. Manning (Washington, Govt. Printing Office, 1905), and [**699a**] J. M. Norris, 'The Policy of the British Cabinet in the Nootka Crisis', *English Historical Review*, lxx (1955), 562–80. See Christelow [603] and Armytage [605] for the free ports in the West Indies, and, for Puerto Rico, [**699b**] A. Morales-Carrión, *Puerto Rico and the Non-Hispanic Caribbean: a study in the decline of Spanish exclusivism* (Río Piedras, P.R., Univ. of Puerto Rico Press, 1952).

[**699c**] G. V. Blue examines 'French Interest in Pacific America in the Eighteenth Century', *Pacific Historical Review*, iv (1935), 246–66, and Moses [550] Spanish-Portuguese relations in South America and the boundary treaty of 1750. Compare [**700**] M. W. Williams, 'The Treaty of Tordesillas and the Argentine-Brazilian Boundary Settlement', *Hispanic American Historical Review*, v (1922), 3–23. [**701**] W. G. Schaeffer, 'The Delayed Cession of Spanish Santo Domingo to France, 1795–1801', *ibid.*, xxix (1949), 46–68, deals with events in the Spanish section of the island between its formal cession under the Treaty of Basle and its final surrender to Toussaint Louverture.

For European designs and ambitions in the closing decades of the Spanish empire see Robertson [553, 554] and Rydjord [556, 621]. Note also [**702**] 'Miranda and the British Admiralty, 1804–1806' (unsigned), *American Historical Review*, vi (April 1901), 508–30, which prints Sir Home Popham's memorandum of 1804. Moses [549, 550], Levene [346], and [**703**] Sir John

Fortescue, *A History of the British Army* (13 vols. in 14, London, Macmillan, 1899–1930), vol. v, describe the British invasions of the Río de la Plata in 1806–7, and on these see in particular [**704**] *Minutes of a Court Martial . . . for the Trial of Captain Sir Home Popham* (London, 1807), [**705**] *The Proceedings of a General Court Martial . . . for the Trial of Lieut. Gen. Whitelocke* (2 vols., London, 1808), and [**705a**] Alexander Gillespie, *Gleanings and Remarks: collected during many months of residence at Buenos Ayres, and within the Upper Country . . .* (Leeds, 1818).

[**705b**] Humphreys, R. A., 'Richard Oswald's Plan for an English and Russian Attack on Spanish America, 1781–1782', *Hispanic American Historical Review*, xviii (1938), 95–101.

[**705c**] Kinnaird, Lucia B., 'Creassy's Plan for Seizing Panama, with an Introductory Account of British Designs on Panama', *Hispanic American Historical Review*, xiii (1933), 46–78.

[**705d**] Thomas, M. E., 'Creassy's Plan for Seizing Panama', *Hispanic American Historical Review*, xxii (1942), 82–103.

[**705e**] Mullett, C. F., 'British Schemes against Spanish America in 1806', *Hispanic American Historical Review*, xxvii (1947), 269–78.

VIII

THE PORTUGUESE IN BRAZIL

1. GENERAL

HISTORIES AND ESSAYS

For works covering the colonial history of Brazil as well as the colonial history of Spanish America see Watson [197], Winsor [198], Chapman [211], and, more particularly, Diffie [202].

[**706**] Robert Southey's massive *History of Brazil* (3 vols., London, 1810–19), though in some respects outdated, and prejudiced in others, is still the most comprehensive treatment in English, and Southey's own judgement still stands: 'What I have done is in many parts imperfect; it is nevertheless even now a great achievement'. [**707**] João Pandiá Calógeras, *A History of Brazil* (translated and edited by P. A. Martin. Univ. of North Carolina Press, 1939), covers the colonial as well as the national period. [**708**] Gilberto Freyre, *The Masters and the Slaves* (translated by Samuel Putnam, 2nd ed., New York, Knopf, 1956), is a study both 'in the development of Brazilian civilization' and in the history of Portuguese colonization. [**709**] P. A. Martin, 'Portugal in America', *Hispanic American Historical Review*, xvii (1937), 182–210, is a general essay.

For a comparison between Portuguese and Spanish methods of colonization see [**710**] M. de Oliveira Lima, *The Evolution of Brazil compared with that of Spanish and Anglo-Saxon America* (Stanford Univ. Press, 1914).

SPECIAL ASPECTS

[**711**] J. F. Normano, *Brazil. A study of economic types* (Univ. of North Carolina Press, 1935), is primarily concerned with the economic history of Brazil as an independent state but contains also pertinent comments on colonial economic developments. [**712**] R. E. Poppino discusses the 'Cattle Industry in Colonial Brazil', *Mid-America*, xxxi (1949), 219–47. [**713**] V. M. Shillington and A. B. Wallis Chapman, *The Commercial Relations of England and Portugal* (London, Routledge, 1907), and [**713a**] A. B. Wallis Chapman, 'Commercial Relations of England and Portugal,

1487–1808', Royal Historical Society, *Transactions*, 3rd series, i (1907), 157–79, illustrate English interest in the Brazil trade. [**714**] Samuel Putnam, *Marvelous Journey. A survey of four centuries of Brazilian writing* (New York, Knopf, 1948), deals with literary history and much else besides. On the fine arts see [**715**] R. C. Smith, 'Baroque Architecture', in *Portugal and Brazil. An introduction* [1347].

2. THE SIXTEENTH CENTURY

DISCOVERY

See Prestage, *Portuguese Pioneers* [237], and Morison, *Portuguese Voyages* [236]. [**716**] Fidelino de Figueiredo, 'The Geographical Discoveries and Conquests of the Portuguese', *Hispanic American Historical Review*, vi (1926), 47–70, is a useful general article which illustrates Portuguese opinion. [**717**] C. E. Nowell, 'The Discovery of Brazil—Accidental or Intentional?' *ibid.*, xvi (1936), 311–38, discusses the voyage of Pedro Alvares Cabral and pleads for intention, as also do Figueiredo and Prestage. But contrast Morison [236] and Greenlee [733].

For the demarcation line between Portuguese and Spanish possessions see Davenport [225] and Vander Linden [321]. Note also Williams [700] and [**718**] W. B. Greenlee, 'The Background of Brazilian History', *Americas*, ii (Oct. 1945), 151–64.

SETTLEMENT

[**719**] W. B. Greenlee provides an excellent summary of 'The First Half Century of Brazilian History', *Mid-America*, xxv (1943), 91–120. The character of the early captaincies is examined by [**720**] Alexander Marchant, 'Feudal and Capitalistic Elements in the Portuguese Settlement of Brazil', *Hispanic American Historical Review*, xxii (1942), 493–512, and R. L. Butler deals with the early governors-general: [**721**] 'Thomé de Sousa, First Governor-General of Brazil, 1549–1553', [**722**] 'Duarte da Costa, Second Governor-General of Brazil', and [**723**] 'Mem de Sá, Third Governor-General of Brazil, 1557–1572', *Mid-America*, xxiv (1942), 229–51, xxv (1943), 163–79, xxvi (1944), 111–37.

[**724**] The scope of Alexander Marchant's useful *From Barter to Slavery. The economic relations of Portuguese and Indians in the settlement of Brazil, 1500–1580* (Johns Hopkins Press, 1942), is sufficiently indicated by its title. Consult, also, on the treatment of the Indians,

Kieman [741, 742]. J. V. Jacobsen and J. M. Espinosa discuss the work of the Jesuits. See J. V. Jacobsen, [**725**] 'Jesuit Founders in Portugal and Brazil', and [**726**] 'Nóbrega of Brazil', *Mid-America*, xxiv (1942), 3–26, 151–87; and J. M. Espinosa, [**727**] 'Gouvéia: Jesuit Lawgiver in Brazil', *ibid.*, xxiv (1942), 27–60; [**728**] 'Luiz da Grã, Mission Builder and Educator of Brazil', *ibid.*, xxiv (1942), 188–216; [**729**] 'José de Anchieta: "Apostle of Brazil" ', *ibid.*, xxv (1943), 250–74, xxvi (1944), 40–61; and, dealing with the seventeenth as well as the sixteenth century, [**730**] 'Fernão Cardim, Jesuit Humanist of Colonial Brazil', *ibid.*, xxiv (1942), 252–71.

[**731**] C. E. Nowell, 'The French in Sixteenth-Century Brazil', *Americas*, v (April 1949), 381–93, discusses foreign intrusion. Note also Marsden [505], and, for the adventures of Aleixo Garcia, Nowell [305].

[**732**] Virginia Rau and Bailey W. Diffie, 'Alleged Fifteenth-Century Joint-Stock Companies and the Articles of Dr Fitzler', *Bulletin of the Institute of Historical Research*, xxvi (1953), 181–99, is a devastating exposure which should be read by all students of Portuguese commercial expansion.

CONTEMPORARY NARRATIVES

[**733**] *The Voyage of Pedro Alvares Cabral to Brazil and India, from contemporary narratives and documents*, is examined by W. B. Greenlee (Hakluyt Soc. Pubns., 2nd series, No. 81, London, 1938). [**733a**] R. G. Marsden has edited 'The Voyage of the *Barbara* to Brazil, Anno 1540' (Navy Record Society Pubns., xl: *The Naval Miscellany II*, London, 1912), and [**734**] Richard F. Burton *The Captivity of Hans Stade of Hesse, in* A.D. *1547–1555, among the wild tribes of eastern Brazil* (translated by Albert Tootal. Hakluyt Soc. Pubns., 1st series, No. 51, London, 1874). For the English attack on Pernambuco see [**735**] *The Voyages of Sir James Lancaster to Brazil and the East Indies, 1591–1603* (edited by Sir William Foster, *ibid.*, 2nd series, No. 85, London, 1940). The *Documents and Narratives concerning the Discovery and Conquest of Latin America* published by the Cortés Society contain the two histories of Pero de Magalhães de Gandavo edited by J. B. Stetson under the title [**736**] *The Histories of Brazil* (2 vols., New York, 1922). See also nos. 214–15, 318–19, 353, and 519–20.

The Portuguese in Brazil

3. THE SEVENTEENTH CENTURY

The importance of the seventeenth-century history of Brazil is fully demonstrated in two excellent studies by C. R. Boxer, [737] *Salvador de Sá and the Struggle for Brazil and Angola, 1602–1686* (London, Athlone Press, 1952), and [738] *The Dutch in Brazil, 1624–1654* (Oxford, Clarendon Press, 1957), which supersedes the early series of articles [739] by G. Edmundson, 'The Dutch Power in Brazil (1624–1654)', *English Historical Review*, xi (1896), 231–59, xiv (1899), 676–99, xv (1900), 38–57. See also C. R. Boxer, [740] 'Salvador Correia de Sá e Benavides and the Reconquest of Angola in 1648', *Hispanic American Historical Review*, xxviii (1948), 483–513, [740a] 'Padre António Vieira, S.J., and the Institution of the Brazil Company in 1649', *ibid.*, xxix (1949), 474–97, and [740b] *A Great Luso-Brazilian Figure. Padre António Vieira, S.J., 1608–1697* (The Canning House Annual Lecture, London, Hispanic and Luso-Brazilian Councils, 1957).

[741] M. C. Kieman, *The Indian Policy of Portugal in the Amazon Region, 1614–1693* (Washington, Catholic Univ. of America, 1954), is a valuable contribution to the understanding of Portuguese-Indian relations and builds in part on the author's earlier essay, [742] 'The Indian Policy of Portugal in America, with special reference to the old state of Maranhão, 1500–1755', *Americas*, v (1948–9), 131–71, 439–61. [743] A. K. Manchester, 'The Rise of the Brazilian Aristocracy', *Hispanic American Historical Review*, xi (1931), 145–68, examines 'certain permanent characteristics of the social life of Brazil' which were 'definitely established' before 1700. [744] M. S. Cardozo, 'The Last Adventure of Fernão Dias Pais (1674–1681)', *ibid.*, xxvi (1946), 467–79, outlines the career of a celebrated *bandeirante* and explorer. [745] C. R. Boxer discusses 'English Shipping in the Brazil Trade, 1640–65', *Mariner's Mirror*, xxxvii (1951), 197–230. See also nos. 352 and 353.

[745a] Bates, Margaret J., 'A Poet of Seventeenth Century Brazil: Gregório de Matos', *Americas*, iv (July 1947), 83–99.

[745b] Wiznitzer, Arnold, *The Records of the Earliest Jewish Community in the New World* (New York, American Jewish Historical Society, 1954). A minute book of 1648–53.

68

4. THE EIGHTEENTH CENTURY

[746] M. S. Cardozo describes 'The Brazilian Gold Rush', *Americas*, iii (Oct. 1946), 137–60, at the opening of the eighteenth century. See also **[747]** his 'The Collection of the Fifths in Brazil, 1695–1709', *Hispanic American Historical Review*, xx (1940), 359–79, and **[748]** 'The *Guerra dos Emboabas*, Civil War in Minas Gerais, 1708–1709', *ibid.*, xxii (1942), 470–92, and the chapter on Brazil in **[749]** W. P. Morrell, *The Gold Rushes* (London, Black, 1940). **[750]** Luís Edmundo da Costa, *Rio in the Time of the Viceroys* (translated by Dorothea H. Momsen, Rio de Janeiro, J. R. de Oliveira, 1936), is a contribution to social history, and **[751]** Alexander Marchant, 'Aspects of the Enlightenment in Brazil' in Whitaker [617] a contribution to intellectual history. For British interest in the Brazil trade see Christelow [587], and, for Spanish-Portuguese relations, Moses [550] and Williams [700]. Graham [409] discusses the situation in Paraguay.

On the famous *Inconfidência Mineira* (1788), by some regarded as 'um facto históricamente insignificante' and by others as the 'first manifestation of revolutionary principles', see **[752]** Alexander Marchant, 'Tiradentes in the Conspiracy of Minas', *Hispanic American Historical Review*, xxi (1941), 239–57, and **[753]** M. S. Cardozo, 'Another Document on the Inconfidencia Mineira', *ibid.*, xxxii (1952), 540–51.

For contemporary travels see **[754]** G. Edmundson's edition of the *Journal of the Travels and Labours of Father Samual Fritz in the River of the Amazons between 1686 and 1723* (Hakluyt Soc. Pubns., 2nd series, No. 51, London, 1922), **[755]** Richard Walter, ed., *Anson's Voyage Round the World* (new edition, with notes by G. S. Laird Clowes, London, Martin Hopkinson: Boston, Charles E. Lauriat, 1928), and **[756]** John Barrow, *A Voyage to Cochinchina in the years 1792 and 1793 . . .* (London, 1806). Anson was at Santa Catarina in 1740. Barrow has left a description of Rio de Janeiro.

[757] Chandler, C. L., 'List of United States Vessels in Brazil, 1792–1805', *Hispanic American Historical Review*, xxvi (1946), 599–617.

IX

THE FALL OF
THE SPANISH AMERICAN EMPIRE

1. THE REVOLUTIONARY ERA

INTRODUCTORY AND GENERAL

On the political, social, and economic background of the Spanish American revolutions see in particular nos. 549–56, 584–6a, 593, 603–6, 616–21, and 702–5. On the revolutions themselves consult, for a brief conspectus, [**758**] F. A. Kirkpatrick, 'The Establishment of Independence in Spanish America', *The Cambridge Modern History. X. The Restoration* (Cambridge Univ. Press, 1907), pp. 280–309, and, for a more detailed narrative, [**759**] W. S. Robertson, *Rise of the Spanish-American Republics as told in the Lives of their Liberators* (New York and London, Appleton-Century, 1918).

[**760**] R. A. Humphreys, *Liberation in South America, 1806–1827. The career of James Paroissien* (London, Athlone Press, 1952), is designed to present a picture of the coming of independence in the viceroyalties of the Río de la Plata and of Peru and in the captaincy-general of Chile and to illustrate also the efforts of English traders and speculators to exploit the newly opened markets.

[**761**] W. R. Manning, ed., *Diplomatic Correspondence of the United States concerning the Independence of the Latin-American Nations* (3 vols., New York, Oxford Univ. Press, 1925), illustrates both the domestic and the international aspects of the revolutionary period. [**762**] The important collection of documents edited by Sir Charles Webster, *Britain and the Independence of Latin America, 1812–1830. Select documents from the Foreign Office archives* (2 vols., Oxford Univ. Press, 1938), is addressed to diplomatic history, and [**763**] R. A. Humphreys, ed., *British Consular Reports on the Trade and Politics of Latin America, 1824–1826* (Royal Historical Society, Camden Third Series, vol. lxiii, London, 1940), to economic history.

For a discussion of the historiography of the revolutionary period in general and of recent work in particular see [**764**] R. A.

Humphreys, 'The Historiography of the Spanish American Revolutions', *Hispanic American Historical Review*, xxxvi (1956), 81–93.

THE ACTION OF BOLÍVAR AND SAN MARTÍN

[**765**] William Pilling, *The Emancipation of South America* (London, Chapman and Hall, 1893), is a condensed translation of Bartolomé Mitre's classic *Historia de San Martín y de la Emancipación Sudamericana*, a biography first published in 1888–9 and still in many respects unsurpassed. Popular 'lives' of San Martín include [**766**] J. C. J. Metford, *San Martín the Liberator* (Oxford, Blackwell, 1950), sober in tone but inaccurate in detail, and, a romantically idealized treatment, [**767**] Ricardo Rojas, *San Martín, knight of the Andes* (translated by H. Brickell and C. Videla, New York, Doubleday, Doran, 1945).

For Bolivarian literature see [**768**] *Bibliography of the Liberator, Simón Bolívar* (Pan American Union, Bibliographic Series, No. 1, rev. ed., Washington, 1933). [**769**] Gerhard Masur's scholarly *Simón Bolívar* (Univ. of New Mexico Press, 1948) is outstanding. Shorter and more popular studies include [**770**] J. B. Trend, *Bolívar and the Independence of Spanish America* (London, Hodder and Stoughton, 1946), and, among older works, [**771**] F. Loraine Petre, *Simón Bolívar* (London, Lane, 1910). [**772**] Salvador de Madariaga's massive *Bolívar* (London, Hollis and Carter, 1952) is so militantly tendentious that it becomes in effect a piece of special pleading, an indictment not only of Bolívar but of the Spanish American revolutions in general.

On the famous interview between Bolívar and San Martín at Guayaquil in 1822 see [**773**] Gerhard Masur, 'The Conference of Guayaquil', *Hispanic American Historical Review*, xxxi (1951), 189–229, and, a rejoinder to this article, [**774**] Vicente Lecuna, 'Bolívar and San Martín at Guayaquil', *ibid.*, xxxi (1951), 369–93. [**775**] A note by W. S. Robertson on the forged letters purporting to bear on this interview which were published at Buenos Aires in 1940 by E. L. Colombres Mármol is in *ibid.*, xxiii (1943), 154–8.

[**776**] *Selected Writings of Bolívar*, compiled by Vicente Lecuna and edited by H. A. Bierck (2 vols., New York, Colonial Press, 1951), provides translations of letters, speeches, and proclamations, including such notable documents as the Jamaica letter of 1815 and the Address to the Congress of Angostura in 1819. The

famous *Narración* of General D. F. O'Leary, 'el paladín más gallardo de los méritos de Bolívar', though partly written in English, is only available in Spanish. Of a different order, [**777**] H. L. Ducoudray Holstein, *Memoirs of Simon Bolívar, president liberator of the Republic of Colombia* . . . (Boston, 1829), is an example of embittered denigration. For a caustic American opinion see Lewis Hanke, ed., [**778**] 'Baptis Irvine's Reports on Simón Bolívar', *Hispanic American Historical Review*, xvi (1936), 360–73, and [**779**] 'Simón Bolívar and Neutral Rights', *ibid.*, xxi (1941), 258–91.

[**780**] Hoffmann, F. L., 'The Financing of San Martín's Expeditions', *Hispanic American Historical Review*, xxxii (1952), 634–8.

[**781**] Rippy, J. F., 'Bolívar as Viewed by Contemporary Diplomats of the United States', *Hispanic American Historical Review*, xv (1935), 287–97.

[**782**] Shepherd, W. R., 'Bolívar and the United States', *Hispanic American Historical Review*, i (1918), 270–98.

See also nos. 783, 784, 847–9, 867, 870.

SPECIAL ASPECTS

The brief but suggestive essay of Bernard Moses [618] and the detailed analysis of [**783**] V. A. Belaunde, *Bolivar and the Political Thought of the Spanish American Revolution* (Johns Hopkins Press, 1938), open up the field of political ideas. Compare [**784**] C. Parra-Pérez, *Bolívar. A contribution to the study of his political ideas* (Pittsburg, Pittsburg Printing Co., 1935).

On social and economic history see the excellent article [**785**] of C. C. Griffin, 'Economic and Social Aspects of the Era of Spanish-American Independence', *Hispanic American Historical Review*, xxix (1949), 170–87, which discusses 'the destructive force of war' on the one hand and 'the stimulation produced by free intercourse with foreign countries' on the other. Goebel [604] examines British trade with the Spanish colonies between 1796 and 1823, and [**786**] J. F. Rippy, 'Latin America and the British Investment "Boom" of the 1820's', *Journal of Modern History*, xix (1947), 122–9, deals with loans to revolutionary governments and speculations in Latin American mines. Compare Humphreys [760, 763]. See also nos. 585–6a, 591, 611, 797, 803–5, 813, 835, 850, 853–5, 858–9, and 891.

[**787**] Alfred Hasbrouck, *Foreign Legionaries in the Liberation of*

Spanish South America (Columbia Univ. Press, 1928), is less general in scope than its title implies and is mostly concerned with northern South America. See also [**788**] A. C. Wilgus, 'Some Activities of United States Citizens in the South American Wars of Independence, 1808–1824', *Louisiana Historical Quarterly*, xiv (1931), 182–203, [**789**] C. C. Griffin, 'Privateering from Baltimore during the Spanish-American Wars of Independence', *Maryland Historical Magazine*, xxxv (March 1940), 1–25, and Chandler [970.]

[**790**] Browning, W. E., 'Joseph Lancaster, James Thomson, and the Lancasterian System of Mutual Instruction, with special reference to Hispanic America', *Hispanic American Historical Review*, iv (1921), 49–98.

[**791**] King, J. F., 'The Colored Castes and American Representation in the Cortes of Cádiz', *Hispanic American Historical Review*, xxxiii (1953), 33–64.

[**792**] King, J. F., 'The Latin American Republics and the Suppression of the Slave Trade', *Hispanic American Historical Review*, xxiv (1944), 387–411.

2. THE REVOLUTIONS IN SOUTH AMERICA

ARGENTINA, URUGUAY, AND PARAGUAY

GENERAL

See Levene [346] and [**793**] F. A. Kirkpatrick, *A History of the Argentine Republic* (Cambridge Univ. Press, 1931).

[**794**] H. F. Peterson, 'Mariano Moreno: the Making of an Insurgent', *Hispanic American Historical Review*, xiv (1934), 450–76, summarizes the career of the man who has been called 'the soul of the revolutionary movement in Argentina'. [**795**] Benjamin Keen, *David Curtis DeForest and the Revolution of Buenos Aires* (Yale Univ. Press, 1947), illustrates both internal developments in the Río de la Plata and the relations between Buenos Aires and the United States. [**796**] T. B. Davis deals briefly with the early career of *Carlos de Alvear. Man of revolution* (Duke Univ. Press, 1955) and more at length with his later career as Argentina's first minister to the United States. On the work of San Martín in Cuyo see Pilling [765], together with nos. 766 and 767, and, for the reforms of Rivadavia, the important monograph [**797**] of Miron Burgin, *The Economic Aspects of Argentine Federalism, 1820–1852* (Harvard Univ. Press, 1946). [**798**] A few, but not many, crumbs may be gleaned from N. L. Kay Shuttleworth, *A Life of Sir Woodbine Parish* (London, Smith, Elder, 1910).

[799] P. A. Martin, 'Artigas, the Founder of Uruguayan Nationality', *Hispanic American Historical Review*, xix (1939), 2–15, is a useful general essay. Compare **[800]** L. W. Bealer, 'Artigas, Father of Federalism in La Plata', in Wilgus, *South American Dictators during the First Century of Independence* [1006]. Portuguese designs on the Banda Oriental of Uruguay are discussed in Manchester [983]. Compare **[801]** J. Street, 'Lord Strangford and Río de la Plata, 1808–1815', *Hispanic American Historical Review*, xxxiii (1953), 477–510, and Webster [762].

For the separation of Paraguay see Warren [347], and, for the reign of Dr. Francia, the contemporary accounts given by J. P. and W. P. Robertson [819, 820] and by Rengger and Longchamps [821].

[802] L. W. Bealer, 'Contribution to a Bibliography on Artigas and the Beginnings of Uruguay, 1810–1820', *Hispanic American Historical Review*, xi (1931), 108–34, is in part also a guide to the general history of the provinces of the Río de la Plata in this period.

SPECIAL ASPECTS

[803] H. S. Ferns, 'Beginnings of British Investment in Argentina', *Economic History Review*, 2nd series, iv (1952), 341–52, covers the years 1806 to 1830. Compare **[804]** J. B. Williams, 'The Establishment of British Commerce with Argentina', *Hispanic American Historical Review*, xv (1935), 43–64 and **[805]** E. J. Pratt, 'Anglo-American Commercial and Political Rivalry on the Plata, 1820–1830', *ibid.*, xi (1931), 302–35.

[806] S. F. Bemis examines *Early Diplomatic Missions from Buenos Aires to the United States, 1811–1824* (American Antiquarian Society, *Proceedings*, April 1939; reprinted Worcester, Mass., American Antiquarian Society, 1940), and **[807]** Watt Stewart, 'The South American Commission, 1817–18', *Hispanic American Historical Review*, ix (1929), 31–59, describes the mission of Rodney, Graham, and Bland to the Río de la Plata. See also, by the same author, **[808]** 'The Diplomatic Service of John M. Forbes at Buenos Aires', *ibid.*, xiv (1934), 202–18, **[809]** 'United States-Argentine Commercial Negotiations of 1825', *ibid.*, xiii (1933), 367–71, and **[810]** 'Argentina and the Monroe Doctrine, 1824–1828', *ibid.*, x (1930), 26–32. Compare Davis [796]. Two articles by J. C. J. Metford are concerned respectively with **[811]** 'The Recognition by Great Britain of the United Provinces of

Río de la Plata', *Bulletin of Hispanic Studies*, xxix (1952), 201–24, and [**812**] 'The Treaty of 1825 between Great Britain and the United Provinces of Río de la Plata', *ibid.*, xxx (1953), 41–51.

[**813**] Chandler, C. L., 'United States Shipping in the La Plata Region, 1809–1810', *Hispanic American Historical Review*, iii (1920), 159–76. Compare nos. 588 and 589.

[**813a**] Rasmussen, W. D., 'Diplomats and Plant Collectors: The South American Commission, 1817–1818', *Agricultural History*, xxix (1955), 22–31. Compare no. 807.

[**814**] Rubio y Esteban, J. M., 'The First Diplomatic Negotiations with the Revolutionary Junta of Buenos Aires', *Hispanic American Historical Review*, iv (1921), 393–415.
The Guezzi mission from Brazil of 1810.

CONTEMPORARY NARRATIVES AND DESCRIPTIONS

For the reports, printed in 1819, of Rodney, Graham, and Bland, the special commissioners of the United States sent to the Río de la Plata in 1817–18, see Manning [761]. [**815**] H. M. Brackenridge, *Voyage to South America, performed by order of the American Government in the years 1817 and 1818* . . . (2 vols., London, 1820), is the work of the commissioners' secretary. For the reports of Woodbine Parish, the first British consul-general at Buenos Aires, in 1824 see Humphreys [763], and compare [**816**] Parish's notable *Buenos Ayres and the Provinces of the Rio de la Plata* . . . (London, 1839; 2nd ed., enlarged, 1852). [**817**] I. B. Núñez, *An Account, Historical, Political, and Statistical, of the United Provinces of Rio de la Plata* . . . (London, 1825), is a semi-official report drawn up at Parish's request.

The accounts left by the two Scottish merchants, John Parish Robertson and William Parish Robertson, of which Carlyle so vigorously disapproved, are invaluable. See [**818**] J. P. and W. P. Robertson, *Letters on South America* . . . (3 vols., London, 1843), and [**819**] *Letters on Paraguay* . . . (2 vols., London, 1838), continued [**820**] as *Francia's Reign of Terror* . . . (London, 1839), and compare with these last [**821**] J. R. Rengger and M. Longchamps (both Swiss), *The Reign of Doctor Joseph Gaspard Roderick de Francia in Paraguay* . . . (London, 1827).

[**822**] E. E. Vidal, *Picturesque Illustrations of Buenos Ayres and Montevideo* . . . (London, 1820), has fortunately been reprinted (Buenos Aires, Ed. Viau S.R., 1943).

[**823**] Andrews, Joseph, *Journey from Buenos Ayres, through the Provinces of Cordoba, Tucuman, and Salta, to Potosi* . . . *and subsequently, to Santiago de Chili and Coquimbo, undertaken on behalf of the Chilian and Peruvian Mining Association, in the years 1825-1826* (2 vols., London, 1827).

[**824**] Beaumont, J. A. B., *Travels in Buenos Ayres, and the adjacent provinces of Rio de la Plata* . . . (London, 1828).

[**825**] Caldcleugh, Alexander, *Travels in South America, during the years 1819-20-21; containing an account of the present state of Brazil, Buenos Ayres, and Chile* (2 vols., London, 1825).

[**826**] Haigh, Samuel, *Sketches of Buenos Ayres, Chile, and Peru* (London, 1831).

[**827**] Head, F. B., *Rough Notes taken during some rapid Journeys across the Pampas and among the Andes* (London, 1826).

CHILE

GENERAL

See Galdames [345]. [**828**] Agustín Edwards, *The Dawn: being the history of the birth and consolidation of the republic of Chile* (London, Benn, 1931), is a popular account. Compare [**829**] A. S. M. Chisholm, *The Independence of Chile* (Boston, Sherman, French, 1911: London, Werner Laurie, 1912), which is an older summation also addressed to the general reader. [**830**] P. V. Shaw deals with *The Early Constitutions of Chile, 1810–1833* (New York, Chile Publishing Co., 1931). Pilling [765] summarizes Mitre's account of the part played by San Martín. See also nos. 766, 767, and 780. For biographies of O'Higgins and the literature of the revolutionary period in Chile in general see [**831**] R. A. Lord, 'Contribution towards a Bibliography on the O'Higgins Family in America', *Hispanic American Historical Review*, xii (1932), 107–38.

SPECIAL ASPECTS

[**832**] C. W. Centner discusses 'The Chilean Failure to obtain British Recognition, 1823–1828', *Revista de Historia de América*, Núm. 15 (1942), 285–97, and [**833**] J. J. Johnson treats of 'Early Relations of the United States with Chile', *Pacific Historical Review*, xiii (1944), 260–70. [**834**] 'United States Aid to the Chilean Wars of Independence' is examined by W. L. Neumann, *Hispanic American Historical Review*, xxvii (1947), 204–19, and [**835**] 'British American Rivalry in the Chilean Trade, 1817–20' by D. B. Goebel, *Journal of Economic History*, ii (1942), 190–203. For

United States relations with Chile see also Evans [1467]. [**836**]
F. K. Hendricks, 'The First Apostolic Mission to Chile', *Hispanic American Historical Review*, xxii (1942), 644–69, is an account of the Muzi mission of 1824.

CONTEMPORARY NARRATIVES AND DESCRIPTIONS

See Manning [761] for the report of the American commissioner, Theodorick Bland, in 1818. For military and naval history consult [**837**] Thomas Cochrane, Earl of Dundonald, *Narrative of Services in the Liberation of Chili, Peru, and Brazil, from Spanish and Portuguese Domination* (2 vols., London, 1859; vol. i separately printed, 1858, as *Memoranda of Naval Services in the Liberation of Chili and Peru from Spanish Domination*), which is a *mémoire justificatif*, and [**838**] John Miller, ed., *Memoirs of General [William] Miller, in the Service of the Republic of Peru* (2 vols., London, 1828; 2nd ed., enlarged, 2 vols., 1829). [**839**] Maria Graham, *Journal of a Residence in Chile during the year 1822* . . . (London, 1824), [**840**] Captain Basil Hall, *Extracts from a Journal written on the coasts of Chile, Peru, and Mexico in the years 1820, 1821, 1822* (2 vols., Edinburgh, 1824), and [**841**] John Miers, *Travels in Chile and La Plata* . . . (2 vols., London, 1826), are outstanding. See also Andrews [823], Caldcleugh [825], and Haigh [826].

[**842**] Schmidtmeyer, Peter, *Travels into Chile, over the Andes, in the years 1820 and 1821* (London, 1824).

[**843**] Stevenson, W. B., *A Historical and Descriptive Narrative of Twenty Years' Residence in South America* (3 vols., London, 1825–9). Stevenson was Cochrane's secretary.

GREAT COLOMBIA
(VENEZUELA, NEW GRANADA, ECUADOR)

GENERAL

See Henao and Arrubla [348]. On early revolutionary activities in Venezuela see Robertson's studies of Miranda [553, 554] and Warren [555]. For Bolívar and the liberation of northern South America see the *Bibliography of the Liberator, Simón Bolívar* [768] and nos. 769 to 784. There is a short sketch of Sucre, Bolívar's greatest lieutenant, by [**844**] G. A. Sherwell, *Antonio José de Sucre* (Washington, B. S. Adams, 1924), and [**845**] a fuller, popular biography of *José Antonio Páez*, the 'father of Venezuela', by R. B. Cunninghame Graham (London, Heinemann, 1929). [**846**] 'The Assassination of Sucre and its Significance in Colombian History, 1828–48' are examined by Thomas F. McGann, *Hispanic American Historical Review*, xxx (1950), 269–89. [**847**] L. F. Ullrich, 'Morillo's Attempts to Pacify Venezuela', *Hispanic American Historical Review*, iii (1920), 535–65, covers the years 1814 to 1820. [**848**] Hiram Bingham, *The Journal of an Expedition across Venezuela and Colombia, 1906–1907* (New Haven, Yale Publishing Association: London, Fisher Unwin, 1909), is 'an exploration of the route of Bolívar's celebrated march of 1819 and of the battle-fields of Boyacá and Carabobo'. Hasbrouck [787] examines the part played by volunteers from overseas. [**849**] W. H. Gray, 'Bolívar's Conquest of Guayaquil', *Hispanic American Historical Review*, xxvii (1947), 603–22, deals with 'the annexation of the city and province of Guayaquil to the Republic of Colombia in 1822'.

[**850**] David Bushnell, *The Santander Regime in Gran Colombia* (Univ. of Delaware Press, 1954), throws a flood of light on the domestic scene in Great Colombia between 1819 and 1827, and, ignoring military and diplomatic history, attacks instead the problems of political, economic, and social history. For the Constitution of 1821 see [**851**] W. M. Gibson, *The Constitutions of Colombia* (Duke Univ. Press, 1948).

SPECIAL ASPECTS

[**852**] Mary Watters, *A History of the Church in Venezuela, 1810–1930* (Univ. of North Carolina Press, 1933), is a contribution both to the civil and to the ecclesiastical history of the revolutionary period. [**853**] John E. Baur discusses 'Venezuelan Education during Liberation', *Mid-America*, xxxiii (1951), 103–27. [**854**] H. A. Bierck, 'The Struggle for Abolition in Gran Colombia', *Hispanic American Historical Review*, xxxiii (1953), 365–86, is a definitive treatment of the problem of manumission. [**855**] David Bushnell examines 'The Development of the Press in Great Colombia', *ibid.*, xxx (1950), 432–52.

On international relations see [**856**] E. Taylor Parks, *Colombia and the United States, 1765–1934* (Duke Univ. Press, 1935), and, principally concerned with 'the diplomacy of Venezuela towards the United States and Europe' between 1810 and 1812, [**857**] W. S. Robertson, 'The Beginnings of Spanish-American Diplomacy', in *Essays in American History dedicated to Frederick Jackson Turner* (New York, Holt, 1910).

[**858**] Gilmore, R. L., and Harrison, J. P., 'Juan Bernardo Elbers

78

The Revolutions in South America

and the Introduction of Steam Navigation on the Magdalena River', *Hispanic American Historical Review*, xxviii (1948), 335-59.

[859] King, J. F., ed., 'A Royalist View of the Colored Castes in the Venezuelan War of Independence', *Hispanic American Historical Review*, xxxiii (1953), 526-37.

CONTEMPORARY NARRATIVES AND DESCRIPTIONS

[860] Charles Stuart Cochrane, *Journal of a Residence and Travels in Colombia, during the years 1823 and 1824* (2 vols., London, 1825), by a naval officer, **[861]** J. P. Hamilton, *Travels through the Interior Provinces of Columbia* (2 vols., London, 1827), by one of the commissioners sent from Britain to Colombia in 1824, and **[862]** Francis Hall, *Colombia: its present state* . . . (London, 1824), by a soldier who was also a disciple of Jeremy Bentham, are British impressions. For a United States commentary see **[863]** William Duane, *A Visit to Colombia in the years 1822 and 1823* (Philadelphia, 1826), and, for a French, **[864]** G. T. Mollien, *Travels in the Republic of Colombia, in the years 1822 and 1823* (London, 1824). For further references to the literature of travel, including the narratives of soldiers who served with the patriot armies, see Hasbrouck [787].

[865] *The Present State of Colombia* . . . By an Officer late in the Colombian Service (London, 1827).

[866] [Walker, Alexander], *Colombia: being a geographical, statistical, agricultural, commercial, and political account of that country* . . . (2 vols., London, 1822).

PERU AND BOLIVIA

GENERAL

See Markham [343]. On the liberating expedition of 1820 and the protectorate of San Martín consult Pilling [765] and nos. 766, 767, and 780, on the interview between San Martín and Bolívar at Guayaquil nos. 773 and 774, and on the work of Bolívar and Sucre nos. 769 to 772 and 844. San Martín's protectorate and Bolívar's dictatorship are unsympathetically dealt with by **[867]** N. A. N. Cleven, 'The Dictators of Peru, Bolivia, and Ecuador', in Wilgus, *South American Dictators during the First Century of Independence* [1006]. See also the same author's *Political Organization of Bolivia* [1323], and, for a discussion of the Bolivian Constitution of 1826, Belaunde [783] and Parra-Pérez [784].

79

CONTEMPORARY NARRATIVES AND DESCRIPTIONS

See Andrews [823], Haigh [826], Dundonald [837], Miller [838], Hall [840], and Stevenson [843], together with [**868**] Robert Proctor, *Narrative of a Journey across the Cordillera of the Andes, and of a Residence in Lima . . .* (London, 1825), and [**869**] Edmond Temple, *Travels in Various Parts of Peru, including a year's residence in Potosí* (2 vols., London, 1830).

[**870**] Humphreys, R. A., ed., 'James Paroissien's Notes on the Liberating Expedition to Peru, 1820', *Hispanic American Historical Review*, xxxi (1951), 253–73.

[**871**] Humphreys, R. A., ed., 'Letters of William Miller, Lord Cochrane, and Basil Hall to James Paroissien, 1821–1823', *Fénix: Revista de la Biblioteca Nacional* [Peru], x (1954), 203–34.

3. THE REVOLUTIONS IN SPANISH NORTH AMERICA
Mexico

GENERAL

See Bancroft [251], [**872**] H. I. Priestley, *The Mexican Nation, a history* (New York, Macmillan, 1923), and [**873**] H. B. Parkes, *A History of Mexico* (rev. ed., Boston, Houghton Mifflin, 1950).

[**874**] J. A. Caruso, *The Liberators of Mexico* (New York, Pageant Press, 1954), summarizes from the printed sources the careers of Hidalgo, Morelos, and Iturbide. Compare Robertson [759]. For the guerrilla leader, Vicente Guerrero, see [**875**] W. F. Sprague's brief biography, *Vicente Guerrero, Mexican Liberator. A study in patriotism* (Chicago, R. R. Donnelley, 1939), for 'el pensador Mexicano', Fernández de Lizardi, [**876**] J. R. Spell, *The Life and Works of José Joaquín Fernández de Lizardi* (Philadelphia, Univ. of Pennsylvania Pubns. in Romantic Languages and Literature, 1931), and, for Iturbide himself, the major study [**877**] of W. S. Robertson, *Iturbide of Mexico* (Duke Univ. Press, 1952). See also [**878**] Robertson's article, 'The Memorabilia of Agustín de Iturbide', *Hispanic American Historical Review*, xxvii (1947), 436–55.

Fisher [552, 616] and Rydjord [556, 621] relate to pre-revolutionary conditions. [**879**] N. L. Benson, 'The Contested Mexican Election of 1812', *Hispanic American Historical Review*, xxvi (1946), 336–50, discusses the election of deputies to represent New Spain in the Cortes of Cadiz, and [**880**] W. H. Timmons examines the activities between 1810 and 1814 of 'Los Guadalupes: a Secret

Society in the Mexican Revolution for Independence', *ibid.*, xxx (1950), 453–79.

[**881**] H. G. Warren, *The Sword was their Passport. A history of American filibustering in the Mexican Revolution* (Louisiana State Univ. Press, 1943), covers the years 1810 to 1821 and is a comprehensive account of plots, expeditions, and depredations. On Gutiérrez de Lara and the establishment of the so-called 'Republic of Texas' in 1813 see also Garrett [638] and Castañeda [635],[1] and, on Mina's invasion of 1817, [**882**] H. G. Warren, 'Xavier Mina's Invasion of Mexico', *Hispanic American Historical Review*, xxiii (1943), 52–76, which is a continuation of [**883**] the same author's 'The Origin of General Mina's Invasion of Mexico', *Southwestern Historical Quarterly*, xlii (July 1938), 1–20, subsequently incorporated in no. 881. [**884**] H. A. Bierck, 'Pedro Gual and the Patriot Effort to Capture a Mexican Port, 1816', *Hispanic American Historical Review*, xxvii (1947), 456–66, is a later addition to the very considerable literature on filibustering.

[**885**] H. E. Bolton illustrates 'The Iturbide Revolution in the Californias', *Hispanic American Historical Review*, ii (1919), 188–242. [**886**] N. L. Benson corrects common errors in the interpretation of 'The Plan of Casa Mata' of 1823, which heralded Iturbide's fall, *ibid.*, xxv (1945), 45–56, and in [**887**] 'Servando Teresa de Mier, Federalist', *ibid.*, xxviii (1948), 514–25, seeks to explain why Mier has mistakenly been regarded as a centralist. [**888**] 'The Origins of Federalism in Mexico' are discussed by J. L. Mecham, *ibid.*, xviii (1938), 164–82. See also [**889**] W. H. Callcott, *Church and State in Mexico, 1822–1857* (Duke Univ. Press, 1926).

SPECIAL ASPECTS

[**890**] K. M. Schmitt, 'The Clergy and the Independence of New Spain', *Hispanic American Historical Review*, xxxiv (1954), 289–312, distinguishes the differing attitudes of the upper and lower clergy.

On economic history see Humphreys [763], Smith [591], and [**891**] C. A. True, 'British Loans to the Mexican Government, 1823–1832', *Southwestern Social Science Quarterly*, xvii (March 1937), 353–62. Howe [611] discusses the later history of the mining

---

[1] For Texas and the northern frontiers prior to the establishment of Mexican independence see The Northern Frontiers of New Spain, 1700–1819, *ante*, pp. 57–62.

guild and its *Tribunal General*, and R. S. Smith [424] deals with the extinction of the *consulados*. See also [**892**] his 'The Puebla Consulado', *Revista de Historia de América*, Núm. 21 (1946), 19–28.

[**893**] John Rydjord, 'Napoleon and the Independence of New Spain', in *New Spain and the Anglo-American West*, i, 289–310 [467], discusses French designs and the activities of French agents between 1808 and 1811. [**894**] I. J. Cox, 'Monroe and the Early Mexican Revolutionary Agents', American Historical Association, *Annual Report*, 1911 (2 vols., Washington, Govt. Printing Office, 1913), i, 199–215, should be compared with Warren [881]. [**895**] J. F. Rippy, 'Britain's Role in the Early Relations of the United States and Mexico', *Hispanic American Historical Review*, vii (1927), 2–24, considers the part played by H. G. Ward. [**896**] W. R. Manning, *Early Diplomatic Relations between the United States and Mexico* (Johns Hopkins Press, 1916), is a standard work. See also [**897**] J. H. Smith, 'Poinsett's Career in Mexico', American Antiquarian Society, *Proceedings*, n.s., xxiv, pt. i (1914), 77–92, and Parton [969]. [**898**] Ohland Morton, *Terán and Texas: a chapter in Texas-Mexican relations* (Austin, Texas State Historical Association, 1948), dealing with Manuel de Mier y Terán, covers the years 1821 to 1832, and for the Texan issue see also [**899**] E. C. Barker, *The Life of Stephen F. Austin* (2nd ed., Austin, Texas State Historical Association, 1949), and [**900**] Barker's *Mexico and Texas, 1821–1835* (Dallas, P. L. Turner, 1928). For further references consult Bemis and Griffin, *Guide* [60].

[**901**] Gardiner, C. H., 'The Role of Guadalupe Victoria in Mexican Foreign Relations', *Revista de Historia de América*, Núm. 26 (1948), 379–92.

[**902**] Salit, C. R., 'Anglo-American Rivalry in Mexico, 1823–1830', *Revista de Historia de América*, Núm. 16 (1943), 65–84.

CONTEMPORARY NARRATIVES AND DESCRIPTIONS

[**903**] H. G. Ward, *Mexico in 1827* (2 vols., London, 1828), by the British chargé d'affaires, and [**904**] J. R. Poinsett, *Notes on Mexico* . . . (Philadelphia, 1824), by the American Minister (though published before his appointment), are of special interest. See also [**905**] Mark Beaufoy, *Mexican Illustrations, founded upon facts* . . . (London, 1828), [**906**] William Bullock, *Six Months' Residence and Travels in Mexico* . . . (2nd ed., 2 vols., London, 1825), [**907**] R. W. H. Hardy, *Travels in the Interior of Mexico* . . . (London, 1829), [**908**] G. F. Lyon, *Journal of a Residence and Tour in the Republic of Mexico in the year 1826* . . . (2 vols., London, 1828),

The Revolutions in Spanish North America

[**909**] W. D. Robinson, *Memoirs of the Mexican Revolution; including a narrative of the expedition of General Xavier Mina* . . . (Philadelphia, 1820), and Hall [840].

CENTRAL AMERICA

GENERAL

See Bancroft [252], Slade [1687], and Munro [1672].

[**910**] F. M. Stanger, 'National Origins in Central America', *Hispanic American Historical Review*, xii (1932), 18–45, is a commentary upon the events of 1820 to 1825. The brief period of annexation to Mexico is summarized by [**911**] T. E. Downey, 'Central America under Mexico, 1821–1823' in *Greater America* [134]. [**912**] F. D. Parker appraises the career of 'José Cecilio del Valle: Scholar and Patriot', *Hispanic American Historical Review*, xxxii (1952), 516–39, though failing to note the influence upon Valle of Jeremy Bentham, and there is a brief sketch [**913**] of *Francisco Morazán, champion of Central American federation*, by R. S. Chamberlain (Univ. of Miami Press, 1950).

SPECIAL ASPECTS

[**914**] M. W. Williams, 'The Ecclesiastical Policy of Francisco Morazán and the other Central American Liberals', *Hispanic American Historical Review*, iii (1920), 119–43, and [**915**] Mary P. Holleran, *Church and State in Guatemala* (Columbia Univ. Press, 1949), deal with the Church-State conflict. On the Belize settlement see Burdon [697], and for the disreputable Poyais scheme on the Mosquito Shore [**916**] A. Hasbrouck, 'Gregor McGregor and the Colonization of Poyais, between 1820 and 1824', *Hispanic American Historical Review*, vii (1927), 438–59.

CONTEMPORARY NARRATIVES AND DESCRIPTIONS

[**917**] Dunn, Henry, *Guatimala, or, the United Provinces of Central America, in 1827–28* (New York, 1828).

[**918**] Roberts, Orlando W., *Narrative of Voyages and Excursions on the East Coast and in the Interior of Central America* (Edinburgh, 1827).

[**919**] Thompson, G. A., *Narrative of an Official Visit to Guatemala from Mexico* (London, 1829).
By the translator of Alcedo's *Dictionary* [226].

SANTO DOMINGO AND HAITI

See Schaeffer [701] on the delayed cession of the old Spanish colony of Santo Domingo to France under the Treaty of Basle (1795).

[**920**] T. L. Stoddard, *The French Revolution in San Domingo* (Boston and New York, Houghton Mifflin, 1914), analyses the situation which led ultimately to the transformation of the old French colony of Saint Domingue into the independent state of Haiti in 1804. The disastrous British intervention in the affairs of the colony is detailed in Fortescue [703], vol. iv, part i. [**921**] Ralph Korngold, *Citizen Toussaint* (Boston, Little, Brown, 1944), is one of the better biographies of 'the first of the blacks', Toussaint Louverture.

[**922**] H. B. L. Hughes, 'British Policy towards Haiti, 1801–1805', *Canadian Historical Review*, xxv (Dec. 1944), 397–408, examines the attitude of the British Government (and of the Governor of Jamaica) to events in Haiti and to French retention of Santo Domingo. On the expulsion of the French and the re-establishment of Spanish rule in 1809 see [**923**] William Walton, *Present State of the Spanish Colonies; including a particular report on Hispañola, or the Spanish part of Santo Domingo . . .* (2 vols., London, 1810).

[**924**] E. L. Griggs and C. H. Prator, eds., *Henry Christophe and Thomas Clarkson. A correspondence* (Univ. of California Press, 1952), is a valuable and extremely interesting contribution to Haitian history at the time of the division of the country into the State of Haiti, under Christophe, in the north, and the Republic of Haiti, under Pétion, in the south. See also [**925**] W. W. Harvey, *Sketches of Hayti; from the expulsion of the French, to the death of Christophe* (London, 1827). For contemporary accounts after the union of the two states under Boyer and the annexation, in 1822, of Santo Domingo, see [**926**] James Franklin, *The Present State of Hayti . . .* (London, 1828), and [**927**] Charles Mackenzie, *Notes on Haiti, made during a residence in that republic* (2 vols., London, 1830).

See also Davis [1870], Léger [1875], Leyburn [1869], and, for the diplomatic history of the period, Logan [1878], Montague [1872], Tansill [1860], and Treudley [1859].

[**927a**] Esterquest, R. T., 'L'Imprimerie Royale d'Hayti (1817–1819). A little known Royal Press of the Western Hemisphere', *Bibliographical Society of America, Papers*, xxxiv (1940), 171–84.

The Diplomatic History of the Revolutionary Period

4. THE DIPLOMATIC HISTORY OF THE REVOLUTIONARY PERIOD[1]

General

For bibliographies see Bemis and Griffin [60], Bradley [61], Meyer [63], and *Harvard Guide* [249].

[**928**] F. L. Paxson, *The Independence of the South-American Republics* (Philadelphia, Ferris and Leach, 1903), which discusses, in particular, the recognition policies of the United States and Great Britain, is a pioneer work now inevitably superseded. The title of [**929**] J. F. Rippy's *Rivalry of the United States and Great Britain over Latin America, 1808–1830* (Johns Hopkins Press, 1929) speaks for itself.

Spain and her Colonies

[**930**] W. S. Robertson, 'The Juntas of 1808 and the Spanish Colonies', *English Historical Review*, xxxi (1916), 573–85, deals with the repercussions in Spain and America of the Napoleonic invasions of the Spanish peninsula. [**931**] C. W. Crawley discusses 'French and English Influences in the Cortes of Cadiz, 1810–1814', *Cambridge Historical Journal*, vi (1939), 176–208. See also, on the Cortes, King [791] and [**931a**] A. F. Zimmerman, 'Spain and its Colonies, 1808–1820', *Hispanic American Historical Review*, xi (1931), 439–63. [**932**] John Rydjord, 'British Mediation between Spain and her Colonies, 1811–1813', *ibid.*, xxi (1941), 29–50, makes use of Spanish but not of English archives. The story is continued by Webster [762, 938, and 939].

[**933**] W. S. Robertson, 'The Policy of Spain toward its Revolted Colonies, 1820–1823', *Hispanic American Historical Review*, vi (1926), 21–46, examines 'constitutionalist' attempts at reconciliation. [**934**] His 'The Recognition of the Spanish Colonies by the Motherland', *ibid.*, i (1918), 70–91, covers the years 1836 to 1895. See also [**935**] J. T. Lanning, 'Great Britain and Spanish Recognition of the Hispanic American States', *ibid.*, x (1930), 429–56.

Britain and Spanish America

[**936**] W. W. Kaufmann, *British Policy and the Independence of*

[1] Only the more general aspects of the diplomatic history of the period are considered in this section. For works which are specifically concerned with the diplomatic history of a particular Spanish American country or area see the preceding regional sections, pp. 73–84.

Latin America, 1804–1828 (Yale Univ. Press, 1951), is an able synthesis based on secondary materials. Webster, *Britain and the Independence of Latin America* [762] is fundamental. The masterly introduction to this collection of documents has been printed separately (Oxford Univ. Press, 1944).

Sir Charles K. Webster, [**937**] *The Foreign Policy of Castlereagh, 1812–1815* (London, Bell, 1931) and [**938**] *The Foreign Policy of Castlereagh, 1815–1822* (2nd ed., London, Bell, 1934), are diplomatic histories of the first rank. The second volume incorporates the substance of Webster's two important articles, [**939**] 'Castlereagh and the Spanish Colonies, I. 1815–1818', *English Historical Review*, xxvii (1912), 78–95, and [**940**] 'Castlereagh and the Spanish Colonies, II. 1818–1822', *ibid.*, xxx (1915), 631–45.

The complementary treatment of Canning is [**941**] H. W. V. Temperley, *The Foreign Policy of Canning, 1822–1827* (London, Bell, 1925). See also Temperley's earlier articles, [**942**] 'The Later American Policy of George Canning', *American Historical Review*, xi (July 1906), 779–97, showing that Canning's last years were devoted to defeating 'the pretensions' of the Monroe Doctrine, and [**943**] 'Canning, Wellington, and George the Fourth', *English Historical Review*, xxxviii (1923), 206–25, together with his later article [**944**] 'Joan Canning on her Husband's Policy and Ideas', *ibid.*, xlv (1930), 409–26. Compare the very interesting discussion of Canning in [**945**] Élie Halévy, *A History of the English People in the Nineteenth Century—II. The Liberal Awakening 1815–1830* (2nd rev. ed., London, Benn, 1949), and see Perkins [965].

[**946**] Lawson, L. A., *The Relation of British Policy to the Declaration of the Monroe Doctrine* (Columbia Univ. Press, 1922).

[**947**] Lloyd, E. M., 'Canning and Spanish America', Royal Historical Society, *Transactions*, n.s., xviii (1904), 77–105.

See also nos. 801, 805, 811–12, 832, 895, 902, 922, 929, 931, 932, and 935.

THE POLICIES OF THE CONTINENTAL POWERS

The authoritative study of French policy is [**948**] W. S. Robertson, *France and Latin American Independence* (Johns Hopkins Press, 1939). Compare H. W. V. Temperley, [**949**] 'French Designs on Spanish America in 1820–5', *English Historical Review*, xl (1925), 34–53, and [**950**] 'The Instructions to Donzelot,

Governor of Martinique, 17 December, 1823', *ibid.*, xli (1926), 583–5.

[**951**] Dexter Perkins, 'Russia and the Spanish Colonies, 1817–1818', *American Historical Review*, xxviii (July 1923), 656–72, attacks the 'myth' that the Holy Alliance ever intended to subjugate South America. See also [**952**] W. S. Robertson, 'Russia and the Emancipation of Spanish America, 1816–1826', *Hispanic American Historical Review*, xxi (1941), 196–221. [**953**] 'Metternich's Attitude toward Revolutions in Latin America' is analysed, with interesting results, by W. S. Robertson, *ibid.*, xxi (1941), 538–58, and [**954**] Dexter Perkins, 'Europe, Spanish America, and the Monroe Doctrine', *American Historical Review*, xxvii (Jan. 1922), 207–18, argues that the continental powers 'at no time in 1823 or 1824 ever had a practicable policy outlined and ready to be carried out'.

[**955**] 'Protocols of Conferences of Representatives of the Allied Powers respecting Spanish America, 1824–1825', *American Historical Review*, xxii (April 1917), 595–616.

[**956**] Robertson, W. S., 'The Monroe Doctrine abroad in 1823–24', *American Political Science Review*, vi (1912), 545–63.

The Vatican

[**957**] Mecham, J. L., 'The Papacy and Spanish-American Independence', *Hispanic American Historical Review*, ix (1929), 154–75.
See also no. 836.

The United States and Spanish America

[**958**] A. P. Whitaker, *The United States and the Independence of Latin America, 1800–1830* (Johns Hopkins Press, 1941), is of the same order of importance as Robertson [948]. Griffin, *The United States and the Disruption of the Spanish Empire, 1810–1822* [689], traces the part played by the United States in the break-up of that empire 'both on the border and in other regions'. [**959**] J. J. Auchmuty, *The United States Government and Latin American Independence, 1810–1830* (London, P. S. King, 1937), uncritically based on Manning [761], is so misleading and inaccurate that its value is slight.

[**960**] H. L. Hoskins discusses 'The Hispanic American Policy of Henry Clay, 1816–1828', *Hispanic American Historical Review*, vii (1927), 460–78. Three articles by W. S. Robertson are con-

cerned with recognition and recognition policy: [**961**] 'The First Legations of the United States in Latin America', *Mississippi Valley Historical Review*, ii (1915), 183–212; [**962**] 'The United States and Spain in 1822', *American Historical Review*, xx (July 1915), 781–800; and [**963**] 'The Recognition of the Hispanic American Nations by the United States', *Hispanic American Historical Review*, i (1918), 239–69. See also [**964**] Julius Goebel, *The Recognition Policy of the United States* (Columbia Univ. Press, 1915).

[**965**] Dexter Perkins, *The Monroe Doctrine*, 1823–1826 (Harvard Univ. Press, 1927), is the classic exposition. Consult also S. F. Bemis, [**966**] *John Quincy Adams and the Foundation of American Foreign Policy* (New York, Knopf, 1949), and [**967**] *The Latin American Policy of the United States* (New York, Harcourt, Brace, 1943).

[**968**] Laura Bornholdt, *Baltimore and Early Panamericanism. A study in the background of the Monroe Doctrine* (Smith College Studies in History, Northampton, Mass., The College, 1949), brings together 'in microcosm many of the elements that influenced' the Latin American policy of the United States.

For the South American and Mexican missions of Poinsett see [**969**] D. M. Parton, *The Diplomatic Career of Joel Roberts Poinsett* (Washington, Catholic Univ. of America, 1934), for the Adams-Onís treaty Brooks [690], and for the diplomatic correspondence of the United States in general Manning [761]. See also nos. 686–8a, 795, 805–10, 833–4, 856–7, 881, 894, 896–900, and 902.

[**970**] Chandler, C. L., *Inter-American Acquaintances* (2nd ed., Sewanee, Tenn., The University Press, 1917).

[**971**] Craven, W. F., 'The Risk of the Monroe Doctrine (1823–1824)', *Hispanic American Historical Review*, vii (1927), 320–33.

[**972**] Ford, W. C., 'John Quincy Adams and the Monroe Doctrine', *American Historical Review*, vii (July 1902), 676–96; viii (Oct. 1902), 28–52.

[**973**] Robertson, W. S., 'South America and the Monroe Doctrine, 1824–1828', *Political Science Quarterly*, xxx (1915), 82–105.

[**974**] Schellenberg, T. R., 'Jeffersonian Origins of the Monroe Doctrine', *Hispanic American Historical Review*, xiv (1934), 1–31.

THE PANAMA CONGRESS

See the discussion in [**975**] J. B. Lockey, *Pan Americanism: its beginnings* (New York, Macmillan, 1920), and compare [**976**]

C. W. Hackett, 'The Development of John Quincy Adams's Policy with respect to an American Confederation and the Panama Congress, 1822–1825', *Hispanic American Historical Review*, viii (1928), 496–526, and [**977**] F. L. Reinhold, 'New Research on the First Pan-American Congress held at Panama in 1826', *ibid.*, xviii (1938), 342–63. Webster [762] prints the reports of the English observer, Dawkins.

[**978**] International American Conference, *Reports of Committees . . . vol. iv, Historical Appendix. The Congress of 1826, at Panama, and subsequent movements toward a conference of American nations* (Washington, Govt. Printing Office, 1890).

See also no. 1230.

[**978a**] Schoonhaven, Jan, and Jong, C. T. de, 'The Dutch Observer at the Congress of Panama', *Hispanic American Historical Review*, xxxvi (1956), 28–37.

X

THE FOUNDATION OF
THE EMPIRE OF BRAZIL

GENERAL

See Calógeras [707]. [**979**] John Armitage, *The History of Brazil* (2 vols., London, 1836), continues the work of Southey [706] and covers the years between the arrival of the Portuguese Court in 1808 and the abdication of Dom Pedro I in 1831. Armitage was only twenty-nine years old when his book was published. But he had lived for several years in Brazil as a merchant, his information was generally exact, and the high reputation which his history enjoys is well deserved.

[**980**] P. V. Shaw, 'José Bonifacio and Brazilian History', *Hispanic American Historical Review*, viii (1928), 527–50, contains a brief evaluation of the influence upon the establishment of Brazilian independence of José Bonifacio de Andrade e Silva of São Paulo. There is an excellent study of Dom Pedro I by A. K. Manchester, [**981**] 'The Paradoxical Pedro, First Emperor of Brazil', *ibid.*, xii (1932), 176–97, and Manchester discusses also the ideas and aims of the Brazilian aristocracy [743]. The imperial constitution of 1824, which, as *The Times* remarked, 'borrowed and pilfered from all sides', but was nevertheless to survive for sixty-five years, is printed in [**982**] H. G. James, *The Constitutional System of Brazil* (Washington, Carnegie Institution, 1923).

SPECIAL ASPECTS

[**983**] A. K. Manchester, *British Preëminence in Brazil: its rise and decline* (Univ. of North Carolina Press, 1933), is an important contribution both to economic and to diplomatic history. Compare, on Portuguese designs in the Banda Oriental, Street [801] and Humphreys [760], and, on the diplomacy of recognition, Webster [762] and Manchester's article, [**984**] 'The Recognition of Brazilian Independence', *Hispanic American Historical Review*, xxxi (1951), 80–96. See also nos. 936 and 941. [**985**] L. F. Hill, *Diplomatic Relations between the United States and Brazil* (Duke

Univ. Press, 1932), covers the earlier as well as the later history of these relations.

[986] Herbert Heaton, 'A Merchant Adventurer in Brazil', *Journal of Economic History*, vi (1946), 1–23, illustrates the effect of the opening of the ports of Brazil to the trade of the world. The 'merchant adventurer' is John Luccock. See no. 995.

[987] Agan, J., *The Diplomatic Relations of the United States and Brazil. I. The Portuguese Court at Rio de Janeiro* (Paris, Jouve, 1926).

[988] Manning, W. R., 'An Early Diplomatic Controversy between the United States and Brazil', *Hispanic American Historical Review*, i (1918), 123–45.

[989] Whitaker, A. P., 'José Silvestre Rebello: The First Diplomatic Representative of Brazil in the United States', *Hispanic American Historical Review*, xx (1940), 380–401.

CONTEMPORARY SOURCES

See Manning [761] and Webster [762]. A bibliography of travel literature is included in [990] Rubens Borba de Moraes and William Berrien, *Manual Bibliográfico de Estudos Brasileiros* (Rio de Janeiro, Gráfica Editora Souza, 1949).

[991] Maria Graham, *Journal of a Voyage to Brazil, and Residence there, during part of the years 1821, 1822, 1823* (London, 1824), [992] Henry Koster, *Travels in Brazil* (London, 1816), and [993] Lieutenant Henry Chamberlain, *Views and Costumes of the City and Neighbourhood of Rio de Janeiro, Brazil* . . . (London, 1822), are outstanding. Maria Graham (later Lady Callcott) became the tutor of the young Princess Maria da Gloria. Koster, the son of a Liverpool merchant, was a correspondent of Southey, and Chamberlain was the son of the British consul-general at Rio de Janeiro.

For other notable works see [994] John Mawe, *Travels in the Interior of Brazil, particularly in the gold and diamond districts of that country* . . . (London, 1812), [995] John Luccock, *Notes on Rio de Janeiro, and the southern parts of Brazil* (London, 1820), [996] J. B. von Spix and C. F. P. von Martius, *Travels in Brazil in the years 1817–1820* (2 vols., London, 1824), and [997] R. Walsh, *Notices of Brazil in 1828 and 1829* (2 vols., London, 1830), and see also Brackenridge [815], Caldcleugh [825], and Dundonald [837].

XI

MODERN LATIN AMERICA

1. GENERAL
HISTORIES AND ESSAYS

See nos. 118–32.

[**998**] R. A. Humphreys, *The Evolution of Modern Latin America* (Oxford, Clarendon Press: New York, Oxford Univ. Press, 1946), provides an introduction to, or commentary upon, the modern history of the Latin American area. Compare [**999**] the brief and relatively early summation of W. R. Shepherd, *The Hispanic Nations of the New World* ('Chronicles of America', vol. L, Yale Univ. Press, 1919), and, for South America, the admirable short survey [**1000**] of C. H. Haring, *South American Progress* (Harvard Univ. Press, 1934). See also [**1001**] A. C. Wilgus, ed., *Argentina, Brazil and Chile since Independence* (George Washington Univ. Press, 1935), and [**1002**] H. Bernstein, *Modern and Contemporary Latin America* (Philadelphia, Lippincott, 1952), which deals with Mexico, Argentina, Brazil, Chile, Colombia, and, in part also, Peru.

[**1003**] Cecil Jane, *Liberty and Despotism in Spanish America* (Oxford, Clarendon Press, 1929), is stimulating but misleading. [**1004**] F. García Calderón, *Latin America: its rise and progress* (London, Fisher Unwin: New York, Scribner's, 1913), is the interpretation of a then young Peruvian diplomat and is a Latin American classic. Compare, on the phenomenon of *caudillismo*, [**1005**] C. E. Chapman, 'The Age of the Caudillos: a chapter in Hispanic-American History', *Hispanic American Historical Review*, xii (1932), 281–300, reprinted in no. 1052, [**1005a**] R. A. Humphreys, 'Latin America. The Caudillo Tradition', in Michael Howard, ed., *Soldiers and Governments. Nine studies in civil-military relations* (London, Eyre and Spottiswoode, 1957), pp. 151–65, and the biographical studies, uneven in quality, in [**1006**] A. C. Wilgus, ed., *South American Dictators during the First Century of Independence* (George Washington Univ. Press, 1937). For further references see [**1007**] C. E. Chapman, 'List of Books referring to Caudillos in Hispanic America', *Hispanic American Historical Review*, xiii (1933), 143–6.

General

[**1008**] Luis-Alberto Sánchez, 'A New Interpretation of the History of America', *Hispanic American Historical Review*, xxiii (1943), 441–56, and [**1009**] R. A. Humphreys, *The Study of Latin American History* (London, H. K. Lewis, 1948; reprinted in *Inter-American Economic Affairs*, iii, No. 1 (1949), 32–49), are general essays. See also Griffin [136] and [**1010**] A. P. Whitaker, 'The Americas in the Atlantic Triangle', in *Ensayos sobre la Historia del Nuevo Mundo* [138].

[**1011**] Akers, C. E., *A History of South America* (3rd ed., London, Murray, 1930).

A superficial work originally published in 1904, principally concerned with the second half of the nineteenth century.

[**1012**] Chapman, C. E., *Republican Hispanic America: a history* (New York, Macmillan, 1937).

A continuation of no. 211.

NINETEENTH-CENTURY TRAVEL AND EXPLORATION[1]

For a partial guide to the voluminous literature of travel see *The Economic Literature of Latin America* [42].

[**1013**] T. B. Jones, *South America Rediscovered* (Univ. of Minnesota Press, 1949), summarizes travellers' accounts to illustrate social and economic history between 1810 and 1870 and provides a useful index to this kind of writing. For further references see the heterogeneous compilations of [**1014**] M. G. Mulhall, *The English in South America* (Buenos Aires, 1878), and [**1015**] W. H. Koebel, *British Exploits in South America . . .* (New York, Century Co., 1917).

[**1016**] J. P. Harrison, 'Science and Politics: Origins and Objectives of Mid-Nineteenth Century Government Expeditions to Latin America', *Hispanic American Historical Review*, xxxv (1955), 175–202, discusses the United States Exploring Expedition of 1838–42, the Naval Astronomical Expedition of 1849–52, the Amazon explorations of Herndon and Gibbon, and the expedition to explore and survey the waters of the Río de la Plata and its tributaries in 1853–6. For Darwin, Wallace, and Spruce see [**1017**] P. R. Cutright, *The Great Naturalists Explore South America* (New York, Macmillan, 1940), and [**1018**] Victor W. von Hagen, *South America Called Them* (New York, Knopf, 1945: London, Robert Hale, 1949).

[1] For books primarily relating to Central America see below pp. 146–8.

[**1019**] Charles Darwin's famous *Journal* was originally published as vol. iii of *Narrative of the Surveying Voyages of H.M. Ships Adventure and Beagle*, edited by Captain R. Fitzroy (3 vols., London, 1839), and was revised in 1845. Compare [**1020**] Nora Barlow, ed., *Charles Darwin's Diary of the Voyage of H.M.S. Beagle* (Cambridge Univ. Press, 1933), and [**1021**] her edition of Darwin's letters and notebooks, *Charles Darwin and the Voyage of the Beagle* (London, Pilot Press, 1945). To the eighteen-thirties belongs also the first, and South American, volume of [**1022**] Charles Wilkes, *Narrative of the United States Exploring Expedition during the years 1838, 1839, 1840, 1841, 1842* (5 vols., Philadelphia, 1845). Darwin inspired Spruce, who spent fifteen years, from 1849 to 1864, on the Amazon and in Ecuador and Peru. See [**1023**] Richard Spruce, *Notes of a Botanist on the Amazon and Andes . . .* (edited by A. R. Wallace, 2 vols., London, Macmillan, 1908), and compare Wallace [1446], and Bates [1447]. For the successors to Wilkes see Gilliss [1490], [**1024**] W. L. Herndon and L. Gibbon, *Exploration of the Valley of the Amazon* (2 vols., Washington, 1854), an expedition which began in Lima, and Page [1274].

[**1025**] Peabody, G. A., *South American Journals, 1858–1859* (edited by J. C. Phillips, Salem, Mass., Peabody Museum, 1937).

[**1026**] Timins, Douglas, ed., *A Traveller of the Sixties. Being extracts from the diaries kept by the late Frederick James Stevenson of his journeyings and explorations in Brazil, Peru, Argentina, Patagonia, Chile and Bolivia during the years 1867–1869* (London, Constable, 1929).

[**1027**] Orton, James, *The Andes and the Amazon, or, across the continent of South America* (3rd ed., New York, 1876).

TWENTIETH-CENTURY SURVEYS,
DESCRIPTIONS, AND INTERPRETATIONS[1]

See *The Economic Literature of Latin America* [42] and Behrendt [43].

[**1028**] James Bryce, *South America: observations and impressions* (rev. ed., New York, Macmillan, 1914), is outstanding among the travel literature of the early twentieth century. [**1029**] *The Republics of South America* (Oxford Univ. Press, 1937), a report by a study group of the Royal Institute of International Affairs, and [**1030**] W. L. Schurz, *Latin America: a descriptive survey* (rev.

---

[1] For books primarily relating to Central America see below pp. 145–6, 148.

General

ed., New York, Dutton, 1949), are especially noteworthy among later general accounts. Goldsmith [10] provides a critical commentary on books published before 1915. For developments in the period between the two World Wars see [**1031**] J. F. Normano, *The Struggle for South America: economy and ideology* (Boston, Houghton Mifflin: London, Allen and Unwin, 1931); [**1032**] H. K. Norton, *The Coming of South America* (New York, Day, 1932: London, Allen and Unwin, 1933); [**1033**] the widely ranging series of essays in A. C. Wilgus, ed., *Modern Hispanic America* (George Washington Univ. Press, 1933); [**1034**] Frank Tannenbaum, *Whither Latin America? An introduction to its economic and social problems* (New York, Crowell, 1934); [**1035**] Carleton Beals's journalistic *The Coming Struggle for Latin America* (Philadelphia, Lippincott, 1938: London, Cape, 1939); and [**1036**] J. T. Whitaker, *Americas to the South* (New York, Macmillan, 1939).

[**1037**] A. P. Whitaker, ed., *Inter-American Affairs* (5 vols., Columbia Univ. Press, 1942–6), supplies an excellent annual survey for the years 1941 to 1945. [**1038**] Duncan Aikman, *The All-American Front* (New York, Doubleday, Doran, 1940), and [**1039**] S. G. Inman, *Latin America: its place in world life* (rev. ed., New York, Harcourt, Brace, 1942), are general accounts. For further illustrations of contemporary journalism compare [**1040**] Waldo Frank, *South American Journey* (New York, Duell, Sloan and Pearce, 1943); [**1041**] J. F. Privitera, *The Latin American Front* (Milwaukee, Bruce Pub. Co., 1945); [**1042**] Ray Josephs, *Latin America: continent in crisis* (New York, Random House, 1948); [**1043**] Germán Arciniegas, *The State of Latin America* (New York, Knopf, 1952), an exceptionally interesting diagnosis by a distinguished Colombian 'liberal'; and [**1044**] Peter Schmid, *Beggars on Golden Stools. A journey through Latin America* (London, Weidenfeld and Nicolson, 1956).

[**1045**] Bingham, Hiram, *Across South America. An account of a journey from Buenos Aires to Lima by way of Potosí . . .* (Boston and New York, Houghton Mifflin, 1911).

[**1046**] Miller, L. E., *In the Wilds of South America: six years of exploration in Colombia, Venezuela, British Guiana, Peru, Bolivia, Argentina, Paraguay, and Brazil* (New York, Scribner's, 1918: London, Fisher Unwin, 1919).

[**1047**] Tschiffely, A. F., *Southern Cross to Pole Star; Tschiffely's ride* (London, Heinemann, 1933).

[**1048**] Goodspeed, T. H., *Plant Hunters in the Andes* (New York, Farrar and Rinehart, 1941).

2. POLITICS, GOVERNMENT, AND LAW

For the texts of Latin American constitutions consult Fitzgibbon [3] and Rodríguez [4], for a 'Glossary of Latin-American Constitutional Terms' [**1049**] R. H. Fitzgibbon, *Hispanic American Historical Review*, xxvii (1947), 574–90, and for guides to law and legal literature nos. 65–79.

[**1050**] Miguel Jorrín, *Governments of Latin America* (New York, Van Nostrand, 1953), [**1051**] A. F. Macdonald, *Latin American Politics and Government* (2nd ed., New York, Crowell, 1954), and [**1051a**] W. W. Pierson and F. G. Gil, *Governments of Latin America* (New York, McGraw-Hill Book Co., 1957), are general textbooks. [**1052**] A. N. Christensen, ed., *The Evolution of Latin American Government* (New York, Holt, 1951), is a useful collection of essays for the most part previously printed.

[**1053**] J. L. Mecham discusses 'The Ministry of State in Latin America', *Southwestern Political and Social Science Quarterly*, viii (Sept. 1927), 1–26, and [**1054**] W. S. Stokes 'Parliamentary Government in Latin America', *American Political Science Review*, xxxix (June 1945), 522–36, reprinted in Christensen [1052]. See, also reprinted in Christensen, the illuminating general articles of [**1055**] Kingsley Davis, 'Political Ambivalence in Latin America', *Journal of Legal and Political Sociology*, i (Oct. 1942), 127–50, and of A. P. Whitaker, R. H. Fitzgibbon, S. A. Mosk, and W. R. Crawford in [**1056**] the symposium edited by W. W. Pierson, 'Pathology of Democracy in Latin America', *American Political Science Review*, xliv (March 1950), 100–49, and [**1056a**] the interesting essay of R. M. Morse, 'Toward a Theory of Spanish American Government', *Journal of the History of Ideas*, xv (1954), 71–93.

[**1057**] S. F. Simon, 'Anarchism and Anarcho-Syndicalism in South America', *Hispanic American Historical Review*, xxvi (1946), 38–59, is a scholarly contribution and [**1058**] R. J. Alexander, *Labour Movements in Latin America* (London, Fabian Pubns., 1947), reprinted in Christensen [1052], is a general survey. Also reprinted in Christensen, [**1059**] R. J. Alexander, 'The Latin American Aprista Parties', *Political Quarterly*, xx (1949), 236–47, discusses the Alianza Popular Revolucionaria in Peru and related movements elsewhere. [**1060**] R. J. Alexander, *Communism* *in Latin America* (Rutgers Univ. Press, 1957), is a general discussion. Compare the autobiography of an ex-Communist agent in Peru and Chile, [**1061**] Eudocio Ravines, *The Yenan Way* (New York, Scribner's, 1951).

[**1062**] Clagett, H. L., *The Administration of Justice in Latin America* (New York, Oceana Pubns., 1952).

[**1063**] Eder, P. J., *A Comparative Study of Anglo-American and Latin American Law* (New York Univ. Press, 1950).

[**1064**] Recaséns Siches, Luis, *et al.*, *Latin American Legal Philosophy* (Harvard Univ. Press, 1948).

[**1065**] Teeters, N. K., *Penology from Panama to Cape Horn* (Univ. of Pennsylvania Press, 1946).

3. ECONOMIC DEVELOPMENT AND ECONOMIC CONDITIONS

GENERAL

For bibliographies and guides see *The Economic Literature of Latin America* [42], Jones [42a], Behrendt [43], *Bibliography of Selected Statistical Sources of the American Nations* [45], Taeuber [47], Morrison [64], and Phelps [117]. See also [**1066**] Elizabeth Phelps, *Statistical Activities of the American Nations, 1940* (Washington, Inter-American Statistical Institute, 1941), and [**1067**] R. C. Migone *et al.*, *Inter-American Statistical Yearbook* (2nd ed., New York, Macmillan, 1942).

[**1068**] W. C. Gordon, *The Economy of Latin America* (Columbia Univ. Press, 1950), and [**1069**] S. G. Hanson, *Economic Development in Latin America* (Washington, Inter-American Affairs Press, 1951), are important general surveys. [**1070**] The annual *Economic Survey of Latin America* published by the Economic Commission for Latin America [ECLA] of the United Nations Economic and Social Council first appeared in 1949 (Lake Success, New York).[1]

[**1071**] S. A. Mosk, 'Latin America and the World Economy,

[1] ECLA, the Food and Agriculture Organization and other specialized agencies of the United Nations organization, the Inter-American Economic and Social Council of the Organization of American States, the Pan American Union, and, in the United States, the Departments of Agriculture, Commerce, and Labor, the Tariff Commission, and the Bureau of the Census, are all important sources of current information. In the United Kingdom the Export Promotion Department, formerly the Department of Overseas Trade, publishes periodic reports on economic conditions in the Latin American states.

1850–1914', *Inter-American Economic Affairs*, ii, No. 3 (1948), 53–82, calls attention to 'certain propositions about economic development since the middle of the nineteenth century which help to give meaning to the economic history of Latin America'. [**1072**] J. F. Rippy, *Latin America and the Industrial Age* (2nd ed., New York, Putnam's, 1947), sketches the advent of modern technologies. [**1073**] Francis Violich, *Cities of Latin America, housing and planning to the south* (New York, Reinhold, 1944), discusses urban problems.

[**1074**] Behrendt, R. F., *Economic Nationalism in Latin America* (Inter-Americana Short Papers, I. Albuquerque, School of Inter-American Affairs, Univ. of New Mexico, 1941).

[**1075**] Bidwell, P. W., *Economic Defense of Latin America* (Boston, World Peace Foundation, 1941).

[**1076**] Harris, Seymour E., ed., *Economic Problems of Latin America* (New York and London, McGraw-Hill, 1944).

[**1077**] Olson, P. R., and Hickman, C. A., *Pan American Economics* (New York, John Wiley, 1943).

[**1078**] Soule, G. H., Efron, D., and Ness, N. T., *Latin America in the Future World* (New York, Farrar and Rinehart, 1945).

See also Normano [1031], Norton [1032], Tannenbaum [1034], and Whitaker [1037].

AGRICULTURE, INDUSTRY, AND NATURAL RESOURCES

[**1079**] George Wythe traces 'The Rise of the Factory in Latin America', *Hispanic American Historical Review*, xxv (1945), 295–314. Compare Rippy [1072]. [**1080**] D. M. Phelps, *Migration of Industry to South America* (New York and London, McGraw-Hill, 1936), is an important study in economic history. [**1081**] George Wythe, *Industry in Latin America* (2nd ed., Columbia Univ. Press, 1949), and [**1082**] L. J. Hughlett, ed., *Industrialization of Latin America* (New York and London, McGraw-Hill, 1946), are concerned with the general problems and progress of industrialization.

For the sugar industry see [**1083**] Noël Deerr, *The History of Sugar* (2 vols., London, Chapman and Hall, 1949), and, for the banana industry, [**1084**] F. U. Adams, *Conquest of the Tropics. The story of the creative enterprises conducted by the United Fruit Company* (New York, Doubleday, Page, 1914), [**1085**] C. D. Kepner and J. H. Southill, *The Banana Empire: a case study in economic imperialism*

Economic Development and Economic Conditions
(New York, Vanguard Press, 1935), [**1086**] C. D. Kepner, *Social Aspects of the Banana Industry* (Columbia Univ. Press, 1936), and [**1087**] C. M. Wilson, *Empire in Green and Gold: the story of the American banana trade* (New York, Holt, 1947). [**1088**] C. M. Wilson, ed., *New Crops for the New World* (New York, Macmillan, 1945), discusses sixteen crops or groups of crops, including rubber, cinchona, and cane sugar.

[**1089**] Bain, H. F., and Read, T. T., *Ores and Industry in South America* (New York, Council on Foreign Relations, 1934).

[**1090**] Bradley, J. R., *Fuel and Power in Latin America* (Washington, Govt. Printing Office, 1931).

[**1091**] Miller, B. Le R., and Singewald, J. T., *The Mineral Deposits of South America* (New York and London, McGraw-Hill, 1919).

[**1092**] United States Tariff Commission, *Latin America as a Source of Strategic and Other Essential Materials* (Washington, Govt. Printing Office, 1941).

LABOUR

[**1093**] D. H. Blelloch, 'Latin America and the International Labour Standards', *International Labour Review*, xliii (1941), 377–400, is 'intended to show the keen interest in labour and social questions that is felt in the various Latin American countries'. See Bernstein [44], [**1094**] Ernesto Galarza, *Labor Trends and Social Welfare in Latin America, 1941 and 1942* (Washington, Pan American Union, Division of Labor and Social Information, 1943), Soule [1078] and, on labour organization, Alexander [1058].

TRANSPORTATION

[**1095**] R. G. Albion, 'British Shipping and Latin America, 1806–1914', *Journal of Economic History*, xi (1951), 361–74, and [**1096**] J. H. Kemble, 'Mail Steamers Link the Americas, 1840–1890' in *Greater America* [134], are convenient summaries. See also J. H. Kemble, [**1097**] 'The Genesis of the Pacific Mail Steamship Company', *California Historical Society Quarterly*, xiii (1934), 240–54, 386–406, and [**1098**] *The Panama Route, 1848–1869* (Univ. of California Press, 1943). [**1099**] T. A. Bushell, *'Royal Mail': a centenary history of the Royal Mail Line, 1839–1939* (London, Trade and Travel Pubns., [1939]), is a useful company history.

On the history of railways consult [**1100**] G. S. Brady and W. R. Long, *Railways of South America* (3 parts, Washington,

Bureau of Foreign and Domestic Commerce, 1926, 1927, 1930), and W. R. Long's studies, [**1101**] *Railways of Central America and the West Indies* (*ibid.*, 1925), and [**1102**] *Railways of Mexico* (*ibid.*, 1925). [**1103**] W. A. M. Burden deals with *The Struggle for Airways in Latin America* (New York, Council on Foreign Relations, 1943).

[**1104**] Caruso, J. A., 'The Pan American Railway', *Hispanic American Historical Review*, xxxi (1951), 608–39.

[**1105**] Halsey, F. M., *Railway Expansion in Latin America* (New York, Moody Magazine and Book Co., 1916).

[**1106**] Hanson, S. G., 'The Farquhar Syndicate in South America', *Hispanic American Historical Review*, xvii (1937), 314–26.

[**1107**] Rydell, R. A., *Cape Horn to the Pacific. The rise and decline of an ocean highway* (Univ. of California Press, 1952).

DISTRIBUTION, FINANCE, AND TRADE

[**1108**] C. F. Jones, *The Commerce of South America* (Boston and London, Ginn and Co., 1928), was an early general study. [**1109**] *The Foreign Trade of Latin America* (rev. ed., 3 parts in 4 vols., Washington, United States Tariff Commission, 1942), and [**1110**] *The Foreign Trade of Latin America since 1913* (Washington, Pan American Union, Division of Economic Research, 1952), are important works of reference.

[**1111**] *Foreign Capital in Latin America* (New York, United Nations, Department of Economic and Social Affairs, 1955), is a comprehensive survey.

On early British investment see [**1112**] L. H. Jenks, *The Migration of British Capital to 1875* (New York and London, Knopf, 1927: London, Cape, 1937), and a group of short articles by J. F. Rippy: [**1113**] 'Early British Investments in the Latin-American Republics', *Inter-American Economic Affairs*, vi, No. 1 (1952), 40–51, [**1114**] 'British Investments in Latin America, End of 1876', *Pacific Historical Review*, xvii (1948), 11–18, [**1115**] 'The British Investment "Boom" of the 1880's in Latin America', *Hispanic American Historical Review*, xxix (1949), 281–6, amplified in *Inter-American Economic Affairs*, v, No. 4 (1952), 36–45, and [**1116**] 'The British Investment "Boom" of the 1880's in Latin American Mines', *ibid.*, i, No. 4 (1948), 71–78. Compare Rippy [786].

This series is continued by: [**1117**] 'British Investments in Latin America, End of Year 1900', *Inter-American Economic Affairs*, iv, No. 3 (1950), 16–26, [**1118**] 'The Peak of British Investment in Latin American Mines', *ibid.*, ii, No. 1 (1948), 41–48, [**1119**] 'British Investments in Latin America, End of 1913', *ibid.*, v, No. 2 (1951), 90–100, [**1120**] 'British Investments in Latin America at their Peak', *Hispanic American Historical Review*, xxxiv (1954), 94–102, [**1121**] 'British Investments in Latin America, End of 1931', *Journal of Modern History*, xix (1947), 312–19, [**1122**] 'British Investments in Latin America, 1939', *Journal of Political Economy*, lvi (1948), 63–68, and [**1123**] 'British Investments in Latin America: a decade of rapid reduction, 1940–1950', *Hispanic American Historical Review*, xxxii (1952), 285–92.

For French, Italian, and German investments see J. F. Rippy: [**1124**] 'French Investments in Latin America', *Inter-American Economic Affairs*, ii, No. 2 (1948), 52–71, [**1125**] 'Italian Immigrants and Investments in Latin America', *ibid.*, iii, No. 2 (1949), 25–37, and [**1126**] 'German Investments in Latin America', *Journal of Business of the University of Chicago*, xxi (1948), 63–73.

[**1127**] Max Winkler, *Investments of United States Capital in Latin America* (Boston, World Peace Foundation, 1929), and [**1128**] W. Feuerlein and E. Hannan, *Dollars in Latin America* (New York, Council on Foreign Relations, 1941), are both important. See also Hanson [1106] and [**1128a**] A. S. J. Baster, *The International Banks* (London, P. S. King, 1935).

[**1129**] Bratter, H. M., 'Foreign Exchange Control in Latin America', *Foreign Policy Reports*, xiv, No. 23, 15 Feb. 1939.

[**1130**] Fabra Ribas, A., *The Cooperative Movement in Latin America: its significance in hemisphere solidarity* (Inter-Americana Short Papers, III. Albuquerque, School of Inter-American Affairs, Univ. of New Mexico, 1943).

[**1131**] Halsey, F. M., *Investments in Latin America and the British West Indies* (Washington, Govt. Printing Office, 1918).

[**1132**] Hurley, E. N., *Banking and Credit in Argentina, Brazil, Chile and Peru* (Washington, Govt. Printing Office, 1914).

[**1133**] Trueblood, H. J., 'Trade Rivalries in Latin America', *Foreign Policy Reports*, xiii, No. 13, 15 Sept. 1937.

[**1134**] United Nations, Department of Economic Affairs, *A Study of Trade between Latin America and Europe* (Geneva, 1953).

[**1135**] Zimmern, W. H., 'Lancashire and Latin America', *The Manchester School of Economic and Social Studies*, xiii (1944), 45–60. Delightful reminiscences of the trade in cotton piece goods.

4. POPULATION, IMMIGRATION, INTERNAL MIGRATION

POPULATION

[**1136**] Kingsley Davis, 'Population Trends and Policies in Latin America', in *Some Economic Aspects of Postwar Inter-American Relations* (Univ. of Texas Press, 1946), is a detailed analysis. Compare, a more general essay, [**1137**] the same author's 'Latin America's Multiplying Peoples', *Foreign Affairs*, xxv (1947), 643–54, reprinted in Christensen [1052].

[**1138**] John Gillin, 'Mestizo America', in Ralph Linton, ed., *Most of the World. The peoples of Africa, Latin America, and the East today* (Columbia Univ. Press, 1949), discusses those countries which have large mestizo populations. On the native Indian races see *Handbook of South American Indians* [148] and nos. 151–8 generally. See also [**1139**] W. S. Rycroft, ed., *Indians of the High Andes* (New York, Committee on Cooperation in Latin America, 1946), and, historically misleading, [**1140**] Harold Osborne, *Indians of the Andes. Aymaras and Quechuas* (Harvard Univ. Press: London, Routledge and Kegan Paul, 1952). [**1141**] Frank Tannenbaum, 'Agrarismo, Indianismo, y Nacionalismo', *Hispanic American Historical Review*, xxiii (1943), 394–423, is a useful essay. On the negro see Zelinsky [389], nos. 390 to 392b and 792, together with [**1142**] Frank Tannenbaum, *Slave and Citizen: the negro in the Americas* (New York, Knopf, 1947), and [**1143**] C. H. Wesley, ed., *The Negro in the Americas* (Public Lectures of the Division of the Social Sciences of the Graduate School, Howard Univ., Washington, D.C., 1940).

[**1144**] Cohen, J. X., *Jewish Life in South America* (New York, Bloch Pub. Co., 1941).

IMMIGRATION

[**1145**] I. Ferenczi and W. F. Willcox, *International Migrations* (2 vols., New York, National Bureau of Economic Research, 1929, 1931), is an indispensable work of reference. [**1146**] R. F. Foerster, *The Italian Emigration of our Times* (Harvard Univ. Press, 1924), is detailed and thorough. Compare Rippy [1125]. [**1147**] J. F. Normano and Antonello Gerbi, *The Japanese in South America* (New York, Institute of Pacific Relations, 1943), relates in particular to Peru and Brazil. See also [**1148**] J. F. Rippy, 'The Japanese in Latin America', *Inter-American Economic*

Affairs, iii, No. 1 (1949), 50–65. For British enterprise see Mulhall [1014] and Koebel [1015].

[**1149**] Janzen, A. E., *Glimpses of South America* (Hillsboro, Kansas, Mennonite Brethren Pub. House, 1944).
The Mennonite colonies in Paraguay and Brazil.

[**1150**] Maurette, F., and Siewers, E., 'Immigration and Settlement in Brazil, Argentina and Uruguay', *International Labour Review*, xxxv (1937), 215–47, 352–83.

[**1151**] Price, A. G., *White Settlers in the Tropics* (New York, American Geographical Society, 1939).

[**1152**] Thompson, R. W., *Germans and Japs in South America* (London, Faber and Faber, 1942).
Originally published as *Voice from the Wilderness*. Useful for the colonies in Paraguay and Argentine Misiones.

INTERNAL MIGRATION

[**1153**] Bowman, Isaiah, 'Possibilities of Settlement in South America', in Isaiah Bowman, ed., *Limits of Land Settlement* (New York, Council on Foreign Relations, 1937).

[**1154**] Bowman, Isaiah, 'South American Hinterlands', in Isaiah Bowman, *The Pioneer Fringe* (New York, American Geographical Society, 1931).

[**1155**] James, P. E., 'Expanding Frontiers of Settlement in Latin America—a project for future study', *Hispanic American Historical Review*, xxi (1941), 183–95.
Discusses the highlands of Costa Rica, Antioquia, Middle Chile, and South Brazil.

[**1156**] Platt, R. R., 'Opportunities for Agricultural Colonization in the Eastern Border Valleys of the Andes', in *Pioneer Settlement. Coöperative Studies by Twenty-Six Authors* (New York, American Geographical Society, 1932).

[**1157**] Sauer, C. O., 'The Prospects for the Redistribution of Population', in Isaiah Bowman, ed., *Limits of Land Settlement* (New York, Council on Foreign Relations, 1937).

[**1158**] Schurz, W. L., 'Conditions affecting Settlement on the Matto Grosso Highland and in the Gran Chaco', in *Pioneer Settlement. Coöperative Studies by Twenty-Six Authors* (New York, American Geographical Society, 1932).

5. EDUCATION, PHILOSOPHY, RELIGION, SCIENCE

On education see [**1159**] E. E. Brandon, *Latin American Universities and Special Schools* (Washington, Govt. Printing Office, 1913), [**1159a**] H. L. Smith and H. Littell, *Education in Latin America* (New York, American Book Co., 1934), [**1160**] I. L. Kandel, ed., *Education in Latin-American Countries* (Educational Yearbook of the International Institute of Teachers College, vol. xix, Columbia University. Columbia Univ. Press, 1942), and [**1160a**] the symposium edited by Ángel del Río, *Responsible Freedom in the Americas* (New York, Doubleday, 1955). See also Browning [790]. [**1161**] A. A. Moll, *Aesculapius in Latin America* (Philadelphia, W. B. Saunders, 1944), is a pioneer medical history. [**1162**] W. R. Crawford, *A Century of Latin American Thought* (Harvard Univ. Press, 1944), is a valuable collection of essays which opens up the realm of ideas. See also Griffin, *Concerning Latin American Culture* [136].

Mecham, *Church and State in Latin America* [393], is a scholarly history and [**1163**] Edwin Ryan, *The Church in the South American Republics* (Milwaukee, Bruce Pub. Co., 1932), a more popular treatment. [**1164**] P. M. Dunne, *A Padre Views South America* (Milwaukee, Bruce Pub. Co., 1945), presents a Catholic point of view and [**1165**] J. A. Mackay, *The Other Spanish Christ. A study in the spiritual history of Spain and South America* (London, Student Christian Movement, 1932: New York, Macmillan, 1933), a Protestant. For the Mennonites see Janzen [1149].

[**1166**] Howard, G. P., *Religious Liberty in Latin America?* (Philadelphia, Westminster Press, 1944).

[**1167**] Lee, John, *Religious Liberty in South America* (Cincinnati, Jennings and Graham; New York, Eaton and Mains, 1907).

6. LITERATURE AND THE ARTS

See nos. 80–101. Henríquez-Ureña, *Literary Currents in Hispanic America* [455] is a survey of art movements as well as of literature. [**1168**] Alfred Coester, *The Literary History of Spanish America* (2nd ed., New York, Macmillan, 1928), [**1169**] E. Herman Hespelt *et al.*, *An Outline History of Spanish American Literature* (2nd ed., New York, Crofts, 1942), and [**1170**] A. Torres-Ríoseco, *The Epic of Latin American Literature* (rev. ed., New York, Oxford Univ. Press, 1946), are general histories. [**1171**] A. L. Haight, ed., *Portrait of Latin America as seen by her Print Makers* (New York, Hastings House, 1946), illustrates the contemporary scene. See also [**1172**] Lincoln Kirstein, *The Latin American Collection of the Museum of Modern Art* (New York, Museum of Modern Art, 1943). [**1173**] Eleanor Hague, *Latin American Music, past and present* (Santa Ana, California, Fine Arts Press, 1934), is a brief introduction.

[**1174**] Goldberg, Isaac, *Studies in Spanish American Literature* (New York, Brentano's, 1920).

[**1175**] Onís, Harriet de, ed., *The Golden Land. An anthology of Latin American folklore in literature* (New York, Knopf, 1948).

[**1176**] Spell, J. R., *Contemporary Spanish-American Fiction* (Univ. of North Carolina Press, 1944).

[**1177**] Torres-Ríoseco, A., *New World Literature: tradition and revolt in Latin America* (Univ. of California Press, 1949).

7. INTERNATIONAL RELATIONS
GENERAL

See nos. 928-78.

For a partial guide to the diplomatic history of the Latin American states see Bemis and Griffin [60] and for a comprehensive review of international relations [**1178**] J. F. Rippy, *Latin America in World Politics* (3rd ed., New York, Crofts: London, Allen and Unwin, 1938). On contemporary affairs consult the annual volumes of [**1179**] the *Survey of International Affairs*, published for the Royal Institute of International Affairs by the Oxford University Press (1920/23-1938; 1949-), and of [**1180**] *The United States in World Affairs* (New York, Council on Foreign Relations, 1931-41; 1947-).

[**1181**] P. A. Martin, *Latin America and the War* (Johns Hopkins Press, 1925), is a detailed analysis of the effects of the first World War on the diplomatic relations of the Latin American states. The impact of the second World War is best revealed in Whitaker [1037]. See also Bidwell [1075] and, among works of contemporary journalism, [**1182**] N. P. Macdonald, *Hitler over Latin America* (London, Jarrolds, 1940), [**1183**] H. Fernández Artucio, *The Nazi Underground in South America* (New York, Farrar and Rinehart, 1942: London, Hale, as *The Nazi Octopus in South America*, 1943), and [**1184**] Allan Chase, *Falange. The axis secret army in the Americas* (New York, Putnam's, 1943).

[**1185**] W. H. Kelchner discusses *Latin American Relations with the League of Nations* (Boston, World Peace Foundation, 1930), and [**1186**] J. A. Houston *Latin America in the United Nations* (New York, Carnegie Endowment for International Peace, 1956). See also Macedo Soares [1389] and La Foy [1339].
On the Drago Doctrine, formulated in 1902, which repudiates the use of force by European Powers in the collection of public debts, see [**1187**] H. E. Nettles, 'The Drago Doctrine in International Law and Politics', *Hispanic American Historical Review*, viii (1928), 204–23, and on the 'Calvo Clause', which denies the right of a foreigner to appeal to his own government for the enforcement of contracts, [**1188**] D. R. Shea, *The Calvo Clause. A problem of inter-American and international law and diplomacy* (Univ. of Minnesota Press, 1955).

[**1189**] Bradley, Anita, *Trans-Pacific Relations of Latin America* (New York, Institute of Pacific Relations, 1942).

[**1190**] Diffie, B. W., 'The Ideology of *Hispanidad*', *Hispanic American Historical Review*, xxiii (1943), 457–82.
'Pride in liberalism was . . . one of the outstanding characteristics of *Hispanismo* . . . *Hispanidad*, on the other hand, appeals to the Hispanic world on the basis of Spain's traditional, Roman Catholic heritage, to which has been added the ideology of modern Fascism.'

[**1191**] Masters, Ruth D., *Handbook of International Organizations in the Americas* (Washington, Carnegie Endowment for International Peace, 1945).

INTRA-LATIN AMERICAN RELATIONS

Gordon Ireland, [**1192**] *Boundaries, Possessions and Conflicts in South America* (Harvard Univ. Press, 1938), and [**1193**] *Boundaries, Possessions and Conflicts in Central and North America and the Caribbean* (*ibid.*, 1941), are indispensable works of reference and deal with disputes with the United States and Great Britain as well as with controversies between the Latin American states themselves. See also Burr and Hussey [1231].

[**1194**] Burr, R. N., 'The Balance of Power in Nineteenth-Century South America: an exploratory essay', *Hispanic American Historical Review*, xxxv (1955), 37–60.

[**1195**] Frazer, R. W., 'The Role of the Lima Congress, 1864–1865, in the Development of Pan-Americanism', *Hispanic American Historical Review*, xxix (1949), 319–48.

[**1196**] Manning, W. R., *Arbitration Treaties among the American Nations*, *to the close of the year 1910* (New York, Carnegie Endowment for International Peace, 1924).

[**1197**] Nuermberger, G. A., 'The Continental Treaties of 1856: an American Union "exclusive of the United States" ', *Hispanic American Historical Review*, xx (1940), 32–55.

LATIN AMERICA AND THE UNITED STATES

See Bemis and Griffin [60], Bradley [61], Meyer [63], and nos. 958–78.

Bemis, *The Latin American Policy of the United States* [967] and [**1198**] Graham H. Stuart, *Latin America and the United States* (5th ed., New York and London, Appleton-Century-Crofts, 1955), which supersedes [**1199**] J. H. Latané, *The United States and Latin America* (New York, Doubleday, Page, 1920), are general accounts. See also the comprehensive survey [**1200**] of W. S. Robertson, *Hispanic American Relations with the United States* (New York, Carnegie Endowment for International Peace, 1923), which embraces commercial and cultural as well as political and diplomatic relations. [**1201**] A. P. Whitaker, *The United States and South America: the northern republics* (Harvard Univ. Press, 1948), emphasizes the recent past.

[**1202**] A. C. Wilgus discusses 'Official Expression of Manifest Destiny Sentiment concerning Hispanic America, 1848–1871', *Louisiana Historical Quarterly*, xv (1932), 486–506, as exemplified in congressional debates, messages of the presidents, etc., and [**1203**] N. L. Ferris examines 'The Relations of the United States with South America during the American Civil War', *Hispanic American Historical Review*, xxi (1941), 51–78. [**1204**] A. W. Eister, *The United States and the A.B.C. Powers, 1889–1906* (Dallas, Southern Methodist Univ., 1950), which sets out, in short compass and with negative results, to examine the effects upon the relations of these Powers of the Spanish American War of 1898, deserves no more than passing mention.

[**1205**] W. F. Sands, *Our Jungle Diplomacy* (Univ. of North Carolina Press, 1944), is an entertaining indictment of State Department policy between 1904 and 1912 based on the author's experiences in Mexico, Guatemala, Panama, and Ecuador. Also severely critical, [**1206**] Scott Nearing and Joseph Freeman, *Dollar Diplomacy. A study in American imperialism* (New York, B. W. Huebsch and Viking Press, 1926), is primarily concerned, in its Latin American aspects, with Central America and the Caribbean.[1] [**1207**] S. W. Livermore, 'Battleship Diplomacy in South America: 1905–1925', *Journal of Modern History*, xvi (1944), 31–48, examines United States participation in the competition for naval armaments.

[**1208**] C. H. Haring, *South America Looks at the United States* (New York, Macmillan, 1928), analyses Latin American opinion on the eve of the adoption of the Good Neighbour policy. Compare [**1209**] Manuel Ugarte, *The Destiny of a Continent* (ed. J. F. Rippy, New York, Knopf, 1925), and contrast [**1210**] Carleton Beals, Bryce Oliver, Herschel Brickell, and S. G. Inman, *What the South Americans Think of Us* (New York, McBride, 1945).

[**1211**] Alexander DeConde, *Herbert Hoover's Latin-American Policy* (Stanford Univ. Press, 1951), and [**1212**] E. O. Guerrant, *Roosevelt's Good Neighbor Policy* (Univ. of New Mexico Press, 1950), are complementary studies. The former is concerned to explain that the Good Neighbour policy had its roots in the Hoover administration. See also [**1213**] Laurence Duggan, *The Americas. The search for hemisphere security* (New York, Holt, 1949), and, for the contemporary record, no. 1180.

[**1214**] J. W. Gantenbein, ed., *The Evolution of our Latin American Policy. A documentary record* (Columbia Univ. Press, 1950), is a valuable source book. See also the annual volumes of [**1215**] *Documents on American Foreign Relations* (Boston, World Peace Foundation, 1939–52; New York, Council on Foreign Relations, 1953–). [**1216**] The *Diplomatic Correspondence of the United States. Inter-American Affairs, 1831–60* has been edited by W. R. Manning (12 vols., Washington, Carnegie Endowment for International Peace, 1932–9). The great series [**1217**] of *Papers relating to the Foreign Relations of the United States*, published by the State Department, begins in 1861. See also Manning [1196].

[**1218**] Onís, José de, *The United States as seen by Spanish American Writers, 1776–1890* (New York, Hispanic Institute in the United States, 1952).

THE MONROE DOCTRINE

The classic study of Dexter Perkins on the origin of the Monroe Doctrine [965] is continued by [**1219**] his *The Monroe Doctrine, 1826–1867* (Johns Hopkins Press, 1933) and [**1220**] *The Monroe*

---

[1] For the United States, Central America, and the Caribbean area see below pp. 145–8.

Doctrine, 1867–1907 (ibid., 1937), and the results of these detailed investigations are summarized and the history of the doctrine itself is carried forward in his [**1221**] *A History of the Monroe Doctrine* (new ed., Boston, Little, Brown, 1955, originally published in 1941 as *Hands Off: a history of the Monroe Doctrine*). [**1222**] Alejandro Alvarez, *The Monroe Doctrine* (New York, Carnegie Endowment for International Peace, 1924), presents a variety of Latin American and United States views.

[**1223**] Inman, S. G., 'The Monroe Doctrine and Hispanic America', *Hispanic American Historical Review*, iv (1921), 635–76. Reprinted in no. 1236.

[**1224**] Pierson, W. W., 'Alberdi's Views on the Monroe Doctrine', *Hispanic American Historical Review*, iii (1920), 362–74.

[**1225**] Robertson, W. S., 'Hispanic American Appreciations of the Monroe Doctrine', *Hispanic American Historical Review*, iii (1920), 1–16.

The 'reactions produced in Hispanic America by the application of the Monroe Doctrine to the boundary dispute between Venezuela and Great Britain'.

[**1226**] Young, G. B., 'Intervention under the Monroe Doctrine: the Olney Corollary', *Political Science Quarterly*, lvii (June 1942), 247–80.

See also nos. 60, 61, 63, 966, and 971–4.

THE INTER-AMERICAN SYSTEM

On the Panama Congress of 1826 see nos. 975–8a, on the first international congress of American states in 1889 [**1227**] J. B. Lockey, *Essays in Pan-Americanism* (Univ. of California Press, 1939), [**1228**] A. C. Wilgus, 'James G. Blaine and the Pan American Movement', *Hispanic American Historical Review*, v (1922), 662–708, and McGann [1282a, 1292], and, on the Pan American Union, [**1229**] C. B. Casey, 'The Creation and Development of the Pan American Union', *ibid.*, xiii (1933), 437–56. For the conventions, recommendations, resolutions, and motions of the first eight of the International Conferences of American States and of the first and second meetings of American ministers of foreign affairs see [**1230**] J. B. Scott, ed., *The International Conferences of American States, 1889–1928* (New York, Carnegie Endowment for International Peace, 1931), and the *First Supplement, 1933–1940* to this volume (*ibid.*, Washington, 1940). The Charter of the Organization of American States adopted at the Ninth Conference held at Bogotá in 1948 is in Gantenbein [1214] and in the useful collection of documents edited by [**1231**] R. N. Burr and R. D. Hussey, *Documents on Inter-American Cooperation* (2 vols., Univ. of Pennsylvania Press, 1955). These cover the years 1810 to 1948. See also Masters [1191] and Manning [1196]. [**1232**] M. M. Ball, *The Problem of Inter-American Organization* (Stanford Univ. Press, 1944), and [**1233**] John P. Humphrey, *The Inter-American System. A Canadian view* (Toronto, Macmillan, 1942), describe the character and operation of the inter-American regional system. [**1234**] C. G. Fenwick, *The Inter-American Regional System* (New York, D. X. McMullen, 1949), takes brief account of developments at the Bogotá Conference of 1948. See also Houston [1186].

[**1235**] A. P. Whitaker, *The Western Hemisphere Idea: its rise and decline* (Cornell Univ. Press, 1954), is a penetrating examination of the origin of the idea that the peoples of the Western Hemisphere 'stand in a special relationship to one another which sets them apart from the rest of the world' and of the fluctuations of this idea in the nineteenth and twentieth centuries. [**1236**] S. G. Inman, *Problems in Pan Americanism* (2nd ed., New York, Doran, 1925: London, Allen and Unwin, 1926), is a general discussion.

[**1237**] 'An Appraisal of the Inter-American System—a symposium', *Inter-American Economic Affairs*, ii, No. 4 (1949), 45–95.

Papers presented at a round table meeting of the American Political Science Association by J. L. Mecham, F. G. Gil, W. Manger, W. F. Barber, J. F. Rippy, S. G. Hanson, and A. N. Christensen.

XII

THE REPUBLICS OF
SOUTH AMERICA SINCE 1830

1. ARGENTINA

GENERAL

For bibliographies and guides see nos. 38, 42, 65, 66, and 83. Levene, *A History of Argentina* [346], is principally concerned with the colonial and revolutionary periods. Kirkpatrick, *A History of the Argentine Republic* [793], a short introduction, emphasizes nineteenth-century development. The chapters by [**1238**] J. F. Rippy in Wilgus, *Argentina, Brazil and Chile since Independence* [1001], provide a general sketch. [**1239**] Ysabel F. Rennie, *The Argentine Republic* (New York, Macmillan, 1945), carries the story forward but considers also past evolution.

[**1240**] Pendle, George, *Argentina* (London, Royal Institute of International Affairs, 1955).
An excellent brief summary, which pays much attention to recent history.

[**1240a**] White, J. W., *Argentina: the life story of a nation* (New York, Viking Press, 1942).
Comprehensive, semi-popular, undocumented.

SPECIAL ASPECTS

POLITICS, GOVERNMENT, AND LAW

[**1241**] Amadeo, Santos P., *Argentine Constitutional Law* (Columbia Univ. Press, 1943).

[**1242**] Macdonald, A. F., *Government of the Argentine Republic* (New York, Crowell, 1942).

[**1243**] Rowe, L. S., *The Federal System of the Argentine Republic* (Washington, Carnegie Institution, 1921).

ECONOMIC DEVELOPMENT AND ECONOMIC CONDITIONS

On the pastoral industries see [**1244**] S. G. Hanson's excellent *Argentine Meat and the British Market* (Stanford Univ. Press, 1938), and [**1245**] Herbert Gibson, *The History and Present State of the Sheep-breeding Industry in the Argentine Republic* (Buenos Aires,

Ravenscroft and Mills, 1893); on the railway network Brady and Long [1100] and [**1246**] J. S. Duncan, 'British Railways in Argentina', *Political Science Quarterly*, lii (1937), 559–82; and on foreign investment and trade [**1247**] H. S. Ferns, 'Investment and Trade between Britain and Argentina in the Nineteenth Century', *Economic History Review*, 2nd series, iii (1950), 203–18, [**1248**] J. F. Rippy, 'Argentina: late major field of British overseas investment', *Inter-American Economic Affairs*, vi, No. 3 (1952), 3–13, [**1249**] H. E. Peters, *The Foreign Debt of the Argentine Republic* (Johns Hopkins Press, 1934), and [**1250**] V. L. Phelps, *The International Economic Position of Argentina* (Univ. of Pennsylvania Press, 1938). See also Ferns [803, 1284], Salera [1303], and Williams [1287].

POPULATION, IMMIGRATION, SETTLEMENT,
SOCIAL INSTITUTIONS

[**1251**] Mark Jefferson, *Peopling the Argentine Pampa* (New York, American Geographical Society, 1926), is outstanding. See also Foerster [1146], Maurette and Siewers [1150], and Bowman [1154]. On the problems of landownership, tenant farming, and standards of living consult [**1252**] C. C. Taylor's admirable *Rural Life in Argentina* (Baton Rouge, Louisiana State Univ. Press, 1948), on Jewish agricultural settlement [**1253**] E. Schwarz and J. C. Te Velde, 'Jewish Agricultural Settlement in Argentina: the ICA experiment', *Hispanic American Historical Review*, xix (1939), 185–203, and on the Welsh colonizers of Chubut [**1254**] J. E. Baur, 'The Welsh in Patagonia: an example of nationalistic migration', *ibid.*, xxxiv (1954), 468–92.

[**1255**] Dodds, James, *Records of the Scottish Settlers in the River Plate and their Churches* (Buenos Aires, Grant and Sylvester, 1897).

[**1256**] Murray, Thomas, *The Story of the Irish in Argentina* (New York, P. J. Kenedy and Sons, 1919).

See also Thompson [1152].

INTERNATIONAL RELATIONS

[**1257**] C. H. Haring, *Argentina and the United States* (Boston, World Peace Foundation, 1941), is a good short survey. The subject is more fully explored in [**1258**] A. P. Whitaker, *The United States and Argentina* (Harvard Univ. Press, 1954), which is focused, in the main, however, on more recent history.

Argentina

For the dispute over the Falkland Islands (Las Islas Malvinas) see the massive study of Julius Goebel, *The Struggle for the Falkland Islands* [698], and for Antarctica [**1259**] E. W. H. Christie, *The Antarctic Problem: an historical and political study* (London, Allen and Unwin, 1951).

[**1260**] Dickens, P. D., 'The Falkland Islands Dispute between the United States and Argentina', *Hispanic American Historical Review*, ix (1929), 471–87.

[**1261**] Wright, A. R., 'Argentina and the Papacy, 1810–1927', *Hispanic American Historical Review*, xviii (1938), 15–42.

THE AGE OF ROSAS, 1829–52

Burgin, *The Economic Aspects of Argentine Federalism, 1820–1852* [797], is fundamental. [**1262**] J. F. Cady, *Foreign Intervention in the Río de la Plata, 1838–50* (Univ. of Pennsylvania Press, 1929), is an important study in the diplomacies of Britain, France, and the United States. Rosas and his policies are dealt with briefly by [**1262a**] L. W. Bealer, 'Juan Manuel de Rosas...', and [**1262b**] A. R. Wright, 'Juan Manuel de Rosas and the Church', in Wilgus [1006], and [**1263**] W. S. Robertson discusses 'Foreign Estimates of the Argentine Dictator, Juan Manuel de Rosas', *Hispanic American Historical Review*, x (1930), 125–37.

See also Nichols [626], Davis [796], Manning [1216], Bunkley [1278], and Jeffrey [1277], and, for the Falkland Islands dispute of the early thirties, nos. 698 and 1260.

[**1264**] D. F. Sarmiento, *Life in the Argentine Republic in the Days of the Tyrants: or civilization and barbarism* (translated by Mrs. Horace Mann, New York, 1868), first published in 1845, is one of the classics of Argentine literature as [**1265**] W. H. Hudson's *Far Away and Long Ago* (New York, Dutton, 1918), with its reminiscences of life on the pampa, is one of the classics of English literature. See also Parish [816], Darwin [1019], [**1266**] J. A. King, *Twenty-Four Years in the Argentine Republic...* (London, 1846), [**1267**] L. B. Mackinnon, *Steam Warfare in the Paraná* (2 vols., London, 1848), and [**1268**] William MacCann, *A Two Thousand Miles' Ride through the Argentine Provinces...* (2 vols., London, 1853).

THE CONFEDERATION AND THE CONSTITUTION, 1852–61

For the Constitution of 1853 see Rowe, *The Federal System of the Argentine Republic* [1243], and, for the general political and economic history of the period, [**1269**] A. J. Walford, 'Economic Aspects of the Argentine War of Secession (1852–1861)', *Inter-American Economic Affairs*, i, No. 2 (1947), 70–96, by the same author [**1270**] 'General Urquiza and the Battle of Pavón (1861)', *Hispanic American Historical Review*, xix (1939), 464–93, [**1271**] W. H. Jeffrey, *Mitre and Urquiza. A chapter in the unification of the Argentine Republic* (Drew Univ. Studies, No. 4, Madison, N.J., 1952), and [**1272**] J. R. Scobie, 'The Aftermath of Pavón', *Hispanic American Historical Review*, xxxv (1955), 153–74. See also Bunkley [1278], Jeffrey [1277], and for contemporary accounts [**1273**] William Hadfield, *Brazil, the River Plate, and the Falkland Islands* (London, 1854), and [**1274**] T. J. Page, *La Plata, the Argentine Confederation, and Paraguay* (New York, 1859).

[**1275**] Bunkley, A. W., 'Sarmiento and Urquiza', *Hispanic American Historical Review*, xxx (1950), 176–94.

[**1276**] Scobie, J. R., 'Monetary Developments in Argentina, 1852–1865', *Inter-American Economic Affairs*, viii, No. 2 (1954), 54–83.

THE RISE OF MODERN ARGENTINA, 1861–1930

[**1277**] W. H. Jeffrey, *Mitre and Argentina* (New York, Library Publishers, 1952), useful but pedestrian, and [**1278**] A. W. Bunkley, *The Life of Sarmiento* (Princeton Univ. Press, 1952), nearly but not quite a first-rate biography, cover the decades of the 'sixties and 'seventies. See also [**1279**] A. W. Bunkley, ed., *A Sarmiento Anthology* (Princeton Univ. Press, 1948), and [**1280**] Watt Stewart and W. M. French, 'The Influence of Horace Mann on the Educational Ideas of Domingo Faustino Sarmiento', *Hispanic American Historical Review*, xx (1940), 12–31. For the catastrophe of the Paraguayan War see Box [1569], for the Río Negro campaign of General Roca [**1281**] A. Hasbrouck, 'The Conquest of the Desert', *Hispanic American Historical Review*, xv (1935), 195–228, and for politics after 1880 [**1282**] T. F. McGann, 'The Generation of "Eighty"', *Americas*, x (Oct. 1953), 141–57, and [**1282a**] the same author's *Argentina, the United States, and the Inter-American System, 1880–1914* (Harvard Univ. Press, 1957). [**1283**] R. A. Gómez, 'Intervention in Argentina, 1860–1930', *Inter-American Economic Affairs*, i, No. 3 (1947), 55–73, examines the frequency with which the federal government intervened in the affairs of the provinces.

Jefferson's classic study [1251] and Hanson's analysis of the changing nature of the Argentine economy [1244] are fundamental for an understanding of the transformation of the Argentine pampa. See also [**1284**] H. S. Ferns, 'The Establishment of the British Investment in Argentina', *Inter-American Economic Affairs*, v, No. 2 (1951), 67–89, principally concerned with the decades of the 'sixties and 'seventies, [**1285**] A. F. Zimmerman, 'The Land Policy of Argentina, with particular reference to the conquest of the Southern Pampas', *Hispanic American Historical Review*, xxv (1945), 3–26, not much more than a summary sketch, and, of incidental interest, [**1286**] V. L. Johnson, 'Edward A. Hopkins and the Development of Argentine Transportation and Communication', *ibid.*, xxvi (1946), 19–37.

Peters [1249] discusses early financial history but concentrates on the years after 1880. See also [**1287**] J. H. Williams, *Argentine International Trade under Inconvertible Paper Money, 1880–1900* (Harvard Univ. Press, 1920), and [**1288**] A. G. Ford, 'Argentina and the Baring Crisis of 1890', *Oxford Economic Papers*, n.s., viii (1956), 127–50. For the impact of the first World War consult [**1289**] L. B. Smith, H. T. Collings, and E. Murphey, *The Economic Position of Argentina during the War* (Washington, Govt. Printing Office, 1920), and, for the post-war years, Phelps [1250]. Much statistical material is available in [**1290**] *The Economic Development of the Argentine Republic in the last Fifty Years* (Buenos Aires, E. Tornquíst and Co., 1919).

[**1291**] P. D. Dickens, 'Argentine Arbitrations and Mediations with reference to United States participation therein', *Hispanic American Historical Review*, xi (1931), 464–84, takes note of the Middle Chaco arbitration, 1867, the Andean boundary, 1899, the Misiones arbitration, 1892–5, and the A.B.C. mediation of 1914–15, See also no. 700. [**1292**] T. F. McGann, 'Argentina at the First Pan American Conference', *Inter-American Economic Affairs*, i, No. 2 (1947), 21–53, concludes that the 'Pan American Union was born with a South as well as a North Pole'. Compare no. 1282a. For the first World War see Martin [1181].

The literature of travel and description is extensive. Nineteenth-century accounts include [**1293**] T. J. Hutchinson, *Buenos Ayres and Argentine Gleanings* . . . (London, 1865), [**1294**] Wilfrid Latham, *The States of the River Plate: their industries and commerce* (London, 1866), [**1295**] R. A. Seymour, *Pioneering in the Pampas, or the first four years of a settler's experience in the La Plata camps* (London, 1870), [**1296**] Sir Horace Rumbold, *The Great Silver*

River. Notes of a residence in Buenos Ayres in 1880 and 1881 (London, 1887), and [**1297**] T. A. Turner, *Argentina and the Argentines. Notes and impressions of a five years' sojourn in the Argentine republic, 1885–90* (London, 1892). Among later publications see [**1298**] Sir Thomas H. Holdich, *The Countries of the King's Award* (London, Hurst and Blackett, 1904), [**1299**] W. A. Hirst, *Argentina* (London, Fisher Unwin, 1910), [**1300**] Walter Larden, *Argentine Plains and Andine Glaciers* (London, Fisher Unwin, 1911), and, more particularly to be noted, [**1301**] Pierre Denis, *The Argentine Republic: its development and progress* (London, Fisher Unwin, 1922).

NEW COMPLEXITIES, 1930–

On the general history of the period between the revolution of 1930 and the coup d'état of 1943 see Rennie [1239], on changes in economic structure [**1302**] Félix J. Weil, *Argentine Riddle* (New York, John Day, 1944), and on foreign trade Phelps [1250] and [**1303**] Virgil Salera, *Exchange Control and the Argentine Market* (Columbia Univ. Press, 1941). Taylor's analysis of rural life [1252] is excellent. [**1304**] Alfred Hasbrouck, 'The Argentine Revolution of 1930', *Hispanic American Historical Review*, xviii (1938), 285–321, is a descriptive account.

[**1305**] Ray Josephs, *Argentine Diary* (New York, Random House, 1944), records the impressions of a journalist eye-witness of the events of 1943. See also Whitaker [1037], [**1305a**] Ruth and Leonard Greenup, *Revolution before Breakfast: Argentina, 1941–1946* (Univ. of North Carolina Press, 1947), and for the Perón régime [**1306**] R. J. Alexander, *The Perón Era* (Columbia Univ. Press, 1951: London, Gollancz, 1952), which pays particular attention to organized labour, [**1307**] G. I. Blanksten's detailed analysis, *Perón's Argentina* (Univ. of Chicago Press, 1953), Whitaker [1258], and Pendle [1240]. [**1308**] A. P. Whitaker, *Argentine Upheaval: Perón's fall and the new régime* (New York, Praeger: London, Atlantic Press, 1956), supplements no. 1258. [**1309**] F. L. Hoffmann, 'Perón and After: a review article', *Hispanic American Historical Review*, xxxvi (1956), 510–28, contains useful bibliographical information.

[**1310**] Bruce, James, *Those Perplexing Argentines* (New York, Longmans, Green, 1953: London, Eyre and Spottiswoode, 1954).
By an ex-United States ambassador.

[**1311**] United States, Department of State, *Consultation among the*

American Republics with respect to the Argentine Situation. Memorandum of the United States Government (Washington, Govt. Printing Office, 1946). The United States 'Blue Book' published in February 1946.

PATAGONIA AND TIERRA DEL FUEGO

[**1312**] Musters, G. C., *At Home with the Patagonians. A year's wanderings over untrodden ground from the Straits of Magellan to the Río Negro* (London, 1871).

[**1313**] Beerbohm, J., *Wanderings in Patagonia: or, life among the ostrich-hunters* (London, 1879).

[**1314**] Hudson, W. H., *Idle Days in Patagonia* (London, 1893).

[**1315**] Prichard, H. Hesketh, *Through the Heart of Patagonia* (London, Heinemann, 1902).

[**1316**] Skottsberg, C., *The Wilds of Patagonia. A narrative of the Swedish expedition to Patagonia, Tierra del Fuego and the Falkland Islands in 1907–1909* (London, Edward Arnold, 1911).

[**1317**] Willis, Bailey, *Northern Patagonia* (New York, Scribner's, 1914).

[**1318**] Simpson, G. G., *Attending Marvels; a Patagonian journal* (New York, Macmillan, 1934).

[**1319**] Tschiffely, A. F., *This Way Southward. The account of a journey through Patagonia and Tierra del Fuego* (London, Heinemann, 1940).

[**1320**] Bridges, E. L. E., *Uttermost Part of the Earth* (London, Hodder and Stoughton, 1948).

2. BOLIVIA

GENERAL

For bibliographies and guides see nos. 38, 42, 68, and 84.

[**1321**] Harold Osborne, *Bolivia: a land divided* (2nd ed., London, Royal Institute of International Affairs, 1955), is a succinct general survey, and [**1322**] Olen E. Leonard, *Bolivia: land, people and institutions* (Washington, Scarecrow Press, 1952), a detailed sociological investigation.

There is no general history of the country in English. But [**1323**] N. A. N. Cleven, *The Political Organization of Bolivia* (Washington, Carnegie Institution, 1940), is a study in constitutional and administrative history.

The illustrations in [**1324**] Herbert Kirchoff, *Bolivia: its people and scenery* (2nd ed., Buenos Aires, Guillermo Kraft, 1944), are excellent.

SPECIAL ASPECTS

On social and economic problems in general see [**1325**] *Labour Problems in Bolivia. Report of the Joint Bolivian-United States Labour Commission* (Montreal, International Labour Office, 1943), and [**1326**] *Report of the United Nations Mission of Technical Assistance to Bolivia* (London, H.M.S.O., for United Nations, 1951); on economic geography, [**1327**] Alan G. Ogilvie, *Geography of the Central Andes* (New York, American Geographical Society, 1922), and on demographic and racial aspects Leonard [1322]. See also nos. 148, 1139, 1140, 1156, and 1158.

[**1328**] Adams, A. A., *The Plateau Peoples of South America* (London, Routledge: New York, Dutton, 1915).

[**1329**] La Barre, Weston, *The Aymara Indians of the Lake Titicaca Plateau, Bolivia* (Menasha, Wis., American Anthropological Association, 1948).

[**1330**] McBride, G. M., *The Agrarian Indian Communities of Highland Bolivia* (New York, American Geographical Society, 1921).

[**1331**] Métraux, A., *The Native Tribes of Eastern Bolivia and Western Matto Grosso* (Washington, Govt. Printing Office, 1942).

THE NINETEENTH CENTURY

See Cleven [1323]. [**1332**] L. C. Kendall, 'Andrés Santa Cruz and the Peru-Bolivian Confederation', *Hispanic American Historical Review*, xvi (1936), 29–48, discusses the attempt, which collapsed with the fall of Santa Cruz, to unite Peru and Bolivia in a single state. For Santa Cruz see also Cleven [867]. There is a brief note [**1333**] by E. M. Crampton and L. F. Ullrick on the 'Administration of José Ballivián in Bolivia', *Hispanic American Historical Review*, i (1918), 403–14. Manning [1216] provides a running commentary on Bolivian affairs from 1848 to 1860, and Cleven [867] deals with the dictatorship of Mariano Melgarejo (1864–70). For Bolivia's alliance with Chile and Peru in the war with Spain of 1864–6 see Davis [1478], and for her participation in the War of the Pacific (1879–83), resulting in the loss of her Pacific littoral, nos. 1479–83.

[**1334**] Bonelli, L. Hugh de, *Travels in Bolivia . . .* (2 vols., London, 1854).

[**1335**] Conway, Sir William Martin, *The Bolivian Andes. A record of climbing and exploration in the Cordillera Real in the years 1898 and 1900* (New York and London, Harper, 1901).

Bolivia

THE TWENTIETH CENTURY

[**1336**] F. W. Ganzert, 'The Boundary Controversy in the Upper Amazon between Brazil, Bolivia and Peru, 1903–9', *Hispanic American Historical Review*, xiv (1934), 427–49, discusses the Acre question. [**1337**] M. A. Marsh, *The Bankers in Bolivia. A study in American foreign investments* (New York, Vanguard Press, 1928), is a contribution to the economic history of the nineteen-twenties. See also [**1338**] C. A. McQueen, *Bolivian Public Finance* (Washington, Bureau of Foreign and Domestic Commerce, 1925). For the controversy with Paraguay culminating in the Chaco War of the nineteen-thirties see [**1339**] Margaret La Foy, *The Chaco Dispute and the League of Nations* (Ann Arbor, Edwards, 1946), and nos. 347, 1192, 1582, and 1583, and for later history Whitaker [1201] and Osborne [1321].

The travel literature of the twentieth century includes [**1340**] Colonel P. H. Fawcett's account of his explorations between 1906 and 1914, *Exploration Fawcett*, edited by Brian Fawcett (London, Hutchinson, 1953), [**1341**] the entertaining *Adventures in Bolivia* (1903–7) of C. H. Prodgers (London, Lane, 1922), and [**1342**] Julian Duguid, *Green Hell: adventures in the mysterious jungles of eastern Bolivia* (London, Cape, 1931).

[**1343**] Walle, Paul, *Bolivia: its people and its resources . . .* (London, Fisher Unwin, 1914).

[**1344**] Schurz, W. L., *Bolivia: a commercial and industrial handbook* (Washington, Govt. Printing Office, 1921).

3. BRAZIL

GENERAL

For bibliographies and guides see nos. 38, 42, 46, 65, and 85, [**1345**] P. Lee Phillips, *A List of Books, Magazine Articles, and Maps relating to Brazil, 1800–1900* (Washington, Govt. Printing Office, 1901), and the very full *Manual Bibliográfico de Estudos Brasileiros* [990].

Calógeras, *A History of Brazil* [707], originally published in Portuguese in 1930, contains an additional chapter by the translator, P. A. Martin, which carries the story to 1938. There is a good short account [**1345a**] by P. A. Martin in Wilgus, *Argentina, Brazil and Chile since Independence* [1001], and there are useful summaries of nineteenth- and twentieth-century history in [**1346**] L. F. Hill, ed., *Brazil* (Univ. of California Press, 1947), and

[**1347**] H. V. Livermore, ed., *Portugal and Brazil. An introduction* (Oxford, Clarendon Press, 1953). See also Nash [1422] and, for economic history, Normano [711].

[**1348**] Fernando de Azevedo, *Brazilian Culture. An introduction to the study of culture in Brazil* (translated by W. R. Crawford, New York, Macmillan, 1950), is a massive and detailed investigation, indispensable to the serious student. [**1349**] Gilberto Freyre, *Brazil, an interpretation* (New York, Knopf, 1945), is a short but stimulating set of lectures on history, sociology, foreign policy, and literature. [**1350**] T. Lynn Smith and Alexander Marchant, eds., *Brazil. Portrait of half a continent* (New York, Dryden Press, 1951), consists of a widely-ranging series of essays appealing to the general reader and to the specialist alike.

[**1351**] Camacho, J. A., *Brazil. An interim assessment* (2nd ed., London, Royal Institute of International Affairs, 1954).

A comprehensive review in short compass.

[**1352**] Hunnicutt, B. M., *Brazil, world frontier* (New York, Van Nostrand, 1949: London, Macmillan, 1950).

An encyclopaedic survey, essentially a revision of a book published in 1945 under the title *Brazil Looks Forward*.

Special Aspects

politics, government, and law

The imperial constitution of 1824 and the federal constitution of 1891 are contained in James, *The Constitutional System of Brazil* [982]. For later political and constitutional history see Lowenstein [1439], Hill [1346], and Smith [1350].

[**1353**] Hambloch, E., *His Majesty the President. A study of constitutional Brazil* (London, Methuen, 1935).

A critique of the presidential system by an ex-British consul.

[**1353a**] Lipson, Leslie, 'Government in Contemporary Brazil', *Canadian Journal of Economics and Political Science*, xxii (1956), 183–98.

A valuable article which discusses the working of the Constitution of 1946 and relates politics to economics and both to social structure.

[**1354**] Manchester, A. K., 'Constitutional Dictatorship in Brazil', in Wilgus [1006].

[**1355**] Martin, P. A., 'Federalism in Brazil', *Hispanic American Historical Review*, xviii (1938), 143–63.

economic development and economic conditions

[**1356**] H. W. Spiegel, *The Brazilian Economy, chronic inflation*

Brazil

and sporadic industrialization (Philadelphia, Blakiston, 1949), [**1357**] G. Wythe, R. A. Wight, and H. M. Midkiff, *Brazil. An expanding economy* (New York, Twentieth Century Fund, 1949), and [**1358**] the report of the official Abbink mission, *Report of the Joint Brazil-United States Technical Commission* (Washington, Dept. of State, 1949), are comprehensive studies which, between them, embrace every aspect of the Brazilian economy. See also the important papers by George Wythe, Preston E. James, T. Lynn Smith, B. J. Siegel, H. W. Spiegel, and S. J. Stein in [**1359**] Simon Kuznets, W. E. Moore, and J. J. Spengler, eds., *Economic Growth: Brazil, India, Japan* (Duke Univ. Press, 1955).

Normano, *Brazil. A study of economic types* [711] is 'a study of the *typical* in the Brazilian economic history' and is both brilliant and suggestive. Manchester [983] discusses British economic pre-eminence in Brazilian shipping, markets, and investments throughout the nineteenth century, but with particular reference to the first half of the century. See also [**1360**] J. F. Rippy, 'A Century and a Quarter of British Investment in Brazil', *Inter-American Economic Affairs*, vi, No. 1 (1952), 83–92. On railways see [**1361**] J. S. Duncan, *Public and Private Operation of Railways in Brazil* (Columbia Univ. Press, 1932), which surveys developments since 1835, and on the textile industry [**1362**] S. J. Stein, *The Brazilian Cotton Manufacture. Textile enterprise in an underdeveloped area, 1850–1950* (Harvard Univ. Press, 1957), and no. 1359. Three articles by R. M. Morse deal with the rise of São Paulo: [**1363**] 'São Paulo in the Nineteenth Century: Economic Roots of the Metropolis', *Inter-American Economic Affairs*, v, No. 3 (1951), 3–39; [**1364**] 'São Paulo in the Twentieth Century: Social and Economic Aspects', *ibid.*, viii, No. 1 (1954), 3–60; and [**1365**] 'São Paulo since Independence: a cultural interpretation', *Hispanic American Historical Review*, xxxiv (1954), 419–44.

[**1366**] Leão, Josias, *Mines and Minerals in Brazil* (Rio de Janeiro, Centro de Estudos Económicos, 1939).
Supplementary to Bain and Read [1089].

[**1366a**] Schurz, W. L., *Rubber Production in the Amazon Valley* (Washington, Govt. Printing Office, 1925).

[**1367**] Simonsen, R. C., *Brazil's Industrial Evolution* (São Paulo, Escola Livre de Sociologia e Política, 1939).
A brief summary.

[**1368**] Spiegel, H. W., 'A Century of Prices in Brazil', *Review of Economics and Statistics*, xxx (1948), 57–62.

The Republics of South America since 1830

[1368a] Stein, S. J., *Vassouras. A Brazilian Coffee County, 1850–1900* (Harvard Univ. Press, 1957).

POPULATION, IMMIGRATION, SETTLEMENT,
SOCIAL INSTITUTIONS

See nos. 1348, 1350, and 1352. **[1369]** T. Lynn Smith, *Brazil: people and institutions* (2nd ed., rev., Baton Rouge, Louisiana State Univ. Press, 1954), is a work of sociological analysis, which provides, *inter alia*, a detailed examination of the growth and distribution of the population and of the problems of immigration, land settlement, and land tenure. Compare **[1370]** the same author's 'Demographic Factors related to Economic Growth in Brazil', in Kuznets [1359], the brief but interesting report **[1371]** of Fernand Maurette, *Some Social Aspects of Present and Future Economic Development in Brazil* (Geneva, International Labour Office, 1937), and **[1372]** F. B. de Avila, *Economic Aspects of Immigration: the Brazilian immigration problem* (The Hague, Martinus Nijhoff, 1954).

On German immigration consult **[1373]** the bibliographies by R. Maack and A. Marchant in *Handbook of Latin American Studies*, iv (1938), 399–431 [8], and, on Japanese, Normano and Gerbi [1147] and **[1374]** Henri Hauser, 'Japanese Immigration in Brazil', *New Mexico Quarterly Review*, xii (1942), 5–17. **[1375]** P. H. Price discusses 'Demographic Aspects of the Polish Migration to Brazil', *Inter-American Economic Affairs*, v, No. 4 (1952), 46–58.

Freyre's classic study [708], **[1376]** Arthur Ramos, *The Negro in Brazil* (Washington, Associated Publishers, 1939), and **[1377]** Donald Pierson, *Negroes in Brazil. A study of race contact at Bahia* (Univ. of Chicago Press, 1942), are indispensable. See also Zelinsky [389] and nos. 1142–3.

[1378] Harris, Marvin, *Town and Country in Brazil* (Columbia Univ. Press, 1956).
An analysis of a small rural community in Bahia.

[1379] Pierson, Donald, *Cruz das Almas, a Brazilian village* (Washington, Govt. Printing Office, 1951).
A community near São Paulo.

[1380] Wagley, Charles, *Amazon Town. A study of man in the tropics* (New York, Macmillan, 1953).
A community on the lower Amazon.

[1381] Wagley, Charles, ed., *Race and Class in Rural Brazil* (Paris, Unesco, 1952).
Case studies of four rural communities.

Brazil

LITERATURE AND THE ARTS

See nos. 1347–9 and Putnam, *Marvelous Journey* [714].

[**1382**] Driver, D. M., *The Indian in Brazilian Literature* (New York, Hispanic Institute in the United States, 1942).

[**1383**] Goldberg, Isaac, *Brazilian Literature* (New York, Knopf, 1922).

[**1384**] Goodwin, P. L., *Brazil Builds. Architecture, new and old, 1652–1942* (New York, Museum of Modern Art, 1943).

[**1385**] Hanke, Lewis, 'Gilberto Freyre: Brazilian Social Historian', *Quarterly Journal of Inter-American Relations*, i (1939), 24–44.

[**1386**] Mindlen, H. E., *Modern Architecture in Brazil* (London, Architectural Press, 1956).

[**1387**] Sayers, R. S., *The Negro in Brazilian Literature* (New York, Hispanic Institute in the United States, 1956).

[**1388**] Veríssimo, Erico, *Brazilian Literature: an outline* (New York, Macmillan, 1945).

INTERNATIONAL RELATIONS

See Hill [1346] and Freyre [1349]. Manchester [983] discusses relations with Great Britain, and Hill [985] relations with the United States.

[**1389**] Macedo Soares, J. C. de, *Brazil and the League of Nations* (Paris, Pedone, 1928).

THE EMPIRE OF DOM PEDRO II, 1831–89

[**1390**] M. W. Williams, *Dom Pedro the Magnanimous, Second Emperor of Brazil* (Univ. of North Carolina Press, 1937), is the best biography of the scholar-emperor in any language and outlines also the general history of the empire. Compare, on constitutional history, Manchester [1354].

[**1391**] T. W. Palmer, Jr., 'A Momentous Decade in Brazilian Administrative History, 1831–1840', *Hispanic American Historical Review*, xxx (1950), 209–17, examines the movement towards local autonomy, and the reaction against it, during the years of Dom Pedro's minority and youth, and [**1392**] Manoel Cardozo, 'The Holy See and the Question of the Bishop-Elect of Rio, 1833–1839', *Americas*, x (July 1953), 3–74, discusses an early dispute between the Imperial Government and Rome. [**1393**] William J. Coleman, *The First Apostolic Delegation in Rio de Janeiro and its Influence in Spanish America . . .* (Washington, Catholic Univ. of America, 1950), is 'a study in Papal Policy, 1830–1840', and of the relations of the Nunciature at Rio de Janeiro with neighbouring Spanish American states.

[**1394**] Gilberto Freyre, 'Social Life in Brazil in the Middle of the Nineteenth Century', *Hispanic American Historical Review*, v (1922), 597–630, an admirable discussion, takes the view that the majority of Brazilians were living in the middle ages and an élite only in the eighteenth century. See also his *The Masters and the Slaves* [708], and, on slavery, [**1395**] H. B. Alexander, 'Brazilian and United States Slavery Compared', *Journal of Negro History*, vii (1922), 349–64, [**1396**] M. W. Williams, 'The Treatment of Negro Slaves in the Brazilian Empire: a comparison with the United States of America', *ibid.*, xv (1930), 315–36, [**1397**] M. V. Nelson, 'The Negro in Brazil as seen through the Chronicles of Travellers, 1800–1868', *ibid.*, xxx (1945), 203–18, and Stein [1368a].

[**1398**] J. E. Adams, 'The Abolition of the Brazilian Slave Trade', *Journal of Negro History*, x (1925), 607–37, and [**1399**] L. F. Hill, 'The Abolition of the African Slave Trade to Brazil', *Hispanic American Historical Review*, xi (1931), 169–97, both valuable, cover the years 1808 to 1861. See also Manchester [983]. For the later history of slavery and the rise and final success of the abolition movement see [**1400**] P. A. Martin, 'Slavery and Abolition in Brazil', *Hispanic American Historical Review*, xiii (1933), 151–96, and [**1401**] Carolina Nabuco, *The Life of Joaquim Nabuco* (Stanford Univ. Press, 1950).

[**1402**] Anyda Marchant, 'A New Portrait of Mauá, the Banker: a Man of Business in Nineteenth-Century Brazil', *Hispanic American Historical Review*, xxx (1950), 411–31, illustrates the rise in the 'fifties and 'sixties of forces which contributed ultimately to the undermining of the foundations upon which the empire rested. See also Normano [711]. S. J. Stein's masterly analysis of plantation society and economy in Vassouras [1368a] embodies his earlier studies: [**1403**] 'Middle Paraíba Plantations, 1850–1860; aspects of growth and decline', in *Four Papers Presented in the Institute of Brazilian Studies of Vanderbilt University*, edited by Charles Wagley (Nashville, Vanderbilt Univ. Press, 1951), and [**1404**] 'The Passing of the Coffee Plantation in the Paraíba Valley', *Hispanic American Historical Review*, xxxiii (1953), 331–64. [**1405**] M. C. Thornton, *The Church and Freemasonry in Brazil, 1872–1875* (Washington, Catholic Univ. of America, 1948), discusses the conflict of Church and State which preceded the fall of the empire. [**1406**] T. W. Palmer, 'São Paulo and the Republican Move-

Brazil

ment in Brazil', *Americas*, viii (July 1951), 41–51, is a brief sketch. [**1407**] P. A. Martin, 'Causes of the Collapse of the Brazilian Empire', *Hispanic American Historical Review*, iv (1921), 4–48, is an able argument which neglects, however, the course of economic change. For the foreign policy of the empire see Cady [1262], Manchester [983], Box [1569], Hill [985], and Manning [1216]. [**1408**] P. A. Martin discusses 'The Influence of the United States on the Opening of the Amazon to the World's Commerce', *Hispanic American Historical Review*, i (1918), 146–62, and [**1409**] W. J. Bell 'The Relation of Herndon and Gibbon's Exploration of the Amazon to North American Slavery, 1850–1855', *ibid.*, xix (1939), 494–503. [**1410**] L. F. Hill, 'Confederate Exiles to Brazil', *ibid.*, vii (1927), 192–210, is an interesting footnote to nineteenth-century Brazilian and United States history, revised in no. 985.

For contemporary accounts see, in particular, [**1411**] George Gardner, *Travels in the Interior of Brazil, principally through the northern provinces, and the gold and diamond districts, during the years 1836–1841* (London, 1846); [**1412**] D. P. Kidder, *Sketches of Residence and Travels in Brazil* (2 vols., Philadelphia, 1845), the work of a methodist missionary who first went to Brazil in 1837, elaborated in [**1413**] D. P. Kidder and J. C. Fletcher, *Brazil and the Brazilians* (Philadelphia, 1857, and many later editions); [**1414**] Adalbert, Prince of Prussia, *Travels in the South of Europe and in Brazil* ... (2 vols., London, 1849); [**1415**] Thomas Ewbank, *Life in Brazil; or, a journal of a visit to the land of the cocoa and the palm* (New York, 1856)—the visit took place in 1846; Hadfield [1273]; [**1416**] W. D. Christie, *Notes on Brazilian Questions* (London, 1865); [**1417**] L. and E. C. Agassiz, *A Journey in Brazil* (Boston, 1868); [**1418**] R. F. Burton, *Explorations of the Highlands of the Brazil* ... (2 vols., London, 1869); [**1419**] M. G. Mulhall, *Rio Grande do Sul and its German Colonies* (London, 1873); [**1420**] T. P. Bigg-Wither, *Pioneering in South Brazil. Three years of forest and prairie life in the province of Paraná* (2 vols., London, 1878); [**1421**] H. C. Dent, *A Year in Brazil, with notes on the abolition of slavery, the finances of the empire, religion, meteorology, natural history, etc.* (London, 1886), and [**1421a**] N. B. Craig, *Recollections of an Ill-fated Expedition to the Headwaters of the Madeira River in Brazil* (Philadelphia, Lippincott, 1907). The expedition is the Madeira-Mamoré railway expedition of 1878–9.

THE 'LIBERAL REPUBLIC', 1889–1930

[**1422**] Roy Nash, *The Conquest of Brazil* (New York, Harcourt Brace, 1926: London, Cape, 1927), a work of interpretation but attentive also to general history, is especially valuable. For constitutional history see James [982] and, for economic, Normano [711], Simonsen [1367], and Stein [1362, 1368a].

[**1423**] M. B. McCloskey, 'The United States and the Brazilian Naval Revolt, 1893–1894', *Americas*, ii (Jan. 1946), 296–321, discusses a movement which might well 'have ended the existence of the republic', but for the action of Admiral A. E. K. Benham of the United States navy. See also Hill [985] and [**1424**] Sir William Laird Clowes, *Four Modern Naval Campaigns, historical, strategical, and tactical* (London, Hutchinson, 1906). For the settlement in 1895 of the boundary dispute with Argentina see Williams [700], and for the Canudos rebellion of 1896–7 [**1425**] R. B. Cunninghame Graham, *A Brazilian Mystic: the life and miracles of Antonio Conselheiro* (London, Heinemann, 1920), and [**1426**] Euclides da Cunha's classic *Rebellion in the Backlands* (translated by Samuel Putnam, Univ. of Chicago Press, 1944).

[**1427**] John Melby, 'Rubber River: an account of the rise and collapse of the Amazon Boom', *Hispanic American Historical Review*, xxii (1942), 452–69, is principally concerned with the years between 1890 and 1910. Ganzert [1336] deals briefly with the Acre dispute with Bolivia, and [**1428**] F. W. Kravigny, *The Jungle Route* (New York, Orlin Tremaine, 1940), is an account by an American engineer engaged in the construction of the Madeira-Mamoré railway, completed in 1912.

For relations with the United States see, supplementary to Hill [985], Nabuco [1401], [**1429**] F. W. Ganzert, 'The Baron do Rio Branco, Joaquim Nabuco, and the Growth of Brazilian-American Friendship, 1900–1910', *Hispanic American Historical Review*, xxii (1942), 432–51, and [**1430**] L. F. Sensabaugh, 'The Coffee-Trust Question in United States-Brazilian Relations, 1912–1913', *ibid.*, xxvi (1946), 480–96. [**1431**] Loretta Baum outlines 'German Political Designs with reference to Brazil' before the first World War, *ibid.*, ii (1919), 586–99, and the war itself is discussed in Martin [1181].

On the post-war years see Nash [1422], [**1432**] H. G. James's general survey, *Brazil after a Century of Independence* (New York, Macmillan, 1925), Hambloch [1353], and, for Brazilian relations with the League of Nations, Macedo Soares [1389].

Brazil

The general descriptive literature since 1900 includes, besides Nash [1422] and James [1432], [**1433**] a valuable monograph by Pierre Denis, *Brazil* (London, Fisher Unwin, 1911), the two useful handbooks of E. C. Buley: [**1434**] *North Brazil* . . . (London, Pitman, 1914), and [**1435**] *South Brazil* . . . (London, Pitman, 1914); and [**1436**] L. E. Elliott's journalistic *Brazil Today and Tomorrow* (New York, Macmillan, 1917). [**1437**] Theodore Roosevelt, *Through the Brazilian Wilderness* (London, Murray, 1914), is an account of his expedition with Colonel Rondon through Matto Grosso and Amazonas. [**1438**] Konrad Guenther, *A Naturalist in Brazil: the flora and fauna and the people of Brazil* (London, Allen and Unwin, 1931), relates, more specifically, to Pernambuco. [**1438a**] Henriqueta Chamberlain, *Where the Sabiá Sings. A partial autobiography* (New York, Macmillan, 1947), records the experiences of an American girl living in Brazil and brought up as a Brazilian.

The Vargas Régime and After, 1930–

[**1439**] K. Loewenstein, *Brazil under Vargas* (New York, Macmillan, 1942), is a detailed study in political, legal, and administrative history. [**1440**] Bailey W. Diffie, 'Some Foreign Influences in Contemporary Brazilian Politics', *Hispanic American Historical Review*, xx (1940), 402–29, discusses Japanese, Italian, and German nationalist groups and the rise, in the nineteen-thirties, of the *integralista* movement, and [**1441**] R. J. Alexander, 'Brazilian "Tenentismo" ', *ibid.*, xxxvi (1956), 229–42, the persistence of 'ideas which have given rise to the Aprista parties in other Latin American countries'. See also Lipson [1353a].

[**1442**] Cooke, M. L., *Brazil on the March* (New York and London, McGraw-Hill, 1944).
'Reflections on the report of the American technical mission to Brazil', optimistic in tone.

[**1443**] Sá, H. Tavares de, *The Brazilians: people of tomorrow* (New York, Day, 1947).

The Amazon

The Amazon has a literature of its own. The most notable among nineteenth-century works are [**1444**] H. L. Maw, *Journal of a Passage from the Pacific to the Atlantic* . . . (London, 1829); [**1445**] W. H. Edwards, *A Voyage up the River Amazon, including a residence at Pará* (New York, 1847); Herndon and Gibbon [1024];

[**1446**] A. R. Wallace, *A Narrative of Travels on the Amazon and Rio Negro* (London, 1853); [**1447**] H. W. Bates, *The Naturalist on the River Amazons* (2 vols., London, 1863); Spruce [1023]; Orton [1027]; [**1448**] Franz Keller, *The Amazon and Madeira Rivers. Sketches and descriptions from the note-book of an explorer* (London, 1874); and [**1449**] C. B. Brown and W. Lidstone, *Fifteen Thousand Miles on the Amazon and its tributaries* (London, 1878). See also [**1450**] H. M. Tomlinson, *The Sea and the Jungle* (London, Duckworth, 1912), and [**1451**] Thomas Whiffen, *The North-West Amazons: notes of some months spent among cannibal tribes* (New York, Duffield: London, Constable, 1915).

4. CHILE

GENERAL

For bibliographies and guides see nos. 38, 42, 65, 67, and 87, together with [**1452**] P. Lee Phillips, *A List of Books, Magazine Articles, and Maps relating to Chile* (Washington, Govt. Printing Office, 1903).

Galdames, *A History of Chile* [345], provides an excellent survey, and there is a good short account [**1453**] by I. J. Cox, in Wilgus, *Argentina, Brazil and Chile since Independence* [1001].

For introductions to Chile see [**1454**] Agustín Edwards, *My Native Land* (London, Benn, 1928), and [**1455**] Stephen Clissold, *Chilean Scrap-book* (London, Cresset Press, 1952), a charming and sensitive collection of regional essays.

SPECIAL ASPECTS

[**1456**] G. M. McBride's masterly analysis of the agrarian problem in Chile, *Chile: land and society* (New York, American Geographical Society, 1936), and [**1457**] Isaiah Bowman's fine study, *Desert Trails of Atacama* (New York, American Geographical Society, 1924), are indispensable. [**1458**] Mark Jefferson, *Recent Colonization in Chile* (New York, American Geographical Society, 1921), discusses immigration and settlement in south-central Chile, and [**1459**] G. J. Butland 'Changing Land Occupance in the South Chilean Provinces of Aysen and Magallanes', *Geographical Studies*, i (1954), 27–43. [**1460**] C. J. Lambert, *Sweet Waters: a Chilean farm* (London, Chatto and Windus, 1952), is a delightful and entertaining description of life on a great *hacienda* near Santiago in the early nineteen-twenties.

Chile

[**1461**] G. Subercaseaux, *Monetary and Banking Policy of Chile* (New York, Carnegie Endowment, 1922), is a general history of money and banking from early colonial times. See also Fetter [1498] and Ellsworth [1505]. On railways see Long [1100] and on foreign investments [**1462**] C. W. Centner, 'Great Britain and Chilean Mining, 1830–1914', *Economic History Review*, xii (1942), 76–82, which reaches the conclusion that British investments in mining were less heavy than might have been expected, and two notes by J. F. Rippy: [**1463**] 'A Century of British Investments in Chile', *Pacific Historical Review*, xxi (1952), 341–8, and [**1464**] 'British Investments in the Chilean Nitrate Industry', *Inter-American Economic Affairs*, viii, No. 2 (1954), 3–10. [**1465**] M. B. Donald, 'History of the Chile Nitrate Industry', *Annals of Science*, i (1936), 29–47, 193–216, and [**1466**] A. Bertrand, *The Chilean Nitrate Industry* (Paris, privately printed, 1920), are both useful.

There are two general studies of Chilean-United States relations: [**1467**] H. C. Evans, *Chile and its Relations with the United States* (Duke Univ. Press, 1927), and [**1468**] W. R. Sherman, *The Diplomatic and Commercial Relations of the United States and Chile, 1820–1914* (Boston, Mass., Badger, 1926). For the Antarctic question see Christie [1259].

[**1469**] [Hillman, Charles F.], 'Quien Sabe', *'Old Timers', British and Americans in Chile* (Santiago, Imp. Moderna, 1901?).

[**1469a**] Griffin, C. C., 'Francisco Encina and Revisionism in Chilean History', *Hispanic American Historical Review*, xxxvii (1957), 1–28.

A review of Encina's twenty-volume *Historia de Chile* which is itself a valuable contribution to Chilean historiography.

[**1470**] Roberts, S. E., *José Toribio Medina* (Washington, Inter-American Bibliographical and Library Association, 1941).

A biography of one of the most eminent of Chilean historians and bibliographers (1852–1930).

1830–1891

Edwards, *The Dawn* [828], covers the decade of the 'thirties. [**1471**] A. U. Hancock, *A History of Chile* (Chicago, C. H. Sergel and Co., 1893), ends with the civil war of 1891. For the Constitution of 1833 see Shaw [830], and on Portales, Montt, and Balmaceda [**1472**] the essays by L. W. Bealer in Wilgus, *South American Dictators* [1006].

[**1473**] T. E. Nichols, 'The Establishment of Political Relations between Chile and Great Britain', *Hispanic American Historical Review*, xxviii (1948), 137–43, is a brief sketch, covering the years 1823 to 1854. [**1474**] W. D. Rasmussen discusses 'The United States Astronomical Expedition to Chile, 1849–1852', *ibid.*, xxxiv (1954), 103–13, and [**1475**] J. J. Johnson describes 'Talcahuano and Concepción as seen by the Forty-Niners', passing round Cape Horn to the gold fields of California, *ibid.*, xxvi (1946), 251–62. Manning [1216] prints United States reports from Chile between 1832 and 1860.

[**1476**] J. J. Johnson, *Pioneer Telegraphy in Chile, 1852–1876* (Stanford Univ. Press, 1948), tells the story of the building of the first telegraph line from Santiago to Valparaíso and examines later developments. For the railways see Long [1100] and Stewart [1602]. [**1477**] J. F. Rippy and Jack Pfeiffer contribute 'Notes on the Dawn of Manufacturing in Chile', between 1825 and 1884, *Hispanic American Historical Review*, xxviii (1948), 292–303.

[**1478**] W. C. Davis, *The Last Conquistadores: the Spanish intervention in Peru and Chile, 1863–1866* (Univ. of Georgia Press, 1950), is a thorough study of the war between Spain on the one hand and Chile, Peru, and Bolivia on the other. On the later, and greater, War of the Pacific, see [**1479**] W. J. Dennis, *Tacna and Arica. An account of the Chile-Peruvian boundary dispute and of the arbitrations by the United States* (Yale Univ. Press, 1931), which discusses the origins of the war as well as the later history of the Tacna-Arica dispute; [**1480**] the same author's *Documentary History of the Tacna-Arica Dispute* (Iowa City, Univ. of Iowa, 1927), the documents ranging from 1787 to 1926; [**1481**] Herbert Millington, *American Diplomacy and the War of the Pacific* (Columbia Univ. Press, 1948), pedestrian and unsatisfying; [**1482**] V. G. Kiernan, 'Foreign Interests in the War of the Pacific', *Hispanic American Historical Review*, xxxv (1955), 14–36, which tells against the view of James G. Blaine that the war was an 'English war'; [**1483**] Sir Clements R. Markham, *The War between Peru and Chile, 1879–1882* (London, Sampson Low, Marston, 1882?), strongly Peruvian in sympathy; and Clowes [1424].

Fetter [1498] deals with the beginnings of monetary inflation in the eighteen-seventies and [**1484**] J. F. Rippy, 'Economic Enterprises of the "Nitrate King" and his Associates in Chile', *Pacific Historical Review*, xvii (1948), 457–65, with the nitrate boom in the eighteen-eighties. The 'king' is John Thomas North.

See more particularly, though the argument is inconclusive, [**1485**] Osgood Hardy, 'British Nitrates and the Balmaceda Revolution', *ibid.*, xvii (1948), 165–80, and, for relations with the United States at the time of the civil war of 1891, the same author's two articles: [**1486**] 'The Itata Incident', *Hispanic American Historical Review*, v (1922), 195–226, and [**1487**] 'Was Patrick Egan a "Blundering Minister"?', *ibid.*, viii (1928), 65–81. [**1488**] F. W. Fetter discusses 'The Chilean Debt Payment of 1891', *Economic History (Economic Journal* supplement), ii (1930–3), 609–16. On the civil war itself see Clowes [1424].

Among contemporary writings consult [**1489**] Thomas Sutcliffe, *Sixteen Years in Chile and Peru from 1822 to 1839. By the Retired Governor of Juan Fernandez* (London, 1841?); [**1490**] J. M. Gilliss, *Chile; its geography, climate, government, social conditions, mineral and agricultural resources, commerce, etc.* (Washington, 1855); [**1491**] E. R. Smith, *The Araucanians: or, notes of a tour among the Indian tribes of southern Chili* (New York, 1855); [**1492**] D. J. A. Hunter, *A Sketch of Chili expressly prepared for the Use of Immigrants from the United States and Europe* (New York, 1866); [**1493**] R. N. Boyd, *Sketches of Chili and the Chilians during the War 1879–1880* (London, 1881); [**1494**] W. H. Russell, *A Visit to Chile and the Nitrate Fields of Tarapacá* (London, 1890); and [**1495**] Maurice H. Hervey, *Dark Days in Chile. An account of the revolution of 1891* (London, 1891–2).

1891–1925

On political life after the revolution of 1891 consult [**1496**] P. S. Reinsch, 'Parliamentary Government in Chile', *American Political Science Review*, iii (1908–9), 507–38, Stokes, 'Parliamentary Government in Latin America' [1054], which has an especial reference to Chile, [**1497**] C. H. Haring, 'Chilean Politics, 1920–1928', *Hispanic American Historical Review*, xi (1931), 1–26, and Stevenson [1504].

[**1498**] F. W. Fetter, *Monetary Inflation in Chile* (Princeton Univ. Press, 1931), covers the years between 1878 and 1926. See also, on economic history, [**1499**] Jack B. Pfeiffer, 'Notes on the Heavy Equipment Industry in Chile, 1880–1910', *Hispanic American Historical Review*, xxxii (1952), 139–44, and [**1500**] L. S. Rowe, *Early Effects of the European War upon the Finance, Commerce and Industry of Chile* (New York, Oxford Univ. Press, 1918). Martin [1181] discusses Chile's general position during the first World

War, and Dennis [1479, 1480] deals with the Tacna-Arica question, finally settled in 1929.

Holdich [1298], [**1501**] G. F. Scott Elliot, *Chile: its history and development* . . . (London, Fisher Unwin, 1907), [**1502**] W. H. Koebel, *Modern Chile* (London, Bell, 1913), and Edwards [1454], are useful descriptive works.

1925–

For the Ibáñez dictatorship (1927–31) see [**1503**] C. H. Haring, 'The Chilean Revolution of 1931', *Hispanic American Historical Review*, xiii (1933), 197–203, and for general political and economic developments in the 'twenties and 'thirties [**1504**] J. R. Stevenson, *The Chilean Popular Front* (Univ. of Pennsylvania Press, 1942), and [**1505**] P. T. Ellsworth, *Chile. An economy in transition* (New York, Macmillan, 1945). [**1506**] Herman Finer provides an essay on *The Chilean Development Corporation* (Montreal, International Labour Office, 1947), 'a study in national planning to raise living standards'.

[**1507**] Hanson, E. P., *Chile, land of progress* (New York, Reynal and Hitchcock, 1941).

[**1508**] Fergusson, Erna, *Chile* (New York, Knopf, 1943).

[**1509**] Subercaseaux, B., *Chile: a geographic extravaganza* (New York, Macmillan, 1943).

[**1510**] Butland, G. J., *Chile: an outline of its geography, economics and politics* (3rd ed., London, Royal Institute of International Affairs, 1956). A concise exposition.

5. COLOMBIA
GENERAL

For bibliographies and guides see nos. 38, 42, 69, and 88.

Henao and Arrubla, *History of Colombia* [348], is the only history in English, though few readers are likely to have the fortitude to complete it. Gibson, *The Constitutions of Colombia* [851] is a useful compilation in which the constitutions are translated and their origin and development discussed. Parks [856] surveys relations with the United States between 1765 and 1934, and [**1511**] Kathleen Romoli, *Colombia: gateway to South America* (New York, Doubleday, Doran, 1941), provides a general popular introduction.

On economic life generally see the Currie Report, [**1512**] *The*

Colombia

Basis of a Development Program for Colombia: report of a mission headed by Lauchlin Currie . . . (Washington, International Bank for Reconstruction and Development, 1950), and, for area studies, [**1513**] R. E. Crist, *The Cauca Valley, Colombia: land tenure and land use* (Baltimore, Waverly Press, 1952), [**1514**] Orlando Fals-Borda, *Peasant Society in the Colombian Andes: a sociological study of Saucío* (Univ. of Florida Press, 1955), and [**1515**] J. J. Parsons, *Antioqueño Colonization in Western Colombia* (Ibero-Americana, 32, Univ. of California Press, 1949).

[**1516**] Alain Gheerbrant, *The Impossible Adventure. Journey to the far Amazon* (London, Gollancz, 1953), and [**1517**] W. R. Philipson, *The Immaculate Forest. An account of an expedition to unexplored territories between the Andes and the Amazon* (London, Hutchinson, 1952), are accounts of two expeditions, the one from Bogotá to the Sierra Parima, and the other to the Macarena mountains.

1830–1909

See McGann [846], [**1518**] R. L. Gilmore, 'Nueva Granada's Socialist Mirage', *Hispanic American Historical Review*, xxxvi (1956), 190–210, which describes the 'extraordinary effervescence that sets apart the decade of the 1850's', and on the presidencies of Mosquera, Núñez, and Reyes [**1519**] J. F. Rippy, 'The Dictators of Colombia', in Wilgus [1006]. See also [**1520**] Carey Shaw, Jr., 'Church and State in Colombia as observed by American Diplomats, 1834–1906', *Hispanic American Historical Review*, xxi (1941), 577–613.

On economic developments see Gilmore and Harrison [858], [**1521**] John P. Harrison, 'The Evolution of the Colombian Tobacco Trade to 1875', *Hispanic American Historical Review*, xxxii (1952), 163–74, [**1522**] Theodore E. Nichols, 'The Rise of Barranquilla', *ibid.*, xxxiv (1954), 158–74, [**1523**] J. F. Rippy, 'Dawn of the Railway Era in Colombia', *ibid.*, xxiii (1943), 650–63, [**1524**] David Bushnell, 'Two Stages in Colombian Tariff Policy: the Radical Era and the Return to Protection (1861–1885)', *Inter-American Economic Affairs*, ix, No. 4 (1956), 3–23, and [**1525**] R. C. Beyer, 'Transportation and the Coffee Industry in Colombia', *ibid.*, ii, No. 3 (1948), 17–30. See also Rippy [1531].

[**1526**] W. S. Robertson, 'An Early Threat of Intervention by Force in South America', *Hispanic American Historical Review*, xxiii (1943), 611–31, discusses the diplomatic consequences of the ill-treatment of a French consular official in 1833. Lockey [1701] illustrates New Granadan apprehensions in the 'forties. See also Manning [1216]. [**1527**] L. F. Sensabaugh, 'The Attitude of the United States toward the Colombia–Costa Rica Arbitral Proceedings', *ibid.*, xix (1939), 16–30, is concerned with the Colombia–Costa Rica arbitration treaty of 1880, held by the United States to conflict with her own treaty with New Granada signed in 1846. [**1528**] D. C. Miner, *The Fight for the Panama Route. The story of the Spooner Act and the Hay-Herrán Treaty* (Columbia Univ. Press, 1940), detailed and authoritative, tells the story of the loss of Panama. See also Parks [856], Rippy [1531], Dennis [1645], Hill [1717], and nos. 1791–3.

[**1529**] Holton, I. F., *New Granada; twenty months in the Andes* (New York, 1857).

[**1530**] Powles, J. D., *New Granada; its internal resources* (London, 1863).

1909–

[**1531**] J. F. Rippy, *The Capitalists and Colombia* (New York, Vanguard Press, 1931), deals mainly (but not exclusively) with the period since 1903, and is a study in United States investment and in external economic relations. See also Beyer [1525] and Whitaker [1201].

The descriptive literature includes [**1532**] F. L. Petre, *The Republic of Colombia. An account of the country, its people, its institutions and its resources* (London, Stanford, 1906), [**1533**] P. J. Eder, *Colombia* (London, Fisher Unwin, 1913), [**1534**] P. L. Bell, *Colombia: a commercial and industrial handbook* (Washington, Govt. Printing Office, 1921), and [**1535**] the compact analysis of W. O. Galbraith, *Colombia. A general survey* (London, Royal Institute of International Affairs, 1953).

6. ECUADOR

GENERAL

For bibliographies and guides see nos. 38, 42, 71, and 90.

[**1536**] George I. Blanksten, *Ecuador, constitutions and caudillos* (Univ. of California Press, 1951), is an interdisciplinary study as valuable to the historian as to the political scientist. [**1537**] Lilo Linke, *Ecuador. Country of contrasts* (2nd ed., London, Royal Institute of International Affairs, 1955), provides an admirable general survey. The illustrations in [**1538**] Rolf Blomberg, ed.,

Ecuador

Ecuador: Andean mosaic (Stockholm, Hugo Gebers, 1952), are excellent.

[**1539**] John Collier, Jr., and Aníbal Buitrón, *The Awakening Valley* (Univ. of Chicago Press, 1949), is a study of the Otavalo valley, and [**1540**] E. W. C. Parsons, *Peguche: a study of Andean Indians* (Univ. of Chicago Press, 1945), an examination of an Indian community in this same northern region.

For the Galápagos Islands see [**1541**] William Beebe, *Galápagos: world's end* (New York, Putnam's, 1924), and [**1542**] Ainslie and Frances Conway, *The Enchanted Islands* (New York, Putnam's, 1947: London, Geoffrey Bles, 1948).

THE NINETEENTH CENTURY

[**1543**] Haskins, R. W., 'Juan José Flores and the Proposed Expedition against Ecuador, 1846–1847', *Hispanic American Historical Review*, xxvii (1947), 467–95.
See also Lockey [1701].

[**1544**] Howe, G. F., 'García Moreno's Efforts to unite Ecuador and France', *Hispanic American Historical Review*, xvi (1936), 257–62.

[**1545**] Robertson, W. S., 'García Moreno's Dream of a European Protectorate', *Contribuciones para el Estudio de la Historia de América. Homenaje al Dr Emilio Ravignani* (Buenos Aires, Peuser, 1941), pp. 125–43.

See also Cleven [867] and Manning [1216], and, for travel accounts, [**1546**] F. Hassaurek, *Four Years among Spanish-Americans* (London, 1868), and [**1547**] Edward Whymper, *Travels amongst the Great Andes of the Equator* (London, 1892).

THE TWENTIETH CENTURY

See Blanksten [1536], Whitaker [1201], Sands [1205], and Ireland [1192].

[**1548**] L. F. Parks and G. A. Nuermberger, 'The Sanitation of Guayaquil', *Hispanic American Historical Review*, xxiii (1943), 197–221, discuss the eradication of yellow fever in 1919.

The descriptive literature includes [**1549**] C. R. Enock, *Ecuador . . .* (London, Fisher Unwin, 1914), [**1550**] Victor W. von Hagen, *Ecuador, the unknown . . .* (New York, Oxford Univ. Press, 1940), [**1551**] A. B. Franklin, *Ecuador, portrait of a people* (New York, Doubleday, Doran, 1943), and [**1552**] Arturo Eichler, *Ecuador: snow peaks and jungles* (New York, Crowell, 1955). [**1553**] Ludwig Bemelmans, *The Donkey Inside* (New York, Viking Press, 1941), is an entertaining series of sketches.

7. PARAGUAY

GENERAL

For bibliographies and guides see nos. 38, 42, 74, and 92, together with [**1554**] José Segundo Decoud, *A List of Books, Magazine Articles, and Maps relating to Paraguay* (Washington, Govt. Printing Office, 1904). Warren, *Paraguay. An informal history* [347], is an admirable synthesis of Paraguayan history from 1537 to 1948. [**1555**] Philip Raine, *Paraguay* (New Brunswick, N.J., Scarecrow Press, 1956), is partly a historical study. [**1556**] George Pendle's general survey, *Paraguay. A riverside nation* (2nd ed., London, Royal Institute of International Affairs, 1956), is excellent.

SPECIAL ASPECTS

[**1557**] Emma Reh, *Paraguayan Rural Life* (Washington, Institute of Inter-American Affairs, 1946), is a valuable account of rural conditions and of nutritional problems in the Piribebuy district, south-east of Asunción, and [**1558**] E. R. and H. S. Service, *Tobatí: Paraguayan town* (Univ. of Chicago Press, 1954), examines a community in a neighbouring area. Janzen [1149], [**1559**] A. E. Krause, *Mennonite Settlement in the Paraguayan Chaco* (Univ. of Chicago, Dept. of Geography, 1952), [**1560**] J. W. Fretz, *Pilgrims in Paraguay* . . . (Scottdale, Pa., Herald Press, 1953), and [**1561**] Willard H. Smith, *Paraguayan Interlude, observations and impressions* (Scottdale, Pa., Herald Press, 1950), record the progress of Mennonite colonization in the Paraguayan Chaco since 1926.

For German settlements in the Misiones area see Thompson [1152].

1830–1870

On the rule of Dr. Francia see J. P. and W. P. Robertson, *Letters on Paraguay* [819] and *Francia's Reign of Terror* [820], together with Rengger and Longchamps [821]. [**1562**] E. L. White, *El Supremo. A romance of the great dictator of Paraguay* (New York, Dutton, 1916), is a first-rate historical novel dedicated to the Robertsons' 'scandalized and indignant ghosts'. [**1563**] There is a useful essay on Francia by L. W. Bealer in Wilgus [1006], and, in the same volume, Bealer also discusses Francia's successors, Carlos Antonio López and Francisco Solano López.

[**1564**] V. G. Kiernan, 'Britain's First Contacts with Paraguay', *Atlante*, iii (1956), 171–91, is an excellent account covering the years 1823 to 1853. [**1565**] H. F. Peterson, 'Edward A. Hopkins: a Pioneer Promoter in Paraguay' (expelled in 1854), *Hispanic American Historical Review*, xxii (1942), 245–61, and [**1566**] P. M. Ynsfran, 'Sam Ward's Bargain with President López of Paraguay', *ibid.*, xxxiv (1954), 313–31, in part concerned with the United States naval expedition of 1858–9, are important for relations with the United States. See also Page [1274] and Manning [1216]. [**1567**] C. B. Mansfield, *Paraguay, Brazil and the Plate: letters written in 1852–53* (Cambridge, 1856), has some, but no great, interest.

[**1568**] R. B. Cunninghame Graham, *Portrait of a Dictator, Francisco Solano López* (London, Heinemann, 1933), sets the scene for the Paraguayan War, and on this see in particular [**1569**] P. H. Box, *The Origins of the Paraguayan War* (Univ. of Illinois, 'Studies in the Social Sciences', xv, Nos. 3 and 4, Urbana, Illinois, 1929), a masterly analysis, and [**1570**] H. F. Peterson, 'Efforts of the United States to Mediate in the Paraguayan War', *Hispanic American Historical Review*, xii (1932), 2–17. Contemporary accounts include [**1571**] Thomas J. Hutchinson, *The Paraná; with incidents of the Paraguayan war and South American recollections from 1861 to 1868* (London, 1868); [**1572**] George Thompson, *The War in Paraguay . . .* (London, 1869), by an English engineer in the Paraguayan armies; [**1573**] A. J. Kennedy, *La Plata, Brazil and Paraguay, during the present war* (London, 1869); [**1574**] G. F. Masterman, *Seven Eventful Years in Paraguay . . .* (London, 1869), by one who entered the Paraguayan service as chief military apothecary; [**1575**] R. F. Burton, *Letters from the Battlefields of Paraguay* (London, 1870); and [**1576**] C. A. Washburn, *The History of Paraguay, with notes of personal observations, and reminiscences of diplomacy under difficulties* (2 vols., Boston, Mass., 1871), by the United States Minister and inclining to 'the demoniac interpretation of history'.

1870–

On the years between the Paraguayan War and the Chaco War, see, for general descriptive literature, [**1577**] E. de Bourgade la Dardye, *Paraguay: the land and the people . . .* (London, 1892), [**1578**] J. S. Decoud, *Paraguay* (2nd ed., Washington, Govt. Printing Office, 1902), [**1579**] W. H. Koebel, *Paraguay* (London,

Fisher Unwin, 1917), and [**1580**] W. L. Schurz, *Paraguay: a commercial handbook* (Washington, Govt. Printing Office, 1920). [**1581**] H. V. Livermore, 'New Australia', *Hispanic American Historical Review*, xxx (1950), 290–313, examines a utopian venture in colonization from Australia launched in 1893. See also Dickens [1291]. For the Chaco conflict in the nineteen-thirties see [**1582**] P. M. Ynsfran, ed., *The Epic of the Chaco: Marshal Estigarribia's memoirs of the Chaco War, 1932–1935* (Univ. of Texas Press, 1950), La Foy [1339], Warren [347], Ireland [1192], and [**1583**] R. W. Thompson, *Land of To-Morrow: a story of South America* (New York and London, Appleton-Century, 1937).

[**1584**] Warren, H. G., 'Political Aspects of the Paraguayan Revolution, 1936–1940', *Hispanic American Historical Review*, xxx (1950), 2–25.

8. PERU

GENERAL

For bibliographies and guides see nos. 38, 42, 75, and 93, together with [**1585**] Sir Clements R. Markham, 'Bibliography of Peru, 1526–1907', in Hakluyt Soc. Pubns., 2nd series, No. 22 (Cambridge, 1907), pp. 269–320, and [**1586**] Alfredo Saco, 'Aprista Bibliography', *Hispanic American Historical Review*, xxiii (1943), 555–85.

[**1587**] G. R. Johnson and R. R. Platt, *Peru from the Air* (New York, American Geographical Society, 1930), [**1588**] Isaiah Bowman, *The Andes of Southern Peru* (New York, American Geographical Society, 1916), and [**1589**] R. C. Murphy, *Bird Islands of Peru. The record of a sojourn on the west coast* (New York and London, Putnam's, 1925), are at once fascinating and indispensable. [**1590**] Claude Archaud and François Hébert-Stevens, *The Andes: roof of America* (translated by E. E. Smith, London, Thames and Hudson, 1956), and [**1591**] Christopher Sandeman, *A Wanderer in Inca Land* (London, Phoenix House, 1948), are notable for the excellence of their illustrations.

SPECIAL ASPECTS

On the land system and its general social effects see [**1592**] Thomas R. Ford, *Man and Land in Peru* (Univ. of Florida Press, 1955), on the Indian and mestizo populations *Handbook of South American Indians* [148] and [**1593**] George Kubler, *The Indian*

Caste of Peru, 1795–1940 (Smithsonian Institution, Institute of Social Anthropology, Washington, Govt. Printing Office, 1952), and on the effects of high altitudes [**1594**] Carlos Monge, *Acclimatization in the Andes* . . . (trans. by D. F. Brown, Johns Hopkins Press, 1948), a study of ' "climatic aggression" in the development of Andean man'. [**1595**] H. Tschopik, *Highland Communities of Central Peru, a regional survey* (Smithsonian Institution, Institute of Social Anthropology, Washington, Govt. Printing Office, 1947), and [**1596**] John Gillin, *Moche, a Peruvian coastal community* (Smithsonian Institution, Institute of Social Anthropology, Washington, Govt. Printing Office, 1947), are detailed 'area' studies.

[**1597**] Toraji Irie, 'History of Japanese Migration to Peru', translated and edited by William Himel, *Hispanic American Historical Review*, xxxi (1951), 437–52, 648–64, xxxii (1952), 73–82, is the fullest account available. But see also Normano and Gerbi [1147].

[**1598**] *The Peruvian Economy* (Washington, Pan American Union, Division of Economic Research, 1950), is a study of 'characteristics, stage of development and main problems'. [**1599**] C. A. McQueen, *Peruvian Public Finance* (Washington, Govt. Printing Office, 1926), is mainly historical in interest. On railways see Long [1100].

THE NINETEENTH CENTURY

Markham, *A History of Peru* [343], published in 1892, provides a general narrative. [**1600**] F. M. Stanger, 'Church and State in Peru', *Hispanic American Historical Review*, vii (1927), 410–37, is a broad sketch.

For the decade of the 'thirties and the Peru-Bolivian Confederation see Cleven [867] and Kendall [1332]. [**1601**] Watt Stewart, *Chinese Bondage in Peru. A history of the Chinese coolie in Peru, 1849–1874* (Duke Univ. Press, 1951), examines the notorious coolie traffic by which some 90,000 Chinese were brought to Peru to work on the cotton plantations and in the guano fields. [**1602**] The same author's *Henry Meiggs, Yankee Pizarro* (Duke Univ. Press, 1946), tells the story of railway construction in the eighteen-seventies. See also Long [1100] and, on the guano fields, Murphy [1589].

For Peruvian-United States relations see Manning [1216], Martin [1408], and [**1603**] L. C. Nolan, 'The Relations of the

United States and Peru with respect to Claims, 1822–1870',
Hispanic American Historical Review, xvii (1937), 30–66; for the
war with Spain in the eighteen-sixties Davis [1478]; and for the
War of the Pacific nos. 1424 and 1479–83.

The more notable of contemporary accounts include [**1604**]
J. J. von Tschudi, *Travels in Peru during the years 1838–1842*
(London, 1847); [**1605**] G. W. Peck, *Melbourne, and the Chincha
Islands* (New York, 1854); [**1606**] Sir Clements R. Markham,
*Cuzco: a journey to the ancient capital of Peru . . . and Lima: a visit to
the capital and provinces of modern Peru* (London, 1856); [**1607**] by
the same author, *Travels in Peru and India . . .* (London, 1862);
[**1608**] T. J. Hutchinson, *Two Years in Peru . . .* (2 vols., London,
1873); [**1609**] E. G. Squier, *Peru. Incidents of travel and exploration
in the land of the Incas* (New York, 1877); [**1610**] A. J. Duffield,
Peru in the Guano Age . . . (London, 1877), and [**1611**] the same
author's *The Prospects of Peru. The end of the guano age . . .* (London,
1881).

THE TWENTIETH CENTURY

For the Tacna-Arica question see Dennis [1479, 1480], and
for territorial disputes generally Ireland [1192]. See also Ganzert
[1336] and Whitaker [1201].

Irie [1597] traces the movement of Japanese immigration between 1898 and 1936. [**1612**] J. F. Rippy, 'The Dawn of Manufacturing in Peru', *Pacific Historical Review*, xv (1946), 147–57, is
a brief survey which emphasizes twentieth-century developments.

[**1613**] L. S. Rowe examines the *Early Effects of the War upon the
Finance, Commerce and Industry of Peru* (New York, Oxford Univ.
Press, 1920). McQueen [1599] discusses public finance in the
nineteen-twenties and [**1614**] G. H. Stuart analyses *The Governmental System of Peru* (Washington, Carnegie Institution, 1925)
in the same post-war decade.

For the Alianza Popular Revolucionaria Americana see [**1615**]
R. E. McNicoll, 'Intellectual Origins of Aprismo', *Hispanic
American Historical Review*, xxiii (1943), 424–40, and [**1616**]
Harry Kantor, *The Ideology and Program of the Peruvian Aprista
Movement* (Univ. of California Press, 1953). See also no. 1061.

[**1617**] Fred Bronner, 'José de la Riva-Agüero (1885–1944),
Peruvian Historian', *Hispanic American Historical Review*, xxxvi
(1956), 490–502, is a useful note.

[**1618**] W. E. Hardenburg, *The Putumayo, the Devil's Paradise;*

travels in the Peruvian Amazon region and an account of the atrocities committed upon the Indians therein (London, Fisher Unwin, 1912), is the work of the American engineer whose exposure of the appalling conditions in the Putumayo region led to the mission of Sir Roger Casement to inquire into the activities of the Peruvian Amazon Company. The literature of travel and exploration includes also [**1619**] Hiram Bingham, *Inca Land. Explorations in the highlands of Peru* (Boston and New York, Houghton Mifflin, 1922), [**1620**] Christopher Sandeman, *A Forgotten River* (Oxford Univ. Press, 1939), a book of 'travel notes and botanical jottings' on the Huallaga river, [**1621**] Frances Toor, *Three Worlds of Peru* (New York, Crown Publishers, 1949), and [**1622**] Leonard F. Clark, *The Rivers Ran East* (New York, Funk and Wagnalls, 1953), which is concerned with the *montaña* region of the Gran Pajonal.

[**1623**] Martin, P. F., *Peru of the Twentieth Century* (London, Arnold, 1911).

[**1624**] Dunn, W. E., *Peru, a commercial and industrial handbook* (Washington, Govt. Printing Office, 1925).

[**1625**] Beals, Carleton, *Fire on the Andes* (Philadelphia and London, Lippincott, 1934).

9. URUGUAY
General

For bibliographies and guides see nos. 38, 42, 76, and 95.

[**1626**] Russell H. Fitzgibbon, *Uruguay. Portrait of a democracy* (New Brunswick, N.J., Rutgers Univ. Press, 1954), and [**1627**] George Pendle's brief survey, *Uruguay* (2nd ed., rev., Oxford Univ. Press, for Royal Institute of International Affairs, 1957), are both excellent.

[**1628**] International Bank for Reconstruction and Development and Food and Agriculture Organization of the United Nations, *The Agricultural Development of Uruguay* (Washington, I.B.R.D., 1951).

[**1629**] Taylor, Philip B., *The Executive Power in Uruguay* (Berkeley, Calif., The author, 1951).

The Nineteenth Century

[**1630**] L. W. Bealer, 'Fructuoso Rivera, Colorado Caudillo of Uruguay', in Wilgus [1006], discusses the first president. For the interventionist policies of Rosas see Cady [1262] and, for the Paraguayan War, Box [1569]. [**1631**] W. H. Hudson, *The Purple*

The Republics of South America since 1830

Land (London, 1885), is a nineteenth-century classic. See also [**1632**] J. H. Murray, *Travels in Uruguay* . . . (London, 1871).

THE TWENTIETH CENTURY

[**1633**] P. A. Martin, 'The Career of José Batlle y Ordóñez', *Hispanic American Historical Review*, x (1930), 413–28, is a brief biography of the founder of the modern state, and [**1634**] S. G. Hanson's scholarly *Utopia in Uruguay* (New York, Oxford Univ. Press, 1938) a history, in effect, of social and economic development between 1904 and 1934. [**1635**] Philip B. Taylor, 'The Uruguayan Coup d'Etat of 1933', *Hispanic American Historical Review*, xxxii (1952), 301–20, discusses the régime of President Terra.

[**1636**] Koebel, W. H., *Uruguay* (London, Fisher Unwin, 1911).

10. VENEZUELA

GENERAL

For bibliographies and guides see nos. 37, 42, 77, and 96.
[**1637**] W. D. and A. L. Marsland, *Venezuela through its History* (New York, Crowell, 1954), is a popular distillation of Venezuelan history. Watters, *History of the Church in Venezuela* [852], covers the years 1810 to 1930. [**1638**] W. W. Pierson traces 'Foreign Influences on Venezuelan Political Thought, 1830–1930', *Hispanic American Historical Review*, xv (1935), 3–42, and [**1639**] Edwin Lieuwen, *Petroleum in Venezuela: a history* (Univ. of California Press, 1954), surveys the development of the oil industry from its nineteenth-century beginnings to 1953.

[**1640**] Sardá, Juan, ed., *Economic Development in Venezuela* (Inter-American Economic Affairs, vii, No. 4, 1954).

THE NINETEENTH CENTURY

See [**1641**] J. F. Rippy, 'The Dictators of Venezuela', in Wilgus [1006], Graham, *José Antonio Páez* [845], and [**1642**] George S. Wise, *Caudillo. A portrait of Antonio Guzmán Blanco* (Columbia Univ. Press, 1951).
[**1643**] W. H. Gray, 'Steamboat Transportation on the Orinoco', *Hispanic American Historical Review*, xxv (1945), 455–69, discusses the attempts to foster navigation by monopolistic grants to successive steamship companies after 1847. [**1644**] By the same author, 'American Diplomacy in Venezuela, 1835–1865', *ibid.*,

xx (1940), 551–74, examines Venezuelan relations with the United States. See also Manning [1216]. For the Anglo-Venezuelan dispute of 1895 see Perkins [1220], [**1645**] A. L. P. Dennis, *Adventures in American Diplomacy, 1896–1906* (New York, Dutton, 1928); [**1646**] N. M. Blake, 'Background of Cleveland's Venezuelan Policy', *American Historical Review*, xlvii (Jan. 1942), 259–77; [**1647**] P. R. Fossum, 'The Anglo-Venezuelan Boundary Controversy', *Hispanic American Historical Review*, viii (1928), 299–329, and [**1648**] Jennie A. Sloan, 'Anglo-American Relations and the Venezuelan Boundary Dispute', *ibid.*, xviii (1938), 486–506, both based on printed sources only; and [**1649**] an important note, C. J. Child, 'The Venezuela-British Guiana Boundary Arbitration of 1899', *American Journal of International Law*, xliv (1950), 682–93. [**1650**] G. L. Burr, 'The Search for the Venezuela-Guiana Boundary', and [**1651**] 'The Guiana Boundary', *American Historical Review*, iv (April 1899), 470–7, and vi (Oct. 1900), 49–64, relate to the historical work of Cleveland's boundary commission. For further references and for sources see Bemis and Griffin, *Guide* [60], *Harvard Guide* [249], and Ireland [1192].

[**1652**] *Caracas Diary, 1835–1840. The journal of John G. A. Williamson, first diplomatic representative of the United States to Venezuela*, edited by Jane Lucas de Grummond (Baton Rouge, Camellia Pub. Co., 1954), consists of commonplace observations by a commonplace man. [**1653**] J. Hawkshaw, *Reminiscences of South America from two and a half years in Venezuela* (London, 1838), [**1654**] E. B. Eastwick, *Venezuela: or, sketches of life in a South-American republic; with the history of the loan of 1864* (London, 1868), and [**1655**] J. M. Spence, *The Land of Bolivar, or War, Peace, and Adventure in the Republic of Venezuela* (2 vols., London, 1878), are worth note.

[**1656**] Grummond, Jane Lucas de, *Envoy to Caracas. The story of John G. A. Williamson, nineteenth century diplomat* (Baton Rouge, Louisiana State Univ. Press, 1951). See no. 1652. Trivial in interest.

[**1657**] Grummond, Jane Lucas de, 'The Jacob Idler Claim against Venezuela, 1817–1890', *Hispanic American Historical Review*, xxxiv (1954), 131–57.

THE TWENTIETH CENTURY

On the long dictatorship of Juan Vicente Gómez see [**1658**] Thomas Rourke [D. J. Clinton], *Gómez, tyrant of the Andes* (New

York, Morrow, 1936: London, Joseph, 1937), and, a defence of Gómez, [**1659**] P. M. Arcaya, *The Gómez Régime in Venezuela* (Washington, privately printed, 1936). [**1660**] J. F. Rippy and C. E. Hewitt, 'Cipriano Castro, "Man without a Country" ', *American Historical Review*, lv (Oct. 1949), 36–53, discuss the means taken, by the United States Government and other governments, to prevent Castro's return to Venezuela in 1909.

On the Venezuelan debt question see Dennis [1645], Hill, *Roosevelt and the Caribbean* [1717], and [**1661**] S. W. Livermore, 'Theodore Roosevelt, the American Navy, and the Venezuelan Crisis of 1902–1903', *American Historical Review*, li (April 1946), 452–71. See also [**1662**] P. F. Fenton, 'Diplomatic Relations of the United States and Venezuela, 1880–1915', *Hispanic American Historical Review*, viii (1928), 330–56, [**1663**] J. F. Rippy, 'The Venezuelan Claims Settlements of 1903–05', *Inter-American Economic Affairs*, vii, No. 4 (1954), 65–77, and Bemis and Griffin, *Guide* [60].

Two articles by J. C. Rayburn trace [**1664**] the history of 'United States Investments in Venezuelan Asphalt' between 1883 and 1935, *Inter-American Economic Affairs*, vii, No. 1 (1953), 20–36, and [**1665**] the 'Development of Venezuela's Iron Ore Deposits', *ibid.*, vi, No. 1 (1952), 52–70.

See also Whitaker [1201].

Bingham [848] and Gheerbrant [1516] should be noted among the literature of travel. [**1666**] T. R. Ybarra, *Young Man of Caracas* (New York, Washburn, 1941: London, Hale, 1943), is a highly entertaining autobiography. For the descriptive literature see [**1667**] L. V. Dalton, *Venezuela* (London, Fisher Unwin, 1912), [**1668**] P. L. Bell, *Venezuela: a commercial and industrial handbook* (Washington, Govt. Printing Office, 1922), and [**1669**] Erna Fergusson, *Venezuela* (New York and London, Knopf, 1939).

XIII
THE CENTRAL AMERICAN AND
ISLAND REPUBLICS SINCE 1830

1. THE CENTRAL AMERICAN AND CARIBBEAN AREA[1]
GENERAL

For bibliographies and guides see nos. 38, 42, 60, 64, 78, and 86, together with [**1670**] P. L. Phillips, *A List of Books, Magazine Articles, and Maps relating to Central America, including the Republics of Costa Rica, Guatemala, Honduras, Nicaragua, and Salvador, 1800–1900* (Washington, Govt. Printing Office, 1902), and [**1671**] J. C. Frank, *American Interoceanic Canals: a list of references in the New York Public Library* (New York, Public Library, 1916).

[**1672**] Dana G. Munro, *The Five Republics of Central America. Their political and economic development and their relations with the United States* (New York, Oxford Univ. Press, 1918), is in a class by itself and remains the best single volume ever written on the Central American area in general.

[**1673**] C. L. Jones, *Caribbean Backgrounds and Prospects* (New York and London, Appleton, 1931), a study of economic and social problems in the islands and on the mainland, and [**1674**] his *The Caribbean since 1900* (New York, Prentice-Hall, 1936), are outstanding. See also the symposia edited by A. Curtis Wilgus, [**1675**] *The Caribbean Area* (George Washington Univ. Press, 1934), [**1676**] *The Caribbean at Mid-Century* (Univ. of Florida Press, 1951), [**1677**] *The Caribbean: peoples, problems and prospects* (*ibid.*, 1952), and, continuing the series, [**1678**] *The Caribbean: contemporary trends* (*ibid.*, 1953), [**1679**] *The Caribbean: its economy* (*ibid.*, 1954), [**1680**] *The Caribbean: its culture* (*ibid.*, 1955), [**1681**] *The Caribbean: its political problems* (*ibid.*, 1956), and [**1682**] *The Caribbean: contemporary international relations* (*ibid.*, 1957).

[**1683**] Ruhl, A., *The Central Americans: adventures and impressions between Mexico and Panama* (New York and London, Scribner's, 1928). An entertaining travelogue.

---

[1] See also the section on Modern Latin America, above, pp. 92–110.

[**1684**] Beals, Carleton, *Banana Gold* (Philadelphia and London, Lippincott, 1932).
A journalist's provocative impressions.

[**1685**] U.S. Bureau of the Census, *Census Atlas Maps of Latin America. Central America* (Washington, Bureau of the Census, 1955).
Nine maps showing land forms, roads, railways, and distribution of urban and rural populations.

[**1686**] Carr, Archie, *High Jungles and Low* (Univ. of Florida Press, 1953).
A naturalist in Honduras and Nicaragua.

SPECIAL ASPECTS

[**1687**] W. F. Slade, *The Federation of Central America* (Worcester, Mass., 1917; reprinted from *Journal of Race Development*, viii), examines the various attempts to form such a federation between 1823 and 1915. For a further attempt in 1921 see [**1688**] Edward Perry, 'Central American Union', *Hispanic American Historical Review*, v (1922), 30–51. [**1689**] M. O. Hudson, 'The Central American Court of Justice', *American Journal of International Law*, xxvi (1932), 759–86, summarizes the history of the Court between its creation in 1907 and its demise in 1918.

[**1690**] J. P. Young, *Central American Currency and Finance* (Princeton Univ. Press, 1925), deals with monetary policy during the nineteenth century but more particularly in the first quarter of the twentieth century. For railways see Long [1101] and, for the banana industry, Adams [1084], Kepner and Southill [1085], Kepner [1086], and Wilson [1087].

[**1691**] Rippy, J. F., 'British Investments in Central America, the Dominican Republic and Cuba: a story of meagre returns', *Inter-American Economic Affairs*, vi, No. 2 (1952), 89–98.

CENTRAL AMERICA AND THE CENTRAL AMERICAN QUESTION IN THE NINETEENTH CENTURY

Bancroft [252] supplies a narrative history ending in 1887. For the ill-starred Central American Federation which collapsed in 1838–9 see also Stanger [910], Chamberlain [913], Williams [914], and Slade [1687]. [**1692**] J. B. Lockey, 'Diplomatic Futility', *Hispanic American Historical Review*, x (1930), 265–94, reprinted in no. 1227, discusses the misfortunes of the early diplomatic agents of the United States in Central America.

[**1693**] M. W. Williams, *Anglo-American Isthmian Diplomacy, 1815–1915* (Washington, American Historical Association, 1916), is a standard work which supersedes [**1694**] I. D. Travis, *The History of the Clayton-Bulwer Treaty* (Ann Arbor, Michigan Political Science Association, 1900), but is itself in need of revision. For the Central American question in mid-century see, more particularly, R. W. van Alstyne: [**1695**] 'The Central American Policy of Lord Palmerston, 1846–1848', *Hispanic American Historical Review*, xvi (1936), 339–59, [**1696**] 'British Diplomacy and the Clayton-Bulwer Treaty, 1850–60', *Journal of Modern History*, xi (1939), 149–83, and [**1697**] 'Anglo-American Relations, 1853–57', *American Historical Review*, xlii (April 1937), 491–500. Compare Perkins [1219], Manning [1216], and [**1698**] Hunter Miller, ed., *Treaties and Other International Acts of the United States of America, 1788–1863* (8 vols., Washington, Govt. Printing Office, 1931–48), v. [**1699**] G. F. Hickson, 'Palmerston and the Clayton-Bulwer Treaty' and [**1700**] J. D. Ward, 'Sir Henry Bulwer and the United States Archives', *Cambridge Historical Journal*, iii, No. 3 (1931), 295–303, 304–13, are to be taken *cum grano*.

[**1701**] J. B. Lockey, 'A Neglected Aspect of Isthmian Diplomacy', *American Historical Review*, xli (Jan. 1936), 295–305, reprinted in no. 1227, discusses the treaty between the United States and New Granada in 1846. [**1702**] Gavin B. Henderson examines 'German Colonial Projects on the Mosquito Coast, 1844–8', *English Historical Review*, lix (1944), 257–71. Kemble, *The Panama Route* [1098] is a detailed account of the development of the route to the Pacific by way of Panama, used by some fifth of the California emigrants between 1848 and 1869. See also [**1703**] F. N. Otis, *History of the Panama Railroad; and of the Pacific Mail Steamship Company* . . . (New York, 1867), and Du Val [1796]. For filibustering in Central America in the 'fifties the standard work is [**1704**] W. O. Scroggs, *Filibusters and Financiers: the story of William Walker and his associates* (New York, Macmillan, 1916).

[**1705**] W. W. Pierson, 'The Political Influences of an Inter-Oceanic Canal, 1826–1926', *Hispanic American Historical Review*, vi (1926), 205–31, a brief outline, discusses canal projects in the later nineteenth century, and Du Val [1791, 1796] and Mack [1797] provide detailed accounts. [**1706**] J. A. S. Grenville, 'Great Britain and the Isthmian Canal, 1898–1901', *American Historical Review*, lxi (Oct. 1955), 48–69, sees the Hay-Pauncefote Treaty in 1901 as the conscious recognition by Great Britain of eventual United States supremacy in the western hemisphere.

The literature of travel and description contains, besides the classic work of Stephens [160], [**1707**] R. G. Dunlop, *Travels in Central America* . . . (London, 1847), [**1708**] F. Crowe's notable *The Gospel in Central America* (London, 1850), [**1709**] E. G. Squier's *Travels in Central America* (2 vols., New York, 1853), [**1710**] his *Waikna; or adventures on the Mosquito Shore*, published under the pseudonym of Samuel A. Bard (New York and London, 1855), and [**1711**] his *The States of Central America* (New York, 1858), [**1712**] Carl Scherzer, *Travels in the Free States of Central America* . . . (2 vols., London, 1857), and [**1713**] Julius Froebel, *Seven Years' Travel in Central America, Northern Mexico, and the Far West of the United States* (London, 1859).

THE CARIBBEAN AREA SINCE 1900[1]

[**1714**] W. H. Callcott, *The Caribbean Policy of the United States, 1890–1920* (Johns Hopkins Press, 1942), mechanical, pedestrian, and of limited value, [**1715**] D. G. Munro's admirable *The United States and the Caribbean Area* (Boston, World Peace Foundation, 1934), and [**1716**] Dexter Perkins's not wholly satisfactory *The United States and the Caribbean* (Harvard Univ. Press, 1947), are general accounts.

[**1717**] H. C. Hill, *Roosevelt and the Caribbean* (Univ. of Chicago Press, 1927), an excellent and dispassionate survey, Scott Nearing [1206], highly critical of United States policy, Sands [1205], and [**1718**] Selig Adler, 'Bryan and Wilsonian Caribbean Penetration', *Hispanic American Historical Review*, xx (1940), 198–226, cover the opening decades of the twentieth century. See also Miller [1799] and, for territorial disputes, Ireland [1193].

2. COSTA RICA
GENERAL

[**1719**] C. L. Jones, *Costa Rica and Civilization in the Caribbean* (Univ. of Wisconsin Press, 1935), is outstanding. Compare [**1720**] J. and M. Biesanz, *Costa Rican Life* (Columbia Univ. Press, 1944), and, on economic conditions generally, [**1721**] Stacy May *et al.*, *Costa Rica. A study in economic development* (New York, Twentieth Century Fund, 1952).

SPECIAL ASPECTS

[**1722**] Houk, R. J., 'The Development of Foreign Trade and Com-

---

[1] See also above, pp. 105–10.

munication in Costa Rica to the Construction of the first Railway', *Americas*, x (Oct. 1953), 197–209.

[**1723**] Scheips, P. J., 'Gabriel Lafond and Ambrose W. Thompson: Neglected Isthmian Promoters', *Hispanic American Historical Review*, xxxvi (1956), 211–28.

[**1724**] Bischoff, H. C., 'British Investments in Costa Rica', *Inter-American Economic Affairs*, vii, No. 1 (1953), 37–47.

3. EL SALVADOR

GENERAL

[**1725**] Martin, P. F., *Salvador of the Twentieth Century* (New York, Longmans, Green: London, Arnold, 1911).

[**1725a**] Osborne, Lilly de Jongh, *Four Keys to El Salvador* (New York, Funk and Wagnalls, 1956).

[**1726**] Wallich, H. C., and Adler, J. H., *Public Finance in a Developing Country. El Salvador, a case study* (Harvard Univ. Press, 1951).

4. GUATEMALA

GENERAL

See [**1727**] Lázaro Lamadrid, 'A Survey of the Historiography of Guatemala since 1821', *Americas*, viii (Oct. 1951, Jan. 1952), 189–202, 305–20.

[**1728**] C. L. Jones, *Guatemala, past and present* (Univ. of Minnesota Press, 1940), is the outstanding general study. See also, more popular in approach, [**1729**] Erna Fergusson, *Guatemala* (New York, Knopf, 1937), and [**1730**] Vera Kelsey and Lilly de Jongh Osborne, *Four Keys to Guatemala* (New York, Funk and Wagnalls, 1939).

[**1731**] Adler, J. H., Schlesinger, E. R., and Olson, E. C., *Public Finance and Economic Development in Guatemala* (Stanford Univ. Press, 1952).

[**1732**] *The Economic Development of Guatemala. Report of a Mission sponsored by the International Bank for Reconstruction and Development in collaboration with the Government of Guatemala* (Washington, International Bank for Reconstruction and Development, 1951).

SPECIAL ASPECTS

Holleran, *Church and State in Guatemala* [915], academic but useful, is mainly concerned with the national period.

[**1733**] G. C. Shattuck *et al.*, *A Medical Survey of the Republic* *of Guatemala* (Washington, Carnegie Institution, 1938), provides vital statistics and an analysis of the incidence of diseases. For regional and community studies see [**1734**] F. W. McBryde, *Cultural and Historical Geography of Southwest Guatemala* (Smithsonian Institution, Institute of Social Anthropology, Washington, Govt. Printing Office, 1947), [**1734a**] John Gillin, *The Culture of Security in San Carlos; a study of a Guatemalan community of Indians and Ladinos* (New Orleans, Middle American Research Institute, Tulane Univ., 1951), [**1735**] Sol Tax, *Penny Capitalism. A Guatemalan Indian economy* (Smithsonian Institution, Institute of Social Anthropology, Washington, Govt. Printing Office, 1953), and [**1736**] Charles Wagley, *Economics of a Guatemalan Village* (Menasha, Wis., American Anthropological Association, 1941).

[**1737**] La Farge, Oliver, *Santa Eulalia. The religion of a Cuchumatán Indian town* (Univ. of Chicago Press, 1947).

[**1738**] Wisdom, Charles, *The Chorti Indians of Guatemala* (Univ. of Chicago Press, 1940).

The Nineteenth Century

See Jones [1728], Holleran [915], and [**1739**] Paul Burgess, *Justo Rufino Barrios* (Philadelphia, Dorrance, 1926), a biography of the Liberal leader killed in 1885.

[**1740**] Mary P. Chapman discusses 'The Mission of Elisha O. Crosby to Guatemala, 1861–1864', *Pacific Historical Review*, xxiv (1955), 275–86, and [**1741**] J. F. Rippy the 'Relations of the United States and Guatemala during the Epoch of Justo Rufino Barrios', *Hispanic American Historical Review*, xxii (1942), 595–605. See also, by the same author, [**1742**] 'Justo Rufino Barrios and the Nicaraguan Canal', *ibid.*, xx (1940), 190–7. [**1743**] S. A. Mosk, 'The Coffee Economy of Guatemala, 1850–1918: development and signs of instability', *Inter-American Economic Affairs*, ix, No. 3 (1955), 6–20, is a useful outline.

Among contemporary writings consult [**1744**] G. W. Montgomery, *Narrative of a Journey to Guatemala, in Central America in 1838* (New York, 1839), [**1745**] G. F. von Tempsky, *Mitla. A narrative of incidents and personal adventures on a journey in Mexico, Guatemala, and Salvador in the years 1853 to 1855* (London, 1858), [**1746**] C. A. Barker, ed., *Memoirs of Elisha Oscar Crosby. Reminiscences of California and Guatemala from 1849 to 1864* (San Marino, Calif., Huntington Library, 1945), [**1747**] W. T. Brigham,

Guatemala

Guatemala: the land of the quetzal (London, 1887), and [**1748**] A. C. and A. P. Maudslay, *A Glimpse at Guatemala* ... (London, 1899).

THE TWENTIETH CENTURY

See Jones [1728], Holleran [915], Mosk [1743], and, for side lights on the régime of Estrada Cabrera, Sands [1205]. [**1749**] K. H. Silvert, *A Study in Government: Guatemala* (New Orleans, Middle American Research Institute, Tulane Univ., 1954), examines national and local government under the Constitution of 1945. See also [**1750**] L. A. Suslow, *Aspects of Social Reforms in Guatemala, 1944–1949* (Hamilton, New York, Colgate Univ. Area Studies, 1949), and [**1751**] A. C. Bush, *Organized Labor in Guatemala, 1944–1949 (ibid.*, 1950), [**1752**] United States, Department of State, *Intervention of International Communism in Guatemala* (Washington, Govt. Printing Office, 1954), and [**1753**] Great Britain, Foreign Office, *Report on Events leading up to and arising out of the Change of Régime in Guatemala*, 1954 (Cmd. 9277, London, H.M. Stationery Office, 1954), together with [**1753a**] P. B. Taylor, 'The Guatemalan Affair: a critique of United States Foreign Policy', *American Political Science Review*, L (1956), 787–806.

[**1754**] Huxley, Aldous, *Beyond the Mexique Bay: a traveller's journal* (New York and London, Harper, 1934).

[**1755**] Burbank, Addison, *Guatemala Profile* (New York, Coward-McCann, 1939).

THE ANGLO-GUATEMALAN DISPUTE

[**1756**] The *White Book. Controversy between Guatemala and Great Britain relative to the Convention of 1859 on territorial matters. Belize question* (Guatemala, Secretaría de Relaciones Exteriores, 1938. Numerous *Supplements*), and [**1757**] J. L. Mendoza, *Britain and her Treaties on Belize* (Guatemala, Publications by the Ministry of Foreign Affairs, 1947), are *ex parte* statements.

[**1758**] R. A. Humphreys, 'The Anglo-Guatemalan Dispute', *International Affairs*, xxiv (July 1948), 387–404, is a historical summary based upon the Foreign Office and Colonial Office records. For discussions of the legal issues see [**1759**] J. L. Kunz, 'Guatemala *vs.* Great Britain: *in re* Belice', *American Journal of International Law*, xl (1946), 383–90, and [**1760**] L. M. Bloomfield, *The British Honduras-Guatemala Dispute* (Toronto, Carswell, 1953). See also Ireland [1193].

5. HONDURAS

GENERAL

[**1761**] W. S. Stokes, *Honduras. An area study in government* (Univ. of Wisconsin Press, 1950), a useful discussion, provides also an outline of political history.

Nineteenth-century accounts include [**1762**] W. V. Wells, *Explorations and Adventures in Honduras* . . . (New York, 1857), and, based upon no. 1711, [**1763**] E. G. Squier, *Honduras; descriptive, historical and statistical* (London, 1870). [**1764**] H. B. Deutsch, *The Incredible Yanqui: the career of Lee Christmas* (London, Longmans, Green, 1931), and [**1765**] A. Díaz Lozano's charming reminiscences, *Enriqueta and I* (translated by Harriet de Onís, New York, Farrar and Rinehart, 1944: London, Dennis Dobson, 1945), should be noted among twentieth-century works. See also Carr [1686].

6. NICARAGUA

GENERAL

See [**1766**] V. L. Minor, 'A Brief Classified Bibliography relating to United States Intervention in Nicaragua', *Hispanic American Historical Review*, xi (1931), 261–77.

[**1767**] *The Economic Development of Nicaragua. Report of a Mission organized by the International Bank for Reconstruction and Development at the request of the Government of Nicaragua* (Johns Hopkins Press, 1953).

THE NINETEENTH CENTURY

W. O. Scroggs [1704] and [**1768**] 'William Walker and the Steamship Corporation in Nicaragua', *American Historical Review*, x (July 1905), 792–811, tell the story of filibustering in mid-century. See also [**1769**] W. V. Wells, *Walker's Expedition to Nicaragua; a history of the Central American war* (New York, 1856), and, Walker's own account, [**1770**] William Walker, *The War in Nicaragua* (Mobile, 1860).

[**1771**] L. M. Keasbey, *The Nicaragua Canal and the Monroe Doctrine* . . . (New York, 1896), and [**1772**] R. R. Hill, 'The Nicaraguan Canal Idea to 1913', *Hispanic American Historical Review*, xxviii (1948), 197–211, are general reviews. See, more particularly, Du Val [1791] and Mack [1797], together with, for the 'fifties, [**1773**] Cyril Allen, 'Félix Belly: Nicaraguan Canal Promoter', *Hispanic American Historical Review*, xxxvii (1957), 46–59, and, in the 'eighties, Rippy [1742].

Nicaragua

[**1774**] R. L. Morrow, 'A Conflict between the Commercial Interests of the United States and its Foreign Policy', *Hispanic American Historical Review*, x (1930), 2–13, is concerned with the final incorporation of the Mosquito Shore into Nicaragua.

[**1775**] Squier, E. G., *Nicaragua; its people, scenery, monuments, and the proposed interoceanic canal* (2 vols., New York, 1852).

[**1776**] Stout, Peter F., *Nicaragua; past, present and future* (Philadelphia, 1859).

[**1777**] Belt, Thomas, *The Naturalist in Nicaragua* (London, 1874).

THE TWENTIETH CENTURY

See Hill [1772], [**1778**] T. A. Bailey, 'Interest in a Nicaragua Canal, 1903–1931', *Hispanic American Historical Review*, xvi (1936), 2–28, which discusses the Bryan-Chamorro Treaty of 1914 and subsequent developments, and, no more than a sketch, [**1779**] A. I. Powell, 'Relations between the United States and Nicaragua, 1898–1916', *ibid.*, viii (1928), 43–64.

[**1780**] I. J. Cox, *Nicaragua and the United States, 1909–1927* (Boston, World Peace Foundation, 1927), a scholarly account, [**1781**] H. N. Denny, *Dollars for Bullets: the story of American rule in Nicaragua* (New York, Dial Press, 1929), and [**1782**] Floyd Cramer, *Our Neighbor Nicaragua* (New York, Stokes, 1929), both by journalists, deal with the period of United States intervention. See also [**1783**] H. L. Stimson (the special representative of President Coolidge), *American Policy in Nicaragua* (New York and London, Scribner's, 1927), [**1784**] R. R. Hill's valuable *Fiscal Intervention in Nicaragua* (New York, Paul Maisel, 1933), and, an intemperate indictment of United States policy, [**1785**] Rafael de Nogales, *The Looting of Nicaragua* (New York, Robert M. McBride, 1928).

[**1786**] Virginia L. Greer, 'State Department Policy in regard to the Nicaraguan Election of 1924', *Hispanic American Historical Review*, xxxiv (1954), 445–67, exploits United States archives to good effect. J. O. Baylen [**1787**] 'Sandino: Patriot or Bandit?', *ibid.*, xxxi (1951), 394–419, and [**1788**] 'Sandino: Death and Aftermath', *Mid-America*, xxxvi (1954), 116–39, discuss the situation between 1926 and Sandino's assassination in 1934 and the rise of Somoza.

[**1789**] Cumberland, W. W., *Nicaragua: an economic and financial survey* (Washington, Govt. Printing Office, 1928).

7. PANAMA

GENERAL

For bibliographies and guides see nos. 38, 42, 60, 64, and 91.
[**1790**] J. and M. Biesanz, *The People of Panama* (Columbia Univ. Press, 1955), is a sociological analysis.

On the birth of the republic see Parks [856] and Rippy [1531], but, more particularly, Miner [1528], Dennis [1645], Hill [1717], and [**1791**] Miles P. Du Val, *Cádiz to Cathay: the story of the long diplomatic struggle for the Panama Canal* (2nd ed., Stanford Univ. Press, 1947). [**1792**] Philippe Bunau-Varilla, *Panama: the creation, destruction and resurrection* (London, Constable, 1913: New York, McBride, Nast, 1914), is an *ex parte* account, of great interest, by the former chief engineer of the New Panama Canal Company who played a prominent rôle in the events of 1903 and became Panama's first representative in the United States.

Two full-length studies review foreign relations: [**1793**] W. D. McCain, *The United States and the Republic of Panama* (Duke Univ. Press, 1937), and [**1794**] L. O. Ealy, *The Republic of Panama in World Affairs, 1903–1950* (Univ. of Pennsylvania Press, 1951). [**1795**] A. R. Wright discusses 'German Interest in Panama's Piñas Bay, 1910–1938', *Journal of Modern History*, xxvii (1955), 61–65.

THE PANAMA CANAL

[**1796**] Miles P. Du Val, *And the Mountains Will Move: the story of the building of the Panama Canal* (Stanford Univ. Press, 1947), continues no. 1791. [**1797**] Gerstle Mack, *The Land Divided: a history of the Panama Canal and other isthmian canal projects* (New York, Knopf, 1944), takes up in turn the Spanish, the French, and the American eras.

[**1798**] Abbot, W. J., *Panama and the Canal. . .* (New York, Dodd, Mead, 1914).

[**1799**] Miller, H. G., *The Isthmian Highway: a review of the problems of the Caribbean* (New York, Macmillan, 1929).

[**1800**] Padelford, N. J., *The Panama Canal in Peace and War* (New York, Macmillan, 1942).

See also Sands [1205].

8. CUBA

GENERAL

For bibliographies and guides see nos. 38, 42, 60, 70, and 89,

Cuba

together with [**1801**] A. P. C. Griffin, *List of Books relating to Cuba* (*including references to collected works and periodicals*) . . . *with a bibliography of maps by P. Lee Phillips* (Washington, Govt. Printing Office, 1898), continued, in effect, by [**1802**] L. Castro de Morales, *Impresos relativos a Cuba editados en los Estados Unidos de Norteamérica* (La Habana, Pubns. de la Biblioteca Nacional, 1956).

SPECIAL ASPECTS

[**1803**] Lowry Nelson, *Rural Cuba* (Univ. of Minnesota Press, 1950), an outstanding survey, analyses the structure and problems of rural society. [**1804**] Fernando Ortiz, *Cuban Counterpoint: tobacco and sugar* (translated by Harriet de Onís, New York, Knopf, 1947), is as valuable to the sociologist as to the historian. [**1805**] *Report on Cuba. Findings and Recommendations of an Economic and Technical Mission organized by the International Bank for Reconstruction and Development in collaboration with the Government of Cuba in 1950* (Washington, International Bank for Reconstruction and Development, 1951) is a comprehensive investigation covering all aspects of the Cuban economy.

[**1806**] Corbitt, D. C., '*Mercedes* and *Realengos*: a Survey of the Public Land System in Cuba', *Hispanic American Historical Review*, xix (1939), 262–85.

[**1807**] Corbitt, D. C., 'Immigration in Cuba', *Hispanic American Historical Review*, xxii (1942), 280–308.

[**1808**] Wallich, H. C., *Monetary Problems of an Export Economy. The Cuban experience, 1914–1947* (Harvard Univ. Press, 1950).

THE COLONY IN THE NINETEENTH CENTURY

For domestic history see [**1809**] W. F. Johnson, *The History of Cuba* (5 vols., New York, B. F. Buck, 1920), and [**1810**] H. H. S. Aimes, *A History of Slavery in Cuba, 1511–1868* (New York and London, Putnam's, 1907), neither especially satisfactory, and, for international history, [**1811**] J. M. Callahan, *Cuba and International Relations. A historical study in American diplomacy* (Johns Hopkins Press, 1899), and [**1812**] F. E. Chadwick, *The Relations of the United States and Spain. Diplomacy* (New York, Scribner's, 1909).

Rippy [929], Manning [896], and [**1813**] J. M. Callahan, 'Cuba and Anglo-American Relations', American Historical Association, *Annual Report* for 1897 (Washington, Govt. Printing

Office, 1898), pp. 193–215, discuss the Cuban problem at the time of the Spanish American revolutions. [**1814**] W. W. Pierson, 'Francisco de Arango y Parreño', *Hispanic American Historical Review*, xvi (1936), 451–78, is a study of an able administrator who was *intendente* of Cuba in 1824–5 and died in 1837.

[**1815**] R. G. Caldwell examines *The López Expeditions to Cuba, 1848–1851* (Princeton Univ. Press, 1915), and [**1816**] Basil Rauch *American Interest in Cuba, 1848–1855* (Columbia Univ. Press, 1948). For the situation in the 'fifties see also [**1817**] A. A. Ettinger, *The Mission to Spain of Pierre Soulé, 1853–1855: a study in the Cuban diplomacy of the United States* (Yale Univ. Press, 1932), [**1818**] C. Stanley Urban, 'The Africanization of Cuba Scare, 1853–1855', *Hispanic American Historical Review*, xxxvii (1957), 29–45, and [**1819**] G. B. Henderson, 'Southern Designs on Cuba, 1854–1857, and some European Opinions', *Journal of Southern History*, v (1939), 371–85.

[**1820**] C. J. Bartlett, 'British Reaction to the Cuban Insurrection of 1868–1878', *Hispanic American Historical Review*, xxxvii (1957), 296–312, makes excellent use of the Foreign Office archives.

[**1821**] Turnbull, David, *Travels in the West. Cuba: with notices of Porto Rico and the slave trade* (London, 1840).

[**1822**] Madden, R. R., *The Island of Cuba: its resources, progress and prospects* . . . (London, 1849).

[**1823**] Ballou, M. M., *History of Cuba; or notes of a traveller in the tropics* . . . (Boston, 1854).

[**1824**] Humboldt, Alexander von, *The Island of Cuba* (translated from the Spanish, with notes and a preliminary essay by J. S. Thrasher, New York, 1856).
See no. 224.

[**1825**] Atkins, E. F., *Sixty Years in Cuba: reminiscences* (Cambridge, Mass., Riverside Press, 1926).

The Liberation and the Spanish-American War

[**1826**] C. E. Chapman, *A History of the Cuban Republic* (New York, Macmillan, 1927), covers the war and the subsequent American military government. See also Fitzgibbon [1842].

[**1827**] H. S. Rubens, *Liberty, the story of Cuba* (New York, Brewer, Warren, and Putnam, 1932), is the narrative of the New York lawyer who acted as general counsel to the Cuban junta.

See, on an alleged War Department memorandum therein cited, [**1828**] T. M. Spaulding, 'Propaganda or Legend', *American Historical Review*, xxxix (April 1934), 485–8. For biographies of Martí see [**1829**] Jorge Mañach, *Martí: apostle of freedom* (translated by Coley Taylor, New York, Devin-Adair, 1950), and [**1830**] Félix Lizaso, *Martí. Martyr of Cuban independence* (translated by Esther E. Shuler, Univ. of New Mexico Press, 1953), and, for a selection from Martí's writings, [**1831**] *The America of José Martí; selected writings* (translated by Juan de Onís, New York, Noonday Press, 1953).

[**1832**] G. W. Auxier, in a valuable article, examines 'The Propaganda Activities of the Cuban *Junta* in Precipitating the Spanish-American War, 1895–1898', *Hispanic American Historical Review*, xix (1939), 286–305, and American opinion is analysed by [**1833**] J. W. Pratt, *Expansionists of 1898. The acquisition of Hawaii and the Spanish islands* (Johns Hopkins Press, 1936). See also [**1834**] Walter Millis, *The Martial Spirit. A study of our war with Spain* (Boston, Houghton Mifflin, 1931), and further references in Bemis and Griffin [60] and *Harvard Guide* [249].

[**1835**] F. E. Chadwick, *The Relations of the United States and Spain; the Spanish-American war* (2 vols., Scribner's, 1911), and [**1836**] E. J. Benton, *International Law and Diplomacy of the Spanish-American War* (Johns Hopkins Press, 1908), are the classical studies. But see also, on European opinion and diplomacy, Rippy [1178], [**1837**] Orestes Ferrara, *The Last Spanish War: revelations in 'diplomacy'* (translated by W. E. Shea, New York, Paisley Press, 1937), [**1838**] R. G. Neale, 'British-American Relations during the Spanish-American War: some problems', *Historical Studies. Australia and New Zealand*, vi (Nov. 1953), 72–89, [**1839**] L. B. Shippee, 'Germany and the Spanish American War', *American Historical Review*, xxx (July 1925), 754–77, and [**1840**] L. M. Sears, 'French Opinion of the Spanish-American War', *Hispanic American Historical Review*, vii (1927), 25–44.

[**1841**] A. G. Robinson, *Cuba and the Intervention* (New York and London, Longmans, Green, 1905), is an account of American military government by a journalist who witnessed both its beginning and its end. See also no. 1825.

THE REPUBLIC

Chapman, *History of the Cuban Republic* [1826], carries the story to 1925.

[**1842**] R. H. Fitzgibbon, *Cuba and the United States, 1900–1935* (Menasha, Wis., George Banta Publishing Co., 1935), is the best general study of Cuban-American relations between the appointment of General Wood as military governor in 1900 and the abrogation of the Platt amendment in 1934. See also [**1843**] H. F. Guggenheim, *The United States and Cuba: a study in international relations* (New York, Macmillan, 1934), a review of treaty relations by an ex-United States ambassador to Cuba, [**1844**] P. G. Wright, *The Cuban Situation and our Treaty Relations* (Washington, The Brookings Institution, 1931), especially concerned with the sugar problem, and [**1844a**] L. H. Jenks, *Our Cuban Colony: a study in sugar* (New York, Vanguard Press, 1928), highly critical of United States policy. [**1845**] D. A. Lockmiller, *Magoon in Cuba: a history of the second intervention, 1906–1909* (Univ. of North Carolina Press, 1938), is the authoritative account. See also [**1846**] his 'The Settlement of the Church Property Question in Cuba' and [**1847**] 'The Advisory Law Commission of Cuba', *Hispanic American Historical Review*, xvii (1937), 488–98, 2–29, of which the last is reprinted in no. 1845. [**1848**] L. J. Meyer discusses 'The United States and the Cuban Revolution of 1917', *Hispanic American Historical Review*, x (1930), 138–66, and [**1849**] J. D. Frost 'Cuban-American Relations concerning the Isle of Pines', *ibid.*, xi (1931), 336–50.

[**1850**] R. L. Buell *et al.*, *Problems of the New Cuba* (New York, Foreign Policy Association, 1935), a report drawn up by an *ad hoc* commission of the Foreign Policy Association at the request of President Mendieta, is a comprehensive survey of the Cuban situation, social and economic, after the fall of Machado. For later history see [**1851**] Edmund A. Chester, *A Sergeant Named Batista* (New York, Holt, 1954), and the scholarly articles of W. S. Stokes, [**1852**] 'The Cuban Parliamentary System in Action, 1940–47', *Journal of Politics*, xi (1949), 335–64, and [**1853**] 'The "Cuban Revolution" and the Presidential Elections of 1948', *Hispanic American Historical Review*, xxxi (1951), 37–79.

[**1854**] Wright, Irene A., *Cuba* (New York, Macmillan, 1910).

[**1855**] Forbes-Lindsay, C. H. A., and Winter, N. O., *Cuba and her People of Today* (2nd ed., Boston, Page, 1928).

[**1856**] Barbour, Thomas, *A Naturalist in Cuba* (Boston, Little, Brown, 1945).

[**1857**] Fergusson, Erna, *Cuba* (New York, Knopf, 1946).

The Dominican Republic

9. THE DOMINICAN REPUBLIC

GENERAL

For bibliographies and guides see nos. 38, 42, 60, 70, and 94.

[**1858**] Sumner Welles, *Naboth's Vineyard: the Dominican Republic, 1844–1924* (2 vols., New York, Payson and Clarke, 1928), covers the years between the establishment of independence from Haiti and the ending of twentieth-century American military intervention.

[**1859**] Mary Treudley, *The United States and Santo Domingo, 1789–1866* (Worcester, Mass., 1916; reprinted from *Journal of Race Development*, vi, July and Oct. 1916, pp. 83–145, 220–74), and [**1860**] C. C. Tansill, *The United States and Santo Domingo, 1798–1873: a chapter in Caribbean diplomacy* (Johns Hopkins Press, 1938), are the major studies in nineteenth-century diplomatic history. See also [**1861**] C. C. Hauch, 'Attitudes of Foreign Governments towards the Spanish Reoccupation of the Dominican Republic', *Hispanic American Historical Review*, xxvii (1947), 247–68, Logan [1878], and Montague [1872].

[**1862**] J. F. Rippy discusses 'The Initiation of the Customs Receivership in the Dominican Republic', in 1905, *Hispanic American Historical Review*, xvii (1937), 419–57, and [**1863**] Carl Kelsey *The American Intervention in Haiti and the Dominican Republic* (Philadelphia, 1922; reprinted from *Annals* of the American Academy of Political and Social Science, vol. 100, March 1922, pp. 109–22). See also, highly critical of United States policy, [**1864**] M. M. Knight, *The Americans in Santo Domingo* (New York, Vanguard Press, 1928), and, for the rise of Trujillo, [**1865**] C. A. Thomson, 'Dictatorship in the Dominican Republic', *Foreign Policy Reports*, xii, No. 3, 15 April 1936.

[**1866**] Hazard, Samuel, *Santo Domingo, past and present, with a glance at Hayti* (New York, 1873).

[**1867**] Schoenrich, Otto, *Santo Domingo: a country with a future* (New York, Macmillan, 1918).

[**1868**] *Refugee Settlement in the Dominican Republic* (Washington, Brookings Institution, 1942).
Far more general in scope than its title implies.

10. HAITI

GENERAL

For bibliographies and guides see nos. 38, 42, 60, 70, and 94.

[**1869**] J. G. Leyburn, *The Haitian People* (Yale Univ. Press, 1941), is an outstanding contribution not only to social history but to political and economic history also. [**1870**] H. P. Davis, *Black Democracy: the story of Haiti* (rev. ed., New York, Dodge, 1936), provides a general historical sketch, and [**1871**] Selden Rodman, *Haiti: the black republic* (New York, Devin-Adair, 1954), a popular survey.

[**1872**] L. L. Montague, *Haiti and the United States, 1714–1938* (Duke Univ. Press, 1940), is indispensable.

[**1873**] Herskovits, M. J., *Life in a Haitian Valley* (New York, Knopf, 1937).

[**1874**] *Mission to Haiti. Report of the United Nations Mission of Technical Assistance to the Republic of Haiti* (Lake Success, New York, 1949).

THE NINETEENTH CENTURY

See nos. 920–7, and, for a partial representation of nineteenth-century history, [**1875**] J. N. Léger, *Haiti, her history and her detractors* (New York and Washington, Neale Pub. Co., 1907).

Two articles by J. E. Baur deal with [**1876**] 'Faustin Soulouque, Emperor of Haiti: his character and his reign', *Americas*, vi (Oct. 1949), 131–66, and [**1877**] 'The Presidency of Nicolas Geffrard of Haiti', *ibid.*, x (April 1954), 425–61. [**1878**] R. W. Logan, *The Diplomatic Relations of the United States with Haiti, 1776–1891* (Univ. of North Carolina Press, 1941), supplements Treudley [1859], Tansill [1860], and Montague [1872]. See also [**1879**] W. D. Boyd, 'James Redpath and American Negro Colonization in Haiti, 1860–1862', *Americas*, xii (Oct. 1955), 169–82, and [**1880**] L. M. Sears, 'Frederick Douglass and the Mission to Haiti, 1889–1891', *Hispanic American Historical Review*, xxi (1941), 222–38.

[**1881**] Brown, Jonathan, *The History and Present Condition of St. Domingo* (2 vols., Philadelphia, 1837).

[**1882**] Candler, John, *Brief Notices of Hayti: with its conditions, resources, and prospects* (London, 1842).

[**1883**] St. John, Sir Spencer, *Hayti, or the black republic* (London, 1884).

THE TWENTIETH CENTURY

On the central event of United States intervention see [**1884**] A. C. Millspaugh, *Haiti under American Control, 1915–30* (Boston, World Peace Foundation, 1931), Kelsey [1863], Davis [1870], and [**1885**] E. G. Balch, ed., *Occupied Haiti* (New York, Writers Pub. Co., 1927). [**1885a**] R. W. Logan, 'The United States Mission in Haiti, 1915–1952', *Inter-American Economic Affairs*, vi, No. 4 (1953), 18–28, provides a supplementary note.

XIV

MEXICO SINCE 1830

GENERAL

For bibliographies and guides see nos. 39, 42, 54, 60, 64, 72, and 73, together with [**1885b**] *List of Works in the New York Public Library relating to Mexico* (New York, Public Library, 1909), [**1886**] C. H. Gardiner, 'Foreign Travelers' Accounts of Mexico, 1810–1910', *Americas*, viii (Jan. 1952), 321–51, which lists 394 items, and [**1887**] H. F. Cline, 'Remarks on a Selected Bibliography of the Caste War and Allied Topics', in Alfonso Villa R., *The Maya of East Central Quintana Roo* [1954], pp. 165–78, which provides a guide to Yucatecan history between 1840 and 1910. See also Bancroft's *Works* [251, 465, 466, 651, and 652].

Bancroft's *History of Mexico* [251] ends in 1887 and Priestley's *The Mexican Nation* [872], now outdated, in 1920. The lively narrative of H. B. Parkes, *A History of Mexico* [873] and Simpson's illuminating commentary on Mexican history, *Many Mexicos* [340], cover the decades of the nineteen-thirties and nineteen-forties.

Among general interpretative syntheses [**1888**] Ernest Gruening, *Mexico and its Heritage* (New York and London, Century, 1928), and [**1889**] Frank Tannenbaum, *Mexico. The struggle for peace and bread* (New York, Knopf, 1950), are outstanding.

[**1889a**] Justo Sierra, ed., *Mexico, its social evolution* . . . (2 vols. in 3, Mexico, J. Ballescá y Cía, 1900–4), contains, vilely translated, the editor's own classic study of the political evolution of the Mexican people and Pablo Macedo's three well-known monographs on commercial development, communications and public works, and public finance.

SPECIAL ASPECTS
ECONOMIC DEVELOPMENT

See [**1890**] *The Economic Development of Mexico. Report of the Combined Mexican Working Party* (Johns Hopkins Press, for the International Bank for Reconstruction and Development, 1953), and [**1891**] Sanford A. Mosk, *Industrial Revolution in Mexico* (Univ. of California Press, 1950).

Mexico since 1830

[**1892**] J. R. Powell, *The Mexican Petroleum Industry, 1938–1950* (Univ. of California Press, 1956), examines the industry after the expropriation of the foreign oil companies. On railways see Long [1102], [**1893**] F. W. Powell, *The Railroads of Mexico* (Boston, The Stratford Co., 1921), [**1894**] David M. Pletcher, 'The Building of the Mexican Railway' (the line between Vera Cruz and Mexico City, inaugurated in 1873), *Hispanic American Historical Review*, xxx (1950), 26–62, [**1895**] the same author's 'The Development of Railroads in Sonora', *Inter-American Economic Affairs*, i, No. 4 (1948), 3–45, and [**1896**] E. B. Glick, 'The Tehuantepec Railroad: Mexico's White Elephant', *Pacific Historical Review*, xxii (1953), 373–82.

[**1897**] M. R. Clark, *Organized Labor in Mexico* (Univ. of North Carolina Press, 1934), traces the early history of the labour movement.

On the history of public finance see W. F. McCaleb, [**1898**] *Present and Past Banking in Mexico* (New York, Harper, 1920), which covers the period 1884 to 1919, and [**1899**] *The Public Finances of Mexico* (New York, Harper, 1921). See also Conant [2031] and Turlington [1936].

Land and Society

[**1900**] G. M. McBride, *The Land Systems of Mexico* (New York, American Geographical Society, 1923), and [**1901**] Helen Phipps, *Some Aspects of the Agrarian Question in Mexico: a historical study* (Univ. of Texas *Bulletin*, No. 2515, Austin, Univ. of Texas, 1925), were pioneer works, of which the first is more significant than the second. [**1902**] E. N. Simpson, *The Ejido, Mexico's way out* (Univ. of North Carolina Press, 1937), a classic statement, and [**1903**] Nathan L. Whetten, *Rural Mexico* (Univ. of Chicago Press, 1948), an encyclopaedic survey, are major contributions. See also Tannenbaum [2052], and, by way of footnotes, [**1904**] H. F. Infield and Koka Freier, *People in Ejidos. A visit to the co-operative farms of Mexico* (New York, Frederick A. Praeger, 1954), and [**1905**] Tom Gill, *Land Hunger in Mexico* (Washington, Charles Lathrop Pack Forestry Foundation, 1951), the view of a soil conservationist.

[**1906**] H. F. Cline, 'Mexican Community Studies', *Hispanic American Historical Review*, xxxii (1952), 212–42, reviews some two dozen such studies beginning with [**1907**] the pioneer work of Robert Redfield, *Tepoztlán, a Mexican Village: a study of folk-life*

Special Aspects

(Univ. of Chicago Press, 1930), and concluding with [**1908**] Oscar Lewis's revisionist interpretation, *Life in a Mexican Village: Tepoztlán restudied* (Univ. of Illinois Press, 1951).[1]

[**1909**] Rodney Gallop, *Mexican Mosaic* (London, Faber, 1939), is a charming description of village ways.

EDUCATION AND PHILOSOPHY

[**1910**] Sánchez, G. I., *Mexico: a revolution by education* (New York, Viking Press, 1936).

[**1911**] Booth, G. C., *Mexico's School-Made Society* (Stanford Univ. Press, 1941).

[**1912**] Wilson, Irma, *Mexico, a century of educational thought* (New York, Hispanic Institute, 1941).

[**1913**] Sánchez, G. I., *The Development of Higher Education in Mexico* (New York, King's Crown Press, 1944).

[**1914**] Kneller, G. F., *The Education of the Mexican Nation* (Columbia Univ. Press, 1951).

[**1915**] Romanell, Patrick, *Making of the Mexican Mind. A study in recent Mexican thought* (Lincoln, Nebraska, Univ. of Nebraska Press, 1952).

LITERATURE, THE ARTS, FOLKLORE

[**1916**] Carlos González Peña, *History of Mexican Literature* (rev. ed., translated by G. B. Nance and F. J. Dunstan, Dallas, Southern Methodist Univ. Press, 1943), is a standard work. [**1917**] J. Lloyd Read discusses *The Mexican Historical Novel, 1826–1910* (New York, Instituto de las Españas, 1939), and [**1918**] J. S. Brushwood *The Romantic Novel in Mexico* (Univ. of

---

[1] Compare Robert Redfield and Alfonso Villa R., *Chan Kom: a Maya Village* (Washington, Carnegie Institution, 1934); E. C. Parsons, *Mitla, town of the souls* . . . (Univ. of Chicago Press, 1936); Robert Redfield, *The Folk Culture of Yucatan* (Univ. of Chicago Press, 1941); G. M. Foster, *A Primitive Mexican Economy* (New York, J. J. Augustin, 1942); R. L. Beals, *Cherán: A Sierra Tarascan village* (Smithsonian Institution, Institute of Social Anthropology, Washington, Govt. Printing Office, 1946); G. M. Foster and Gabriel Ospina, *Empire's Children: the people of Tzintzuntzán* (Smithsonian Institution, Institute of Social Anthropology, Mexico, Imp. Nuevo Mundo, 1948); Robert Redfield, *A Village that Chose Progress: Chan Kom revisited* (Univ. of Chicago Press, 1950); and Donald Brand and J. C. Núñez, *Quiroga: a Mexican municipio* (Smithsonian Institution, Institute of Social Anthropology, Washington, Govt. Printing Office, 1951). For related regional studies see, as examples, G. C. Shattuck, ed., *The Peninsula of Yucatan: medical, biological, meteorological and sociological studies* (Washington, Carnegie Institution, 1933), and R. C. West, *Cultural Geography of the Modern Tarascan Area* (Smithsonian Institution, Institute of Social Anthropology, Washington, Govt. Printing Office, 1948).

Missouri Press, 1954). [**1919**] M. G. Martínez, *Don Joaquín García Icazbalceta: his place in Mexican historiography* (Washington, Catholic Univ. of America, 1947), is a useful bio-bibliographical study.

[**1920**] Pál Kelemen, *Battlefield of the Gods: aspects of Mexican history, art and exploration* (London, Allen and Unwin, 1937), ranges from architecture to painting and from pre-Colombian to modern times. [**1921**] Anita Brenner, *Idols behind Altars* (New York, Payson and Clarke, 1929), discusses indigenous influences in Mexican art. [**1922**] L. E. Schmeckebier, *Modern Mexican Art* (Univ. of Minnesota Press, 1939), [**1923**] MacKinley Helm, *Modern Mexican Painters* (New York, Harper, 1941), and [**1924**] B. S. Myers, *Mexican Painting in our Time* (Oxford Univ. Press, 1957), are all concerned with the twentieth century. See also [**1925**] Diego Rivera and B. D. Wolfe, *Portrait of Mexico* (New York, Covici Friede: London, Allen and Unwin, 1937), [**1926**] B. D. Wolfe, *Diego Rivera, his life and times* (New York, Knopf, 1939), and [**1927**] Alma Reed, *Orozco* (New York, Oxford Univ. Press, 1956).

On the art of the silversmith see Anderson [464], on music [**1928**] Robert Stevenson, *Music in Mexico. A historical survey* (New York, Crowell, 1952), and on folk arts and crafts and folklore Frances Toor, [**1929**] *Mexican Popular Arts* (Mexico, Frances Toor Studios, 1939), and [**1930**] *A Treasury of Mexican Folkways* (New York, Crown Publishers, 1947).

INTERNATIONAL RELATIONS

[**1931**] J. M. Callahan, *American Foreign Policy in Mexican Relations* (New York, Macmillan, 1932), is a general study. [**1932**] J. F. Rippy, *The United States and Mexico* (rev. ed., New York, Crofts, 1931), focuses its attention on the second half of the nineteenth century, and [**1933**] H. F. Cline, *The United States and Mexico* (Harvard Univ. Press, 1953), is principally concerned with the twentieth century. On special aspects of United States–Mexican relations see [**1934**] F. S. Dunn's valuable *The Diplomatic Protection of Americans in Mexico* (Columbia Univ. Press, 1933), and [**1935**] S. A. MacCorkle's slender *American Policy of Recognition towards Mexico* (Johns Hopkins Press, 1933), both of which deal with nineteenth- as well as with twentieth-century problems.

[**1936**] Edgar Turlington, *Mexico and her Foreign Creditors*

(Columbia Univ. Press, 1930), covers the history of foreign loans and is supplemented by [**1937**] A. H. Feller's very detailed *The Mexican Claims Commissions, 1923–34* (New York, Macmillan, 1935).

See also Ireland [1193], Kelchner [1185], and Houston [1186].

THE AGE OF SANTA ANNA, 1830–54

GENERAL

For political and constitutional history see Callcott, *Church and State in Mexico* [889], for political biography [**1938**] W. H. Callcott, *Santa Anna: the story of an enigma who once was Mexico* (Univ. of Oklahoma Press, 1936), and [**1939**] T. E. Cotner, *The Military and Political Career of José Joaquín de Herrera, 1792–1854* (Univ. of Texas Press, 1949), principally concerned with Herrera's second presidency, 1848–51, and for diplomatic history [**1940**] G. L. Rives, *The United States and Mexico, 1821–1848* . . . (2 vols., New York, Scribner's, 1913), and [**1941**] N. W. Stephenson, *Texas and the Mexican War: a chronicle of the winning of the southwest* ('Chronicles of America', vol. xxiv, Yale Univ. Press, 1921).

[**1942**] Graebner, N. A., 'United States Gulf Commerce with Mexico, 1822–1848', *Inter-American Economic Affairs*, v, No. 1 (1951), 36–51.

[**1943**] Robertson, W. S., 'French Intervention in Mexico in 1838', *Hispanic American Historical Review*, xxiv (1944), 222–52. The 'Pastry War'.

[**1943a**] Johnson, R. A., 'Spanish-Mexican Diplomatic Relations, 1853–1855', *Hispanic American Historical Review*, xxi (1941), 559–76.

THE TEXAS REVOLUTION

Castañeda [635] supplies a narrative history of events in Texas between 1810 and 1836. Barker's *Life of Stephen F. Austin* [899] and his *Mexico and Texas* [900] are indispensable. They are supplemented by [**1944**] W. C. Binkley, *The Texas Revolution* (Baton Rouge, Louisiana State Univ. Press, 1952), an admirable brief statement. See also E. C. Barker, [**1945**] 'President Jackson and the Texas Revolution', *American Historical Review*, xii (July 1907), 788–809, and [**1946**] 'The United States and Mexico, 1835–1837', *Mississippi Valley Historical Review*, i (June 1914), 3–30. [**1947**] W. C. Binkley has edited the *Official Correspondence of the Texan Revolution, 1835–1836* (2 vols., New York, Appleton-Century, 1936), and [**1948**] C. E. Castañeda, ed., *The Mexican*

Side of the Texan Revolution ... (Dallas, Texas, P. L. Turner, 1928), prints in translation the accounts of five of the chief Mexican participants. See also Manning [1216] and, for earlier phases of the Texan problem, nos. 895, 896, 898, and 929.

YUCATAN

Three articles by H. F. Cline illustrate economic history: [**1949**] 'The "Aurora Yucateca" and the Spirit of Enterprise in Yucatan, 1821–1847', *Hispanic American Historical Review*, xxvii (1947), 30–60; [**1950**] 'The Sugar Episode in Yucatan, 1825–1850', *Inter-American Economic Affairs*, i, No. 4 (1948), 79–100; and [**1951**] 'The Henequen Episode in Yucatan', *ibid.*, ii, No. 2 (1948), 30–51.

For Yucatecan-Mexican relations between 1839 and 1853 see [**1952**] M. W. Williams, 'Secessionist Diplomacy of Yucatan', *Hispanic American Historical Review*, ix (1929), 132–43, and for Yucatecan appeals to the United States [**1953**] Louis de Armond, 'Justo Sierra O'Reilly and Yucatecan-United States Relations, 1847–1848', *ibid.*, xxxi (1951), 420–36.

[**1954**] Alfonso Villa R., *The Maya of East Central Quintana Roo* (Washington, Carnegie Institution, 1945), deals briefly with the war of the castes.

THE MEXICAN-UNITED STATES WAR, 1846–8

See Rives [1940], Stephenson [1941], and [**1954a**] W. F. McCaleb, *The Conquest of the West* (New York, Prentice-Hall, 1947).

On the Texan question see [**1955**] J. H. Smith, *The Annexation of Texas* (New York, Macmillan, 1911), [**1956**] W. C. Binkley, *The Expansionist Movement into Texas, 1836–1850* (Univ. of California Press, 1925), [**1957**] E. D. Adams, *British Interests and Activities in Texas, 1838–46* (Johns Hopkins Press, 1910), [**1958**] G. P. Garrison, ed., *Diplomatic Correspondence of the Republic of Texas* (3 vols., American Historical Association, *Annual Report* for 1907–8, Washington, Govt. Printing Office, 1908–11), and, a convenient summary, [**1959**] E. C. Barker, 'The Annexation of Texas', *Southwestern Historical Quarterly*, L (July 1946), 49–74; on California and the Far West, [**1960**] R. G. Cleland, *A History of California. The American period* (New York, Macmillan, 1939), [**1961**] E. D. Adams, 'English Interest in the Annexation of California', *American Historical Review*, xiv (July 1909), 744–63, reprinted in no. 1957, and [**1962**] N. A. Graebner's excellent *Empire on the Pacific: a study in American continental expansion* (New York, Ronald Press, 1955).

[**1963**] J. H. Smith, *The War with Mexico* (2 vols., New York, Macmillan, 1919), is the classic study. But see also [**1964**] R. S. Henry, *The Story of the Mexican War* (Indianapolis, Bobbs-Merrill, 1950), and, a still more popularized account, [**1965**] A. H. Bill, *Rehearsal for Conflict. The war with Mexico, 1846–1848* (New York, Knopf, 1947).

[**1966**] J. D. P. Fuller discusses *The Movement for the Acquisition of all Mexico, 1846–48* (Johns Hopkins Press, 1936), [**1967**] C. E. Castañeda the 'Relations of General Scott with Santa Anna', *Hispanic American Historical Review*, xxix (1949), 455–73, and [**1968**] Lota M. Spell 'The Anglo-Saxon Press in Mexico, 1846–1848', *American Historical Review*, xxxviii (Oct. 1932), 20–31.

[**1969**] J. Fernando Ramírez, *Mexico during the War with the United States* (Univ. of Missouri Press, 1950), is a contemporary account edited in translation by W. V. Scholes.

On the Trist mission and the Treaty of Guadalupe Hidalgo, compare [**1970**] Louis M. Sears, 'Nicholas P. Trist, a Diplomat with Ideals', *Mississippi Valley Historical Review*, xi (June 1924), 85–98, [**1971**] E. G. Bourne, 'The United States and Mexico, 1847–1848', *American Historical Review*, v (April 1900), 491–502, and [**1972**] J. S. Reeves, 'The Treaty of Guadaloupe-Hidalgo', *ibid.*, x (Jan. 1905), 309–24.

BOUNDARY PROBLEMS AND FILIBUSTERS

J. F. Rippy, [**1973**] 'The Indians of the Southwest in the Diplomacy of the United States and Mexico, 1848–1853', *Hispanic American Historical Review*, ii (1919), 363–96, [**1974**] 'The Boundary of Mexico and the Gadsden Treaty', *ibid.*, iv (1921), 715–42, and [**1975**] 'Anglo-American Filibusters and the Gadsden Treaty', *ibid.*, v (1922), 155–80, are substantially incorporated in his *United States and Mexico* [1932]. On William Walker's raids on Lower California and Sonora see also Scroggs [1704] and [**1976**] R. K. Wyllys, 'The Republic of Lower California, 1853–1854', *Pacific Historical Review*, ii (1933), 194–213. [**1977**] R. K. Wyllys, *The French in Sonora (1850–1854): the story of French adventurers from California into Mexico* (Univ. of California Press, 1932), examines the activities of Count Raousset-Boulbon. [**1978**] E. K. Chamberlin, 'Baja California after Walker: the Zerman

Enterprise', *Hispanic American Historical Review*, xxxiv (1954), 175–89, concludes that Zerman was not a filibuster.
[**1979**] P. N. Garber, *The Gadsden Treaty* (Univ. of Pennsylvania Press, 1923), is the standard work.

CONTEMPORARY ACCOUNTS

For a bibliography of the travel literature of the period see no. 1886. [**1980**] The delightful account of the Scottish wife of the first Spanish ambassador to Mexico, Mme. Calderón de la Barca [Frances Erskine Inglis], *Life in Mexico during a Residence of Two Years in that Country* (2 vols., Boston, 1843: New York, Dutton, 1931), is a classic. [**1981**] Brantz Mayer, *Mexico as It Was and as It Is* (New York, 1844), is also outstanding. For further examples see [**1982**] Charles J. Latrobe, *The Rambler in Mexico, 1834* (London, 1836), [**1983**] George Folsom, *Mexico in 1842* . . . (New York, 1842), [**1984**] Waddy Thompson, *Recollections of Mexico* (London and New York, 1846), [**1985**] W. W. Carpenter, *Travels and Adventures in Mexico* . . . (New York, 1851), [**1986**] William Parish Robertson, *A Visit to Mexico, by the West India Islands, Yucatan and the United States* (2 vols., London, 1853), and von Tempsky [1745].

The most celebrated work on Yucatan is Stephens [160, 161]. [**1987**] J. J. Williams, *The Isthmus of Tehuantepec* . . . (New York, 1852), records 'the results of a survey for a railroad to connect the Atlantic and Pacific Oceans'. As illustrations of the fairly extensive literature relating to California see Wilkes [1022], [**1988**] T. J. Farnham, *Life and Adventures in California* (New York, 1846), and [**1989**] W. H. Ellison and Francis Price, eds., *The Life and Adventures in California of Don Agustín Janssens, 1834–1856* (San Marino, California, Huntington Library, 1953).

REFORM, INTERVENTION, RECONSTRUCTION, 1854–76

GENERAL

[**1990**] W. H. Callcott, *Liberalism in Mexico, 1857–1929* (Stanford Univ. Press, 1931), continues his *Church and State in Mexico* [889]. [**1991**] Ralph Roeder, *Juárez and his Mexico* (2 vols., New York, Viking Press, 1947), is a distinguished 'biographical history' which sweeps through the period of the *reforma* and of the empire of Maximilian but is over-elaborated on the one hand

and undocumented on the other. [**1992**] F. A. Knapp, *The Life of Sebastián Lerdo de Tejada, 1823–1889. A study of influence and obscurity* (Univ. of Texas Press, 1951), assesses Juárez's successor in the presidency in 1872.

[**1993**] Sir Edward Burnett Tylor, *Anahuac, or Mexico and the Mexicans, ancient and modern* (London, 1861), records the impressions of an anthropologist who visited Mexico in 1856. [**1994**] Charles Lempriere, *Notes in Mexico, in 1861 and 1862; politically and socially considered* (London, 1862), is also the work of an English visitor, sent on a private mission to watch British interests. For the end of the period see [**1995**] A. García Cubas, *The Republic of Mexico in 1876* . . . (translated by G. F. Henderson, Mexico, 1876).

[**1996**] Porter, K. W., 'The Seminole in Mexico, 1850–1861', *Hispanic American Historical Review*, xxxi (1951), 1–36.
The Seminole in Coahuila.

[**1997**] Pletcher, D. M., 'A Prospecting Expedition across Central Mexico, 1856–1857', *Pacific Historical Review*, xxi (1952), 21–41.
E. L. Plumb and the Mexican Pacific Coal and Iron Mining and Land Company.

THE '*Reforma*'

[**1998**] R. A. Johnson, *The Mexican Revolution of Ayutla, 1854–1855* (Rock Island, Illinois, Augustana College Library, 1939), examines the movement which brought about the final fall of Santa Anna and initiated the *reforma*. [**1999**] W. V. Scholes, 'A Revolution Falters: Mexico, 1856–1857', *Hispanic American Historical Review*, xxxii (1952), 1–21, assesses the rule of Comonfort. Callcott [889] and [**2000**] W. V. Scholes, 'Church and State at the Mexican Constitutional Convention, 1856–1857', *Americas*, iv (Oct. 1947), 151–74, discuss the Constitution of 1857. See also [**2001**] F. A. Knapp, 'Parliamentary Government and the Mexican Constitution of 1857', *Hispanic American Historical Review*, xxxiii (1953), 65–87.
See also McBride [1900] and Phipps [1901].

FOREIGN INTERVENTION AND THE EMPIRE OF MAXIMILIAN

See Rippy, *United States and Mexico* [1932], Perkins, *Monroe Doctrine* [1219], Callahan [1931], MacCorkle [1935], Turlington [1936], and Manning [1216]. [**2002**] H. L. Wilson discusses

'President Buchanan's Proposed Intervention in Mexico', in 1859, *American Historical Review*, v (July 1900), 687–701, and [**2003**] W. S. Robertson 'The Tripartite Treaty of London', in 1861, *Hispanic American Historical Review*, xx (1940), 167–89.

The major work on the diplomatic history of the empire is [**2004**] Count Egon Caesar Corti, *Maximilian and Charlotte of Mexico* (translated by Mrs. C. A. Phillips, 2 vols., New York, Knopf, 1928), principally based on the Vienna archives. [**2005**] Daniel Dawson, *The Mexican Adventure* (London, Bell, 1935), adds little that is fresh and goes no further than 1864. [**2006**] H. Montgomery Hyde, *Mexican Empire. The history of Maximilian and Carlota of Mexico* (London, Macmillan, 1946), is a readable biography but has nothing significant to say on the empire itself. [**2007**] J. L. Blasio, *Maximilian, Emperor of Mexico. Memoirs of his private secretary* (edited by R. H. Murray, Yale Univ. Press, 1934), is both entertaining and revealing. See also [**2008**] Felix Salm-Salm (who shared Maximilian's imprisonment), *My Diary in Mexico in 1867* . . . (2 vols., London, 1868). [**2009**] Lord Acton, 'The Rise and Fall of the Mexican Empire', in his *Historical Essays and Studies* (edited by J. N. Figgis and R. V. Laurence, London, Macmillan, 1907), is a remarkable contemporary essay, dated 1868.

[**2010**] N. A. N. Cleven discusses 'The Ecclesiastical Policy of Maximilian of Mexico', *Hispanic American Historical Review*, ix (1929), 317–60, [**2011**] R. W. Frazer 'Maximilian's Propaganda Activities in the United States, 1865–1866', *ibid.*, xxiv (1944), 4–29, and [**2012**] R. B. McCornack 'Maximilian's Relations with Brazil', *ibid.*, xxxii (1952), 175–86. For the emperor's colonization schemes see [**2013**] A. J. and K. A. Hanna, 'The Immigration Movement of the Intervention and Empire as seen through the Mexican Press', *ibid.*, xxvii (1947), 220–46, and [**2014**] G. D. Harmon, 'Confederate Migration to Mexico', *ibid.*, xvii (1937), 458–87.

[**2015**] R. W. Frazer, 'Latin-American Projects to aid Mexico during the French Intervention', *Hispanic American Historical Review*, xxviii (1948), 377–88, examines opinion and reactions in 1861 and 1862. [**2016**] J. M. Callahan discusses the *Evolution of Seward's Mexican Policy* (West Virginia Univ. Studies in American History, Morgantown, W.Va., 1909), and [**2016a**] Kathryn A. Hanna 'The Roles of the South in the French Intervention in Mexico', *Journal of Southern History*, xx (1954), 3–21. [**2017**]

N. A. N. Cleven contributes a note and document on 'The Corwin-Doblado Treaty, April 6, 1862', *Hispanic American Historical Review*, xvii (1937), 499–506. [**2018**] Ivie E. Cadenhead, 'González Ortega and the Presidency of Mexico', *ibid.*, xxxii (1952), 331–46, discusses the dispute between Juárez and the President of the Supreme Court over the question of the presidential succession in 1865.

For French opinion see [**2019**] H. L. Hoskins, 'French Views of the Monroe Doctrine and the Mexican Expedition', *Hispanic American Historical Review*, iv (1921), 677–89, [**2020**] L. M. Case, ed., *French Opinion on the United States and Mexico, 1860–1867* (New York, Appleton-Century, 1936), which prints extracts from the reports of the *Procureurs Généraux*, [**2021**] C. A. Duniway, 'Reasons for the Withdrawal of the French from Mexico', American Historical Association, *Annual Report*, 1902 (2 vols., Washington, Govt. Printing Office, 1903), i, 315–28, and [**2022**] F. E. Lally, *French Opposition to the Mexican Policy of the Second Empire* (Johns Hopkins Press, 1931).

[**2023**] B. F. Gilbert, 'French Warships on the Mexican West Coast, 1861–1866', *Pacific Historical Review*, xxiv (1955), 25–38, discusses an attempted French blockade.

RECONSTRUCTION

See Roeder [1991] and Knapp [1992]. Pletcher [1894] describes the inauguration of the Mexican Railway, and for railways see also [**2024**] D. M. Pletcher, 'General William S. Rosecrans and the Mexican Transcontinental Railroad Project', *Mississippi Valley Historical Review*, xxxviii (March 1952), 657–78, [**2025**] F. A. Knapp, 'Precursors of American Investment in Mexican Railroads', *Pacific Historical Review*, xxi (1952), 43–64, and [**2026**] C. H. Gardiner, 'The Mexico-Toluca Railroad and Lottery', *Inter-American Economic Affairs*, ii, No. 4 (1949), 12–28.

THE AGE OF DÍAZ, 1876–1910

See Callcott [1990]. [**2027**] Carleton Beals, *Porfirio Díaz, dictator of Mexico* (Philadelphia and London, Lippincott, 1932), is the fullest biography but falls far short of the strict canons of historical research. [**2028**] C. L. Jones, *Mexico and its Reconstruction* (New York and London, Appleton, 1921), a dispassionate examination, contains much useful information and throws many valuable side-lights on the Díaz régime. See also Gruening [1888]. [**2029**] J. K. Turner, *Barbarous Mexico* (Chicago, C. H. Kerr, 1911), is a contemporary indictment. [**2030**] C. C. Cumberland, 'Precursors of the Mexican Revolution of 1910', *Hispanic American Historical Review*, xxii (1942), 344–56, examines the 'liberal' opposition to Díaz between 1900 and 1910.

On the land question see McBride [1900], on public finance McCaleb [1899], Turlington [1936], and [**2031**] C. A. Conant, *The Banking System of Mexico* (Washington, Govt. Printing Office, 1910), and on transportation Powell [1893]. [**2032**] Osgood Hardy, 'Ulysses S. Grant, President of the Mexican Southern Railroad', *Pacific Historical Review*, xxiv (1955), 111–20, is an interesting footnote, illustrating, in the 'eighties, the ramifications of American interest in Mexican railways. See also Pletcher [1895]. Two brief articles by C. H. Gardiner deal respectively with [**2033**] 'Early Diplomatic Relations between Mexico and the Far East', *Americas*, vi (April 1950), 401–14, and [**2034**] 'Trade between Mexico and the Transpacific World, 1870–1900', *Inter-American Economic Affairs*, iii, No. 3 (1949), 29–40.

[**2035**] C. W. Hackett discusses 'The Recognition of the Díaz Government by the United States', *Southwestern Historical Quarterly*, xxviii (July 1924), 34–55, and [**2036**], a pedestrian exercise, R. D. Gregg *The Influence of Border Troubles on Relations between the United States and Mexico, 1876–1910* (Johns Hopkins Press, 1937). See also Callahan [1931], Rippy [1932], Dunn [1934], MacCorkle [1935], and, also an academic exercise, [**2037**] Pauline S. Relyea, *Diplomatic Relations between the United States and Mexico under Porfirio Díaz, 1876–1910* (Smith College Studies in History, Northampton, Mass., 1924). [**2038**] Matías Romero, *Mexico and the United States* (New York, 1898), is notable as the work of a Mexican diplomat of long experience in the United States. [**2039**] J. W. Foster, *Diplomatic Memoirs* (2 vols., Boston and New York, Houghton Mifflin, 1909), contains, in vol. i, Foster's reminiscences of his Mexican experiences between 1873 and 1880.

[**2040**] F. A. Ober, *Travels in Mexico and Life among the Mexicans* . . . (Boston, 1884), [**2041**] K. S. Lumholtz, *Unknown Mexico; a record of five years' exploration among the tribes of the western Sierra Madre; in the Tierra Caliente of Tepic and Jalisco; and among the Tarascos of Michoacan* (2 vols., New York, Scribner's, 1902: London, Macmillan, 1903), [**2042**] C. M. Flandrau's delightful

Viva Mexico! (New York, Appleton, 1908), [**2043**] Hans Gadow, *Through Southern Mexico. Being an account of the travels of a naturalist* (London, Witherby: New York, Scribner's, 1908), and [**2044**] Frederick Starr, *In Indian Mexico. A narrative of travel and labor* (Chicago, Forbes, 1908), should be noted among the literature of travel and description.

THE MEXICAN REVOLUTION, 1910–34

GENERAL

See Callcott [1990] and, for a general conspectus, Cline, *The United States and Mexico* [1933]. [**2045**] Anita Brenner and George R. Leighton, *The Wind that Swept Mexico: the history of the Mexican Revolution, 1910–1942* (New York and London, Harper, 1943), is notable for its 184 historical photographs.

Two scholarly monographs, [**2046**] C. C. Cumberland, *Mexican Revolution. Genesis under Madero* (Univ. of Texas Press, 1952), and [**2047**] Stanley R. Ross, *Francisco I. Madero. Apostle of Mexican democracy* (Columbia Univ. Press, 1955), do much to elucidate the events of 1910–13.

Of a different order, [**2048**] Edgcumb Pinchon, *Zapata, the unconquerable* (New York, Doubleday, Doran, 1941), a popular biography of the peasant leader who was assassinated in 1919, frankly adopts a 'novelistic technique' and avowedly sacrifices 'strict historical accuracy to tact'. See also, similar in kind, [**2049**] the same author's *Viva Villa! A recovery of the real Pancho Villa . . .* (New York, Harcourt Brace, 1933).

Gruening in 1928 [1888] and [**2050**] Frank Tannenbaum, *Peace by Revolution: an interpretation of Mexico* (Columbia Univ. Press, 1933), gather together the various threads of the Revolution and summarize its constructive aspects. See also Jones [2028].

SPECIAL ASPECTS

[**2051**] E. W. Kemmerer, *Inflation and Revolution: Mexico's experience of 1912–1917* (Princeton Univ. Press, 1940), examines the effects of monetary changes. McCaleb [1898] sketches the treatment meted out to credit institutions by successive revolutionary leaders. For the Constitution of 1917 see Callcott [1990], for agrarian reform [**2052**] Frank Tannenbaum, *The Mexican Agrarian Revolution* (New York, Macmillan, 1929), Simpson [1902], and Whetton [1903], and, for the labour movement, Clark

[1897]. [**2053**] Earle K. James, 'Church and State in Mexico', *Foreign Policy Reports*, xi, No. 9, 3 July 1935, is a convenient summary. See also Mecham, *Church and State in Latin America* [393] and Callcott [1990]. [**2054**] F. C. Kelley, *Blood Drenched Altars: Mexican study and comment* (Milwaukee, Bruce, 1935), presents the views of a Roman Catholic bishop.

For the diplomatic history of the period and for Mexican-United States relations in particular see nos. 1931 to 1935, and, for foreign claims generally, nos. 1936 and 1937. See also Gordon [2075]. On Wilson's Mexican policy consult [**2055**] R. S. Baker, *Woodrow Wilson, life and letters* (8 vols., New York, Garden City, Doubleday, Doran, 1927–39), and [**2056**] A. S. Link, *Woodrow Wilson and the Progressive Era, 1910–1917* ('The New American Nation Series', New York, Harper, 1954). [**2057**] Francisco Bulnes, *The Whole Truth about Mexico; President Wilson's responsibility* (New York, M. Bulnes Book Co., 1916), is the argument of a Mexican publicist. [**2058**] C. W. Hackett, *The Mexican Revolution and the United States, 1910–1926* (Boston, World Peace Foundation, 1926), a brief discussion under too wide a title, is principally concerned with the nineteen-twenties. See also, an interesting symposium presenting a Mexican as well as an American view, [**2059**] J. F. Rippy, José Vasconcelos, and Guy Stevens, *American Policies Abroad. Mexico* (Univ. of Chicago Press, 1928). [**2060**] C. C. Cumberland, 'The Jenkins Case and Mexican-American Relations', *Hispanic American Historical Review*, xxxi (1951), 586–607, is interesting as an illustration of the precarious character of those relations in 1919–20.

MEMOIRS, CONTEMPORARY ACCOUNTS, AND
DESCRIPTION

[**2061**] E. I. Bell, *The Political Shame of Mexico* (New York, McBride, Nast, 1914), by a former newspaper editor, covers the years 1910 to 1914. The views of the American Ambassador, Henry Lane Wilson, who regarded Madero as 'simply a man of disordered intellect who happened to be in the public eye at the psychological moment', are enshrined in [**2062**] his *Diplomatic Episodes in Mexico, Belgium and Chile* (New York, Doubleday, Page: London, Heinemann, 1927). Edith O'Shaughnessy, [**2063**] *Diplomatic Days* (New York and London, Harper, 1917), and [**2064**] *A Diplomat's Wife in Mexico* . . . (New York and London, Harper, 1916), by the wife of the Secretary of the American

Embassy and an admirer of Díaz, are based on letters written between 1911 and 1914 and are supplemented by [**2065**] her *Intimate Pages of Mexican History* (New York, George H. Doran, 1920), containing descriptions of Díaz, Francisco de la Barra, Madero, and Victoriano Huerta. [**2066**] Rosa E. King, *Tempest over Mexico. A personal chronicle* (Boston, Little, Brown, 1935: London, Methuen, 1936), is an Englishwoman's moving account of the Zapatista rising in Morelos.

[**2067**] John Reed, *Insurgent Mexico* (New York and London, Appleton, 1914), affords glimpses of Villa and Carranza. For Villa see, more particularly, [**2068**] Martín Luis Guzmán, *The Eagle and the Serpent* (translated by Harriet de Onís, New York, Knopf, 1930), which reflects the storm and stress of the Carranza epoch, and for Zapata [**2069**] H. H. Dunn, *The Crimson Jester: Zapata of Mexico* (New York, McBride, 1933: London, Harrap, 1934), the memoirs of a press reporter who lived and rode with Zapata. [**2070**] *The Rosalie Evans Letters from Mexico* (edited by Daisy C. Pettus, Indianapolis, Bobbs-Merrill, 1926), cover the years 1918 to 1924, when the writer, long struggling for the recovery of her property, was killed. [**2071**] Vicente Blasco Ibáñez, *Mexico in Revolution* (New York, Dutton, 1920), 'simple impressions, hastily and incompletely jotted down', is a collection of newspaper articles portraying the rebellion against Carranza. The title of [**2072**] E. J. Dillon, *President Obregón. A world reformer* (Boston, Small, Maynard: London, Hutchinson, 1923), speaks for itself.

For later descriptive literature see, in the early 'thirties, [**2073**] Carleton Beals, *Mexican Maze, with illustrations by Diego Rivera* (Philadelphia and London, Lippincott, 1931), and [**2074**] William Spratling, *Little Mexico* (New York and London, Cape, 1932).

THE MEXICAN REVOLUTION, 1934–

See Cline [1933], Brenner and Leighton [2045], and Tannenbaum [1889].

[**2075**] W. C. Gordon, *The Expropriation of Foreign-Owned Property in Mexico* (Washington, American Council on Public Affairs, 1941), discusses the expropriation of mines and agricultural lands as well as of the oilfields. Compare [**2076**] J. L. Kunz, *The Mexican Expropriations* (New York Univ. School of Law, 1940), and [**2077**] R. B. Gaither, *Expropriation in Mexico, the facts and the* *law* (New York, Wm. Morrow, 1940). On the oil industry after expropriation consult Powell [1892], on agrarian problems Whetten [1903], and on economic development generally nos. 1890 and 1891. [**2078**] A. P. Whitaker, ed., *Mexico Today (Annals of the American Academy of Political and Social Science*, vol. 208, Philadelphia, 1940), an informative symposium, contains essays both by Mexican and by American hands.

[**2079**] W. C. Townsend, *Lázaro Cárdenas, Mexican democrat* (Ann Arbor, George Wahr, 1952), reflects a personal friendship. [**2080**] Nathaniel and Sylvia Weyl, *The Re-Conquest of Mexico: the years of Lázaro Cárdenas* (New York, Oxford Univ. Press, 1939), [**2081**] F. L. Kluckhohn, *The Mexican Challenge* (New York, Doubleday, Doran, 1939)—the author was expelled from Mexico, and [**2082**] Betty Kirk, *Covering the Mexican Front . . .* (Univ. of Oklahoma Press, 1942), are the work of journalists. See also, the impressions of a young English resident, [**2083**] R. H. K. Marett, *An Eye-Witness of Mexico* (New York, Oxford Univ. Press, 1939), and, for sidelights on the years between 1933 and 1942, [**2084**] Josephus Daniels, *Shirt-Sleeve Diplomat* (Univ. of North Carolina Press, 1947). [**2084a**] W. P. Tucker, *The Mexican Government Today* (Univ. of Minnesota Press, 1957), examines the organization and structure of administration and government in the decade of the 'fifties.

[**2085**] Miguel Covarrubias, *Mexico South: the isthmus of Tehuantepec* (New York, Knopf, 1946), [**2086**] J. W. Hilton, *Sonora Sketch Book* (New York, Macmillan, 1947), [**2087**] John Skeaping, *The Big Tree of Mexico* (London, Turnstile Press, 1952: Indiana Univ. Press, 1953), [**2088**] Michael Swan, *Temples of the Sun and Moon* (London, Cape, 1954), and [**2089**] George Woodcock, *To the City of the Dead. An account of travels in Mexico* (London, Faber and Faber, 1957), record the impressions of cultivated travellers.

LIST OF
PERIODICAL PUBLICATIONS CITED

Agricultural History (Agricultural History Society), Chicago; Baltimore, 1927–
American Academy of Political and Social Science, Philadelphia, *Annals*, 1890–
American Anthropologist (American Anthropological Association), Menasha, Wis., 1888–9; n.s., 1899–
American Antiquarian Society, Worcester, Mass., *Proceedings*, 1843–80; n.s., 1880–
American Historical Association, Washington, D.C., *Annual Reports*, 1889–
American Historical Review, New York, etc., 1895–
American Journal of International Law (American Society of International Law), New York, etc., 1907–
American Political Science Review (American Political Science Association), Baltimore, 1906–
Americas (Academy of American Franciscan History), Washington, D.C., 1944–
Annals of Science, London, 1936–
Atlante (Hispanic and Luso-Brazilian Councils), London, i–iii, 1953–5.
Bibliographical Society of America, New York, *Papers*, 1906–
Bulletin of Hispanic Studies [formerly *Bulletin of Spanish Studies*] (Institute of Hispanic Studies, University of Liverpool), Liverpool, 1923–
Bulletin of the Institute of Historical Research (University of London), London, 1923–
California Historical Society Quarterly, San Francisco, 1922–
Cambridge Historical Journal, London, 1923–
Canadian Historical Review, Toronto, 1920–
Canadian Journal of Economics and Political Science (Canadian Political Science Association), Toronto, 1935–
Catholic Historical Review (Catholic University of America), Washington, D.C., 1915–
Comparative Ethnographical Studies, Göteborg, i–x, 1919–38.
Connecticut Academy of Arts and Sciences, New Haven, *Transactions*, 1866–
Economic History (Royal Economic Society, Supplement to *Economic Journal*), London, i–iv, 1926–40.
Economic History Review (Economic History Society), London, 1927–48; 2nd series, 1948–
Economica (London School of Economics and Political Science), London, 1921–33; n.s., 1934–
English Historical Review, London, 1886–
Fénix. Revista de la Biblioteca Nacional, Lima, 1944–
Foreign Affairs (Council on Foreign Relations), New York, 1922–
Foreign Policy Reports (Foreign Policy Association), New York, 1931–
Geographical Review (American Geographical Society), New York, 1916–
Geographical Studies (Birkbeck College, University of London), London, 1954–
Harvard Theological Review (Harvard University), Cambridge, Mass., 1908–
Hispanic American Historical Review, Baltimore; Durham, N.C., 1918–
Historical Studies, Australia and New Zealand (Melbourne University), Melbourne, 1940–
History (Historical Association), London, 1912–15; n.s., 1916–

List of Periodical Publications Cited

Inter-American Economic Affairs, Washington, D.C., 1947–
Inter-American Quarterly [*Quarterly Journal of Inter-American Relations*], Cambridge, Mass., 1939–42.
International Affairs (Royal Institute of International Affairs), London, 1922–
International Labour Review (International Labour Office), Geneva, 1921–
Journal of Business of the University of Chicago, Chicago, 1928–
Journal of Economic and Business History (Harvard University), Cambridge, Mass., i–iv, 1928–32.
Journal of Economic History (Economic History Association), New York, 1941–
Journal of the History of Ideas (College of the City of New York), Lancaster, Pa., 1940–
Journal of Legal and Political Sociology, New York, i–iv, 1942–7.
Journal of Modern History (University of Chicago), Chicago, 1929–
Journal of Negro History (Association for the Study of Negro Life and History), Lancaster, Pa.; Washington, 1916–
Journal of Political Economy (University of Chicago), Chicago, 1892–
Journal of Politics (Southern Political Science Association), Gainesville, Fla., 1939–
Journal of Race Development, Worcester, Mass., i–ix, 1910–19; then *Journal of International Relations*; then *Foreign Affairs*, q.v.
Journal of Southern History (Southern Historical Association), Baton Rouge, 1935–
Louisiana Historical Quarterly (Louisiana Historical Society), New Orleans, 1917–
Manchester School of Economic and Social Studies (Department of Economics, University of Manchester), Manchester, 1930–
Mariner's Mirror (Society for Nautical Research), London, 1911–
Maryland Historical Magazine (Maryland Historical Society), Baltimore, 1906–
Mid-America (Loyola University, Institute of Jesuit History), Chicago, 1918–
Mississippi Valley Historical Review (Mississippi Valley Historical Association), Cedar Rapids, Iowa, 1914–
New Mexico Quarterly Review (University of New Mexico), Albuquerque, 1931–
Oxford Economic Papers, Oxford, 1938–48; n.s., 1949–
Pacific Historical Review (American Historical Association, Pacific Coast Branch), Glendale, Calif., 1932–
Peabody Museum of American Archaeology and Ethnology (Harvard University), Cambridge, Mass., *Memoirs*, 1896– ; *Papers*, 1888–
Political Quarterly, London, 1930–
Political Science Quarterly (Academy of Political Science in the City of New York), New York, 1886–
Quarterly Journal of Economics (Harvard University), Cambridge, Mass., 1886–
Quarterly Journal of Inter-American Relations. See *Inter-American Quarterly*.
Review of Economics and Statistics (Harvard University), Cambridge, Mass., 1919–
Revista de Historia de América (Instituto Panamericano de Geografía e Historia), Tacubaya, Mexico, 1938–
Royal Historical Society, London, *Transactions*, 1872–82; n.s., 1884–1906; 3rd series, 1907–17; 4th series, 1918–50; 5th series, 1951–
Southwestern Historical Quarterly (Texas State Historical Association), Austin, Texas, 1897–
Southwestern Social Science Quarterly (Southwestern Social Science Association), Austin, Texas, 1920– [1923–31 as *Southwestern Political and Social Science Quarterly*].
Yale University Library Gazette, New Haven, Conn., 1926–

BIOGRAPHICAL INDEX

(Numbers refer to items)

INDEX OF AUTHORS,
EDITORS, AND TRANSLATORS

(Numbers refer to items)

Index of Authors, Editors, and Translators